The Mystery
of
Charles Dickens

The Mystery
of
Charles Dickens

A. N. Wilson

W F HOWES LTD

This large print edition published in 2021 by
W F Howes Ltd
Unit 5, St George's House, Rearsby Business Park,
Gaddesby Lane, Rearsby, Leicester LE7 4YH

1 3 5 7 9 10 8 6 4 2

First published in the United Kingdom in 2020
by Atlantic Books

ISBN 978 1 00402 311 0

Typeset by Palimpsest Book Production Limited,
Falkirk, Stirlingshire

Printed and bound by

For Amicia and Richard

CONTENTS

CONTENTS

CHAPTER 1

THE MYSTERY OF FIFTEEN POUNDS, THIRTEEN SHILLINGS AND NINEPENCE

'I have no relief, but in action. I am become incapable of rest . . . Much better to die, doing,' the hyper-energetic, over-sexed, tormented, exultant, hilarious, despondent Charles Dickens had written to a friend, thirteen years before he actually died.

Dickens was good at dying. If you want a good death, go to the novels of Dickens. Watch the dwarfish swindler Mr Quilp on the run from the police, slithering into the muddy Thames. Watch Mr Merdle, the financier who cuts his own throat with a penknife in a Turkish bath. Look upwards to the rooftops and see the murderer Bill Sikes trying to make his escape from arrest by clambering over the tiles, missing his footing and hanging himself by accident. See, too, his dog, Bull's Eye, leap to his master's shoulder and fall, dashing his brains out on the stones below. There had been the poignant deaths – little Jo the Crossing Sweeper trying to repeat the, to him unknown, Lord's Prayer; and heroic deaths – none more so than Sydney Carton, voluntarily approaching the guillotine and doing a far, far better thing than he had ever done before.

Sometimes Dickens may be said to have overdone the sob-stuff. Oscar Wilde quipped that it would take a heart of stone to read of the death of Little Nell without laughing. But the thing is, this isn't true: for a start, in *The Old Curiosity Shop* the child is already dead when we find her lying in the schoolmaster's house; her death happens offstage; and – as the thousands who gathered in New York harbour awaiting the latest instalment of the novel attested, with the anxious cry 'Is Little Nell still alive?' – the scene where we find her dead body has astounding power, though sophisticated readers might be disturbed by the vulgarity of that power. Even if you question the story of the Americans shouting, agog on the quayside, for news of Little Nell, the fact remains that the novel was selling 100,000 copies per instalment as it appeared. The public reaction to Little Nell's fate had revealed to Dickens that he possessed what no author in history had ever possessed to such a degree: a mesmeric power. Literature had never before, in the West, attracted the sort of crowds that had hitherto only been drawn to the revivalist meetings of John Wesley.

The poignant deaths were not the only ones at which he was adept, of course. There were grotesque deaths, such as the tall lady eating sandwiches who was decapitated by an unnoticed archway in Rochester; improbable deaths, such as Krook's – by spontaneous combustion; deaths by judicial execution and by mob violence; deaths by accident; deaths, like that of Edwin Drood, in his final novel, unexplained, mysterious. And there is what must be one of the most wonderful deaths in literature – rivalled only by that of Falstaff as described by Mistress Quickly – the death of Barkis: 'and it being low water, he went out with the tide'. [*DC* 30]

But now it was June 1870, and although he was only fifty-eight years old, Dickens was exhausted. His face was ravaged; it could have been the face of an octogenarian. He had been heavily dosing himself with laudanum (a mixture of opium and alcohol) for many months and was opium-dependent. The novel that he was in the middle of writing, *The Mystery of Edwin Drood*, begins with an opium-induced trance. It is the story of a man who drifts into different states of consciousness through the influence of the drug. It is the story of a divided self, a man who is a different person when leading his secret lives – lives hidden from the respectable cathedral town of Cloisterham, a fictionalized version of the same cathedral town, Rochester, that was a brisk hour's walk from Dickens's home at Gad's Hill in Kent. For, ill as he was, Dickens, who all his life was a restless and prodigiously energetic walker, still forced his body into vigorous exercise, on those days when he was capable of it. Now, his heart was weak, his breath was uncertain. He had crammed many lifetimes into one – the lifetime of the most celebrated novelist in the world; the lifetime of a full-time journalist; the lifetime of an actor, and of a public reader; the lifetime of a philanthropist; the lifetime of a family man and of a secret lover. Now, having described and enacted so many deaths, he was going to do it for real.

Enacted, yes, for as well as his unrivalled presence in print, his fame as a writer, he never lost his desire to perform on the public stage. I want to write, in this chapter, about Dickens's debt to the theatre, to burlesque, to pantomime, to the harlequinade, because it is central to his way of functioning as one of the greatest artistic geniuses of the nineteenth century. But although we know so little about the actress Nelly Ternan, she was part of this, obviously she was. So I also want to start with Nelly, and the theatre, before we go back and explore the other mysteries of Charles Dickens – the mystery of his childhood and his past; the mystery of his appalling cruelty to a harmless wife who bore him ten children; the mystery of his passionate, sincere and burning charity, his fury at injustice; the mystery of his relationship with the public, in the first era when there was a truly enormous public with whom to have such a relationship; and the mystery of his last, unfinished novel, *The Mystery of Edwin Drood*, in which he changed direction as an artist and explored the human consciousness in a way that anticipated the developments of psychology and literary modernism. And I want to maintain that Charles Dickens was a writer like no other, a *sui generis* figure, unique in the nineteenth century. It was the glory age of the English novel. In his infancy, Jane Austen was still at work, and Sir Walter Scott. His contemporaries included the Brontë sisters, George Eliot, Anthony Trollope, William Makepeace Thackeray. Dickens was fundamentally different from any one of them, for reasons that we shall explore. Although we call all their works 'novels', he was actually writing books that were quite different in kind from theirs, and it was perhaps only when one of his greatest admirers abroad, Fyodor Mikhailovich Dostoevsky, began to write, partially in homage to Dickens, that the world started to see the kind of novelist he had been. His stories were prodigiously popular, and continue to be so. Unlike so much prose fiction, however, they work on many levels, and it would be as true to describe them as great visionary poems, as fairy tales, as pantomimes, as it would be to talk of them as novels in the prosaic tradition in which, say, Trollope excelled.

This book is entitled *The Mystery of Charles Dickens* because, of all the great novelists, Dickens is the most mysterious. His way of going to work appears to be, on one level, so obvious, so basic: the comedy so crude, often – though, equally often, so hilarious; the pathos so heavily laid on

5

with a trowel. But although he was a journalist, and one of the really great journalists, his novels were not journalistic, like those of Emile Zola. Zola was a camera. He depicted what was there. Dickens, like the illustrators chosen to adorn his early novels, created an alternative universe. He amused, or shamed, his readers into recognizing that this universe was uncommonly like their own, but his techniques were decidedly not those of a realist. He invented, rather, an alternative universe into which we are all drawn, persuaded that it is a real world, of a sort. Those who protest that the Dickensian world is unrealistic are so often forced to confront the pantomimic grotesquerie, the high comedy, the violence and the pathos of 'real life' and recognize that it is 'just like Dickens'. This, however, is not to deny that, almost more than any great artist, he is the puppet-master who pulls the strings and writes the script.

We are now going to his house in Kent, Gad's Hill Place, near Rochester, in June 1870 to watch Charles Dickens die. Before we reach Gad's Hill, however, following a road that was trodden by so many before us, fictitious and semi-fictitious, aware of Chaucer's pilgrims going down to Canterbury, of Falstaff, Bardolph and Poins making their night-foray as highwaymen, and of Mr Pickwick making his more innocent sortie towards Rochester, we are going to return in our mind to a death enacted by Dickens on the stage of the Free Trade Hall in Manchester, thirteen years before. As well as writing up a good death, he loved to act one, and the more the audience sobbed, the better. Thirteen years earlier, then, during the summer of 1857, he was acting in *The Frozen Deep*, a play written by his friend Wilkie Collins, loosely based on the doomed expedition, led by Sir John Franklin, to find the North-West Passage. Dickens, performing on the stage of the Free Trade Hall, had the satisfaction of having 'a couple of thousand people all rigid and frozen together, in the palm of one's hand'. He took particular satisfaction in seeing 'the hardened carpenters at the sides [of the stage] crying and trembling at it night after night'.

He took the part of Richard Wardour, and the actress in whose arms he died was Nelly's sister, 'Miss Maria Ternan – born on the stage, and inured to it from the days when she was the little child'. Dickens wrote *Nicholas Nickleby* before Maria Ternan was even born, but her mother, who had herself been on the stage since childhood, could have echoed the ham actor-manager Mr Vincent Crummles who engages Nicholas Nickleby in his troupe: 'I am in the theatrical profession myself, my wife is in the theatrical profession, my children are in the theatrical profession. I had a dog that lived and died in it from a puppy, and my chaise-pony goes on in Timour the Tartar.' [*NN* 22] Mrs Ternan, a widow, came from a family who had followed the theatrical profession since the eighteenth century.

Continuing to describe Maria's thespian gifts, on display in Manchester, Dickens explained, 'She had to take my head up as I was dying, and to put it in her lap, and give me her face to hold between my two hands. All of which I showed her elaborately . . . that morning. When we came to that point at night, her tears fell down my face, down my beard (excuse my mentioning that hateful appendage), down my ragged dress – poured all over me like rain, so that it was as much as I could do to speak for them.'

Maria Ternan had been a true Infant Phenomenon. In fact she was twenty by now, but she looked much younger. Dickens always liked child-women, little fairies who were betwixt and between, like Little Dorrit or the Marchioness, neither children nor adults. When Mark Lemon, editor of *Punch*, took Maria backstage after the performance, her weeping set him off. Soon they were all crying, and she had to be comforted by her mother and sister, while Dickens gave her sherry. So much for little Maria. Her elder sister Fanny, who would one day marry the brother of the novelist Anthony Trollope and become a popular novelist herself (author of *Aunt Margaret's Trouble*, *That Unfortunate Marriage* and others), really had been an infant prodigy, playing Mamilius in *The Winter's Tale* when she was only three and a half in 1840. All three of the Ternan sisters, like their mother, pursued careers on the stage throughout their childhoods. The summer before they took on the roles in *The Frozen Deep*, Fanny had appeared as Oberon in Edmund Kean's lavish production of *A Midsummer Night's Dream* (in which a ten-year-old Ellen Terry played Puck). Nelly, meanwhile, had been on the stage of the Haymarket Theatre, playing a 'breeches' role – in a show called *Atalanta*. Her part was that of Hippomenes, throwing golden apples in front of the speedy Atalanta to stop her running so fast. It had run every night from April to July 1857, and Nelly had not missed a single performance.

Of the three Ternan girls, it was Nelly – eighteen, the youngest, slightly plump, blonde curls, large blue eyes and, again, the way he liked them, small – who arrested Dickens's attention in that Manchester show some months later.

Even by Dickens's hyper-energetic standards, 1857 had been a phenomenal year. He was deeply involved in running a refuge for women and trying to rehabilitate them, after rocky starts, and prepare them for married life. He was finishing one of his very greatest novels, *Little Dorrit*. He was embarking on a series of public readings from his work. He had a seemingly ceaseless series of charitable dinners at which he was required to make the speech. He was the editor of the weekly *Household Words*. At home, his unhappy marriage seemed to be causing him and his wife Catherine untold strain and misery, and there are few human experiences more exhausting than living with a partner to whom one is unhappily yoked. 'There

9

can be no disparity in marriage like unsuitability of mind and purpose,' [*DC* 45] a manifesto-mantra repeated four times by David Copperfield (twice midway through Chapter 45, once at the end of that chapter and again in Chapter 48).

After *The Frozen Deep* in Manchester, however, he was a changed man. He wrote to Collins seven months later, in March 1858, 'I have never known a moment's peace or content since the last night of *The Frozen Deep*. I do suppose that there never was a Man so seized and rended by one Spirit.'

It was perhaps inevitable that the crisis of his life – the before-and-after experience – should have happened onstage, and that the woman in his life, for its last decade, should have been an actress. Equally inevitable, for Dickens was a divided self whose art depended upon the divisions in his personality, was the fact that Nelly Ternan should become, not his wife, but his secret. When they met he was forty-five and she was eighteen. She was with him to the end, and very nearly at the end, when, thirteen years later, he died in reality. Her relationship with him lasted thirteen creative, energetic, secret years; years in which she was better qualified than most to contemplate the Mystery of Charles Dickens. She did so offstage, away from the lights. As far as the world was concerned, Nelly did not exist. She was unknown to Dickens's devoted public. She was largely unknown to posterity. And when, during the early decades of the twentieth century,

10

rumours of her existence began to emerge, many of his dedicated readers refused to believe in her existence. Even one of the finest late-twentieth-century Dickensian biographers, Peter Ackroyd, claimed it was unthinkable that Dickens and Nelly could have been lovers, as they obviously were.

So in this exploration into the Mystery of Charles Dickens, we begin with the secret Muse, with Nelly, and we return to the bright June day in 1870 when she saw him fully alive for the last time.

He would die on 9 June. On Tuesday 7 June 1870, Charles Dickens was hard at work, in his house at Gad's Hill, writing the next episode of his serial novel *The Mystery of Edwin Drood*. He wrote to Luke Fildes, the young artist who was illustrating the story, telling him that he would be at Gad's Hill from Saturday 11 June onwards. That was to indicate, at the least, that he would be away from home for three days. The next day, on Wednesday 8 June, he breakfasted early, at 7.30 a.m. One of the maids in the house was to be married that day, but Dickens was not intending to be present at the ceremony. He wrote a few other letters, indicating that on the following day, Thursday, he would be in London. He looked in at the Falstaff Inn opposite his house, to cash a cheque for £22 from the landlord, Mr Trood, whose name surely half suggested that of the hero, or anti-hero, of his current fiction.

Dickens never reached London that Thursday. It was the day on which he was destined to die. His scrupulous sister-in-law Georgina, who had kept house for him ever since he separated from her sister Kate, wrote to the solicitor, Frederic Ouvry, on 9 June to relate that she had been through her brother-in-law's pockets after his collapse from a stroke, and found six pounds, six shillings and threepence. In other words, on the previous day he had spent fifteen pounds, thirteen shillings and ninepence. Where had it gone?

The person who emerged from the Falstaff Inn, with £22 in his pocket, on the morning of the 8th was a small, trim, punctiliously neat, whiskery figure who would have been instantly recognized in almost any of the great cities of the world. He was a celebrity. The most famous novelist, but also one of the most famous human beings, alive. The fact that Dickens did not wish the world to know he had a mistress necessitated a life of constant subterfuge and deception, which had been the pattern of his existence for the previous thirteen years. Nelly Ternan could not live with him openly at Gad's Hill. If she had kept rooms in the middle of London, likewise the secret would have been out immediately. He had bought her a house, in 1860, at Ampthill Square, near Mornington Crescent, on the edges of Camden Town. It became the family house of the Ternans, and it was not a place where Dickens could visit Nelly as a lover. It was technically bought by her mother and sisters, but Nelly afterwards admitted that Dickens had bought it himself. She herself had lived a twilit existence, in rented accommodation in France and England. When in England, she had lived in obscure places, villages turning into suburbs, such as Slough – easily reachable from London, but essentially dingy and out of the way; and now the village of Peckham in South London, still a village surrounded by trees and fields, but one that was fast being swallowed up by new jerry-built houses, quickly reachable by railway from the capital. The land of small farms and labourers was giving place to the mean dwellings of obscure clerks and shopkeepers, though the row of villas in which Nelly resided, built on spec because Peckham now had a railway station connecting it with ease to London and the Channel ports, was constructed for respectable professional people.

Dickens, for his own convenience, had moved Nelly (and her mother) from Slough to Peckham, whose new-built station, which connected with his own station of Higham in Kent, enabled him to reach her within less than an hour. They gambled on the fact that there was no one likely to encounter them in Peckham, but it was a risk.

On the morning in question – and if that sounds like the beginning of police evidence in court, how pleased Dickens would be, for if there was anything he liked more than the theatre, it was criminal courts, and if there was a profession that delighted

13

him more than the theatrical profession, it was the police! – he had cashed the cheque, and with the £22 in his pocket he had left for Higham Station. 'It's a singler story, sir,' as Inspector Wield says to him in his marvellous 'Three "Detective" Anecdotes'.

He was making his by now habitual journey, by cab and train and cab, to Windsor Lodge, Nelly's house in Peckham. He did it most weeks. He paid her housekeeping money – which would account for the substantial sum of more than £15 missing from his pockets. Some time after this, he collapsed. One does not need to speculate on what brought on his seizure; clearly Dickens, the father of ten (nine living), was a highly sexed man who brought to the life of love the same exuberant hyper-energy that he also brought to love of life: to acting, writing, walking, charitable work and entertaining.

With the help of two maids, the resourceful Nelly Ternan – and her later life shows her to have been highly resourceful – had to act quickly. One maid was dispatched to the post office, to send a telegram to her friend, Georgina Hogarth, Dickens's sister-in-law at Gad's Hill Place, telling her to expect him back and to have a doctor on hand. She then engaged the help of the caretaker of the church opposite Windsor Lodge, and a hackney-cab driver, to heave the semi-conscious body into a large two-horse brougham. Though Dickens was a small man, inert bodies can appear to double in weight.

What happened after that is not quite clear. Nelly and Dickens, in the two-horse carriage, accomplished the journey of some twenty-four miles in the hot afternoon. They entered a house where the smell of cooking permeated. Dinner was being prepared. The next thing we know is that the famous novelist was lying on the dining-room floor, semi-conscious. A doctor had been sent for, and Georgina, his devoted sister-in-law and housekeeper, was kneeling by his side. Exit Nelly, stage left. She respectably departed, though she would come back the next day, when his family had assembled to watch him die. Two accounts state that she was in the room, with the children and Georgina, when Dickens died at ten past six on the evening of Thursday 9 June 1870. She had waited with them as the breath faded, as the awe-inspiring uncertainty of whether he was dead or alive continued.

Stay! Did that eyelid tremble? . . .
No.
Did that nostril twitch?
No . . .
See! A token of life! An indubitable token of life! The spark may smoulder and go out, or it may glow and expand, but see!
. . . Neither Riderhood in this world, nor Riderhood in the other, could draw tears . . . but a striving human soul between the two can do it easily. [*OMF* III 3]

15

There would be many tears for Dickens, as there had been in his fictitious and dramatic renditions of death, but I quote that passage from *Our Mutual Friend* not because he was like Rogue Riderhood in the smallest degree; rather, that he had been to that No Man's Land with the dying, and described what, for so many, is the most poignant part of witnessing the deathbed experience. And the day of his death altogether possessed that betwixt-and-between quality. Indeed, it may well be that the account just given of the circumstances of that death – the journey to Peckham with £15 in his pocket, and the seizure – did not in fact take place. We'll approach this aspect of the mystery later. What we do know is that, when he died on 9 June in the dining room at Gad's (as it was so often known in the Dickens family), Nelly was there. And we know that fifteen pounds, thirteen shillings and ninepence could not, by the punctilious Georgina, be accounted for.

There had been every reason why those who cared for Dickens's reputation with the public – and that emphatically included his mistress Nelly Ternan, his sister-in-law Georgina and Dickens himself – should wish to create a death which, if not entirely fictitious, was at least a good deal more respectable than the one we just sketched out. That Dickens, the greatest English novelist, and celebrant of family innocence, should have collapsed in the bosom of his mistress in Peckham was not to be countenanced. Nelly was perpetually

16

troubled by the possibility of disgrace. She was a 'respectable' person, and she hated the idea of their relationship being known or acknowledged. The great man must die instead at Gad's Hill in the bosom of his family.

Nelly certainly shared Dickens's wish that their relationship should remain a secret. Unlike Dickens's raffish friend Wilkie Collins, who lived openly with his mistress, and unlike George Eliot (Mary Ann Evans), who lived with her lover George Lewes as if she were his wife, Dickens was a 'respectable' man, and Nelly, although – no, because of – belonging to the theatrical profession, regarded herself as a respectable young woman. They had both had to struggle for their respectability. For many Victorians the acting profession was little better than the low world of the demi-monde. For the Dickens family, respectability was something that had had to be invented for themselves, and however much they clung to it, it had kept blowing away from them, like a flimsy umbrella lost in a gale. Dickens's persistent claim to be a gentleman, a claim on which he had implausibly insisted since childhood, was the first of his great fictions. The English never escape their class. It is one of Dickens's great themes. Social insecurity underpins his comedy and his tragedy, and much of his social life. The great rift with Thackeray, for example, was in part caused by the knowledge that Thackeray was a gentleman and Dickens was only a pretend gentleman, admitted to clubs, for example, because he was a genius, not because his father could ever have been on terms with his fellow clubmen's fathers. With the ambivalences of theatre folk, whose people were professionally involved in pretence, he could feel safe.

Five years before, in June 1865, Nelly Ternan had been travelling with Dickens and her mother in a first-class railway carriage, coming back from France. Dickens had made no fewer than four visits to France to see her that spring, almost certainly because Nelly had gone abroad to give birth to a child. Claire Tomalin, who collected so much of the evidence for Nelly's life with the novelist, shows it was possible that she had two children by Dickens. Gladys Storey, whose book *Dickens and Daughter* is about the author's friendship with Dickens's daughter Katey, states categorically that Nelly had a child, 'a son, who died in infancy'. Storey left a note to say that Dickens's daughter told her in February 1923 that a child had been born. And Madeline House, who spent long periods of conversation with Gladys Storey, left it on record that 'I am convinced that Mrs T[ernan] was with Ellen at the time of the baby's birth.'
  Storey, House and Tomalin all assume that Katey was correct in stating that the baby (or babies) died; and yet, as Tomalin wrote, one of the factors that has made people doubt the story is the non-existence of any death certificates,

especially for the second supposed baby, born in Slough. There could be an obvious explanation for this. That is, that the baby (or babies) did not in fact die, but was given up for adoption. Nelly went on to have two healthy children, in her later, respectable existence as a clergyman's wife. Why should it be assumed that Dickens's babies died? Of his own ten known children, although his wife had some miscarriages, only one of the babies who lived to full term died in infancy, a very low statistic by nineteenth-century standards. Neither Nelly nor Dickens had a medical history of parenting weak children.

The month following the supposed birth of a child in France, accompanied by her mother, Nelly was coming back to England with Dickens in June 1865. The public face of their relationship, in so far as it had a public face at all, was that Dickens was a sort of uncle or godfather figure in her life. The train journey was to make clear to Nelly how completely determined Dickens was to protect his reputation and keep their relationship a secret.

As the train hurtled towards Staplehurst in Kent, it hit a bridge, slithered off the track and fell into the river below. The first-class carriage was at the front, so that although the three of them feared the worst, their lives were spared. They were hurled across the carriage. Nelly, fearing they were about to die, said to her mother and Dickens, 'Let us join hands and die friends', a remark that suggests that there had been an estrangement of some kind.

The evident ruction that the words imply gives the lie to Claire Tomalin's notion that Nelly's baby died in France. If the young woman had just lost a baby through death, her mother and Dickens would surely have been solicitous with a woman in grief. 'Let us join hands and die friends' suggests that Nelly had been angry with Dickens – justifiably angry – and is not the likeliest explanation for such anger that she had been forced, for the sake of appearances, to give away her baby for adoption?

They had to be helped out of the carriage through a window. Nelly's arm and neck were injured and she was frail for weeks afterwards, and Dickens would send his manservant, John, to 'take Miss Ellen' tempting foods: a cold chicken, clotted cream and fruit. Aware of his public, and knowing that it would be impossible to conceal the fact that he had been aboard the train that crashed, he left Mrs Ternan and Nelly to be cared for by the paramedics while he went to offer succour to the second-class passengers. 'I was in the carriage that did not go over, but went off the line, and hung over the bridge in an inexplicable manner. No words can describe the scene,' he would write. Even more revealing (of his character, but unrevealing of the facts of the case) was his preface to *Our Mutual Friend*, the novel he was writing at the time of the accident, the manuscript of which he had in his luggage.

On Friday the ninth of June in the present year Mr and Mrs Boffin (in their manuscript dress of receiving Mr and Mrs Lammle at breakfast) were on the South-Eastern Railway with me, in a terribly destructive accident. When I had done what I could to help others, I climbed back into my carriage – nearly turned over a viaduct, and caught aslant upon the turn – to extricate the worthy couple. They were much soiled, but otherwise unhurt. The same happy result attended Miss Bella Wilfer on her wedding-day and Mr Riderhood inspecting Bradley Headstone's red neckerchief as he lay asleep. I remember with devout thankfulness that I can never be much nearer parting company with my readers for ever, than I was then, until there shall be written against my life the two words with which I have this day closed this book – THE END.

Clearly, Dickens was not going to share with his devoted public the knowledge that, at the time of the Staplehurst railway crash, he had been travelling with a much younger mistress who had borne his child. Nevertheless, given that this *was* what he had been doing – he was certainly with Nelly, whatever truth there is in the story of her having had his babies – there is something more than arch about his speaking about the characters in *Our Mutual Friend* as having been 'on the South-Eastern Railway with me'. It is by no means clear, in the life of a novelist, who are the more 'real': the imagined characters in the books or those who share the supposedly real life of the writer. As we shall discover, the fictions of Dickens, which came from so deep a part of himself, were also capable of swallowing him up, so that in a sense he was absorbed into them. The majority of us have a life that ends in death; Dickens was living a story, whose conclusion was – to quote again from that preface to *Our Mutual Friend* – 'the two words with which I have this day closed this book – THE END'.

After Dickens died, Nelly went to live in Oxford with her mother and sisters, in a house on the Banbury Road just south of the present-day St Hugh's College, where for seven years I used to teach. (Maria the Infant Phenomenon had married an Oxford brewer.)

I often used to think of the Ternans as I cycled past the villa in the late 1970s. The fantasy question would flit in and out of my brain: what would it have been like to teach Nelly? She was the same age, wasn't she, when she lived in that house as the undergraduates with whom I was about to read medieval poetry. Would I have fallen secretly in love with her, as Dickens did, or would she have been one of the pleasant, hard-working majority whose names and personalities one forgot the next year when a new batch of students arrived, clutching Sweet's *Anglo-Saxon Primer*? . . . Nelly at eighteen. But no! She was not, of course, the age of most of my students. Brilliant, loveable Nelly! She had cunningly changed and concealed her age. In *The Life of Charles Dickens* by John Forster, the Will of Charles Dickens is printed as an appendix. After revoking all former wills and codicils and declaring this to be his last Will and Testament, Dickens, with a candour and bravura that had been lacking in life, began: 'I give the sum of £1,000 free of legacy duty to Miss Ellen Lawless Ternan, late of Houghton Place, Ampthill Square, in the county of Middlesex.'

With an inventiveness to match his own, Nelly, who was by now more than thirty, decided to chop a decade or so off her age. Six years later she would marry one of the undergraduates who had visited her mother's house in Oxford, George Wharton Robinson, who had by then become a clergyman. He was twelve years younger than she was, so he had only been eighteen or so when he met the thirty-year-old Nelly. By the time of the 1881 census, she had reduced her age still further, declaring herself to be twenty-eight, when in fact she was forty-two. By now the respectable wife of a clerical schoolmaster, she had left behind the invisible Nelly of Windsor Lodge, Peckham – a figure of the 1860s. Those years had been discarded like a novel, unopened for years. As the years rolled by, she grew ever younger and more respectable.

They had been married, she and Mr Robinson, at St Mary Abbots Church in Kensington. White-clad, virginal Nelly, with flowers in her hair, was by now thirty-seven to her husband's twenty-three. They honeymooned in Italy, and returned to England to run a school in Margate. They had two children, Geoffrey, born in 1879, and Gladys, born in 1884. Nelly helped her husband to run the school, organizing concerts and plays and reading aloud from her favourite novels: *David Copperfield*, *The Old Curiosity Shop*, *A Tale of Two Cities*, *Nicholas Nickleby*, *Bleak House*. She retained her friendships with Georgina Hogarth and Dickens's eldest daughter Mary (Mamie), neither of whom betrayed the secret of her true age. In 1877 Georgina came to have a holiday in Margate and presented the prizes at the school run by Mr Robinson, and in 1882 she had a holiday with Nelly and Mamie.

Nelly Robinson was widowed in 1910 and lived until April 1914, nursed by her son Geoffrey, who subsequently fought a gallant war and remained in the army until 1920, fighting in Persia with Dunster-force. It was only after her death, going through his mother's papers, that he began to piece together the truth. He was horrified by what he discovered and destroyed as many of his mother's letters and papers as he could find. He lived until 1959.

★ ★ ★

A generation ago, John Lucas wrote a book called *The Melancholy Man: A Study of Dickens's Novels.* He took his title from Immanuel Kant, who defined a Melancholy Man as one who:

> is little concerned with the judgements of others, with their opinion of what is good or true; he relies purely on his own insight . . . He regards changes of fashion with indifference and their glitter with contempt . . . He has a lofty sense of the dignity of human nature. He esteems himself and regards man as a creature deserving of respect. He suffers no abject subservience and breathes the noble air of freedom. To him all chains are abhorrent, from the gilded fetters worn at court to the heavy irons of the galley slave.

Lucas's study of the novels was deserving of its status as one of the most perceptive of its time. The notion of Dickens, however, as a man who was not concerned with the judgements of others is not borne out by what we know. In particular in relation to his marriage and his sexual and romantic life, he was intensely occupied not merely with concealment, which is perfectly understandable, but with subterfuge and falsification.

It is easy to mock the desire to be respectable, just as it is easy to label as hypocrites those who wish to keep up appearances. It would be less

25

easy to have been born near the bottom of the heap in the cruel nineteenth century. Charles and Nelly had both gazed into the abyss. The fates of their two fathers could never be forgotten.

Thomas Ternan, one of nineteen children, was the son of a Dublin grocer. Thomas became an actor in England. Even had he aspired, in his dreams, to enter one of the professions, that would have been impossible. He was a Catholic, and in those days the Inns of Court and the universities were reserved for members of the Established Church. A lot of actors, in those Penal Times, were Catholics, from the great Mrs Siddons and her Kemble brothers downwards. Thomas Ternan came to England, joined a troupe of actors in Kent on the Rochester circuit and married a fellow actor, Fanny Jarman, who also came from an Irish theatrical tradition. She was a cut above him, socially and in skill, having played Desdemona to Edmund Kean's Othello, Ophelia to Charles Kemble's Hamlet and having been in her way a minor star. But both Nelly's parents had known the kind of rough-and-tumble life on the road, which we find in the life of Codlin and Short in *The Old Curiosity Shop*, in the Crummles troupe in *Nickleby* and in Jingle, the strolling player in *Pickwick*.

Dickens responded to all this so strongly because, although his parents had not been actors, it was the profession he had always dreamed of following. Pretending to be someone else for a living, being constantly on the road, belonging nowhere – these were all activities he had pursued *faute de mieux*. Thomas Ternan had become an actor-manager in the North of England, with many periods of separation from his wife: that was what the profession demanded – demands – of those who follow it. The family united in Newcastle upon Tyne for the Christmas of 1844. That was the season Maria played Mamilius in *The Winter's Tale* and Fanny performed a duet with her in a melodrama. Shortly thereafter, however, their father became severely ill. The next that was heard of him, he was in London and had been taken to the asylum at Bethnal Green, suffering from 'General Paralysis of the Insane'. He would almost certainly have been kept in chains until, incontinent and skinny, he was too weak to require constraint. He would have been locked up and simply left to die. Which he did when Nelly was only six.

John Dickens, the novelist's father, likewise spent a crucial period locked up – during a (or, rather, *the*) crucial period of Charles Dickens's childhood. We shall investigate all this in the next chapter. Suffice to say here that Charles, like Nelly, had a father who had fallen foul of the nineteenth century in all its monstrous pitilessness. He had been locked up in consequence. Of course, for the Victorians it was a crime to be a thief or a murderer; but also for the Victorians, who bought thousands of copies of Samuel Smiles's *Self-Help* and who believed that they were an Island Empire

27

that had pulled itself up by its own boot-straps, the worst crime was to be a failure. It was the century that reversed the Sermon on the Mount. Cursed were the meek. Cursed were the poor in spirit. Cursed were the merciful.

The respectable professions from which circumstance excluded the parents of Charles and of Nelly were instruments of monstrous cruelty. Dickens's novels dwell repeatedly on the grotesque blundering unkindness of the law. All Victorians knew about it. The other great profession, that of medicine, was something even more to be dreaded. In 1851, when, as usual, Charles Dickens was doing twenty different things at once – tending a sick wife in Malvern (she was suffering from giddiness, occasional loss of eyesight and serious depression, none of which was cured by the quack-water cure recommended by the doctors), preparing a play, *Not So Bad As We Seem*, which Queen Victoria had expressed the desire to see, and editing his weekly *Household Words* – he heard the news that his father was grievously ill. John Dickens was then in his mid-sixties. Ever since he was a young man he had suffered from a urinary complaint, which he had never sufficiently addressed, still less (spendthrift that he was) been in a position to cure. Charles Dickens had rushed back to London from Malvern to make the speech at the annual dinner of the General Theatrical Fund in Covent Garden, a charity devoted to indigent actors. At the same time, in his own house in

Devonshire Terrace, Regent's Park, he had a dying baby – little Dora. In one week he would lose his youngest child and the father who begat him.

When Dickens arrived at Keppel Street in Bloomsbury (just behind the British Museum) it was to see his father, who was in delirious agony.

The doctor was summoned, 'who instantly performed (without chloroform) the most terrible operation known in surgery, as the only chance of saving him'. This involved cutting a vagina-like incision between the anus and the scrotum and unsexing the patient. 'He bore it', wrote Dickens, 'with astonishing fortitude, and I saw him directly afterwards – in his room, a slaughterhouse of blood.' A few days later, when Dickens visited at eleven o'clock at night and sat beside the unconscious figure, 'he died – O so quietly'.

His mother's presence at this scene is scarcely mentioned. Nor is the fact that, present at the death, were Dickens's two brothers Alfred and Augustus, his sister Letitia and her husband Henry Austin. When John Dickens died, Charles did take his mother in his arms and weep, but by the time he described the scene to his biographer, it was a duet, of him and his father alone. For Dickens, it was not the tragedy of a woman losing her husband, or of a family of siblings losing their father. It was the tragedy of severance from a 'zealous, useful and cheerful spirit', as his Micawber-father had become. Dickens had been deeply affected – and, in the middle of so much business, he had visited his father in his affliction. When his mother finally died in 1863, he had not visited her for months.

Dickens's complex relationships with his mother and father were the seedbed of all his art. As far as his relationship with John Dickens is concerned, we watch a huge shift in the artistic problems that Charles was addressing and solving as his imagination came to terms with life-experience.

Dickens did not blame his father for the childhood traumas. It was the mother who bore all the weight of that cruel story. John Dickens remained, for the novelist, the jolly, jokey figure with whom, in early childhood, Charles had enjoyed ramblings in the marsh country along the Medway, and who, in the squalid London houses where they lodged, and from whose rent-collectors they flitted, kept him amused with recitations, imitations and jokes. The two great creations to emerge from the Charles–John Dickens dynamic were Micawber and Dorrit. In *David Copperfield*, the alternative-autobiography composed while John Dickens was still alive, Dickens made his father a figure of benign burlesque. Mr Micawber is the Clown of the old harlequinade. In the original pantomimes, Clown was the speaking part in what was often a mime show and, like all the Dickensian figures who correspond to Clown, Micawber is gifted with the exhilarating power of utterance – "'Now, welcome poverty!" cried Mr Micawber, shedding tears. "Welcome misery, welcome houselessness, welcome hunger, rags, tempest, and beggary! Mutual confidence will sustain us to the end!'" [*DC* 52] Just as Micawber changes his character entirely and becomes a successful farmer and administrator in Australia, so John Dickens after his death – he who had been so conspicuously inept as a clerk and so undistinguished as a hack journalist – was saluted by his son as 'one of the most efficient and respected members of the Press'.

Pantomime, more than serious drama, was the template for Dickens's fiction in the earlier half of his writing life. How an audience responds to comedy and pantomime was central to Dickens's life-view. Grimaldi the Clown, whom John Dickens took his children to see, and whose biography Charles Dickens reworked after writing *Pickwick,* was one of the greatest exponents of the *commedia dell'arte.*

Behind the traditional Christmas pantomime may be seen, even in the debased form in which it is performed in Britain today, a dramatic arche-type which offers much the same *katharsis* that Aristotle sought in Tragedy. The inadequacy of the parents; the frustration of the young lovers; the poverty of the unsympathetic father, and his attempt to force the heroine to marry money against her will; the machinations of the Yellow Dwarf or the Demon King; while the transves-tite Dame or Widow Twanky or Mother Goose projects, and redeems, the eternal dread of Mother. In these garish projections, the audience confronts comic versions of their own fears and griefs – the impossibility of finding domestic happiness in the place where we are programmed to seek it: in the family; the emotional frustrations and financial anxieties of life. It is a world, of course, where misfortune, rather than being something to weep over, is of necessity projected as comic.

Dickens himself, both in his definitive and revealing essay 'The Pantomime of Life', and in a later article for *Household Words* called 'A Curious Dance Round a Curious Tree', made the point trenchantly – that pantomime was a world:

> where a man may tumble into the broken ice, or dive into the kitchen fire, and only be the droller for the accident; where babies may be knocked about and sat upon, or choked with gravy spoons, in the process of feeding, and yet no Coroner be wanted, nor anybody made uncomfortable; where workmen may fall from the top of a house to the bottom, or even from the bottom of a house to the top, and sustain no injury to the brain, need no hospital, leave no young children; where every one, in short, is so superior to all the accidents of life, though encountering them at every turn, that I suspect this to be the secret (though many persons may not present it

to themselves) of the general enjoyment which an audience of vulnerable spectators, liable to pain and sorrow, find in this class of entertainment.

In the great English tragic tradition of the Elizabethan stage, the Clown had his finest manifestation in *King Lear*, the ultimate drama of fathers and children, in which the mad Lear, on the Heath, gathers around him the alternative family, consisting of Edgar disguised as a crazy beggar man, Poor Tom, the loyal Kent and Fool. Most of us, when we first read or see *King Lear*, realize that we have seen the story acted out before – at Christmas, with Cinderella and her Ugly Sisters foreshadowing Cordelia, Goneril and Regan. In the alternative fairy-tale universe of the panto, the inadequate parent – the Lear-like character – is usually a relatively minor figure, Baron Hard-up, as it were, in *Cinderella*, whereas the Clown could sometimes be the dominant figure. This was especially true, in the old harlequinade, if Clown were played by a great figure such as Joseph Grimaldi – later in the century by Dan Leno and in the twentieth century Charlie Chaplin, the conscious heir of this tradition, who carried it into motion pictures.

In *David Copperfield*, Dickens's own favourite among the novels, he recast his own autobiography as a harlequinade. When the Brothers Grimm, whose collection of German fairy stories was published in the year of Dickens's birth, began their researches, they were appalled to discover how many of the folktales related to incest, or to parents in one way or another neglecting, brutalizing or mismanaging their children; so in the published version, the wicked mothers were converted into wicked stepmothers. When he came to write *Copperfield*, one of the central pantomime/fairy-tale themes – that of faulty parents betraying, through weakness or wickedness, their children – was neutralized by making David Copperfield pretty quickly into an orphan. His father is dead before the story starts, and once she has married Murdstone, David's mother has no further role to play and can be allowed conveniently to die. The real John Dickens, whose misfortunes caused the infant Charles so much torment, was transmogrified kindly into a benign father-substitute, a Pantaloon Clown in the figure of Micawber.

After the death of John Dickens in 1851, these burlesque examples no longer worked, for Dickens, as a template for experience. The Micawbers undergo the same horrors that the Dickenses underwent, but they are 'only the droller for the accident'. After he had been ripped by the surgeon and his bedroom had become 'a slaughterhouse of blood', John Dickens could no longer be the clownish Micawber. His life could not be milked for comedy; but then again, nor need his feelings be spared. He could never again read his son's novels and see burlesque versions of himself, pantomimic enactments of his own humiliating inability to cope with life. So a new layer of truth could be unpeeled. In the novel that Charles Dickens was writing in the year before he met Nelly Ternan – *Little Dorrit* – the gloves were off. The full ghastliness of his parents' improvidence, and its consequences – the Marshalsea Prison and abject humiliation – were able to be examined with a cold eye.

If, in his depiction of Mr Dorrit in the Marshalsea, Dickens penetrated a much deeper place than when he had created Mr Micawber, how much more does that novel reveal about the depth of his mother-hatred. In that dark, joyless room of Mrs Clennam – mother of the hero – something extraordinary is going on. It is like the drug-like fantasy world entered by sadomasochists who implore women to enchain them, whip and torture them. It is not, of course, a rational request. It comes from the deepest needs of mother-hate. From this stems the legend of Medusa who turns men to stone, of Circe turning them to pigs. Flintwinch, the horrible old family retainer, is not Mrs Clennam's son, so he can say to her, 'I have been faithful to you, and useful to you, and I am attached to you. But I can't consent, and I won't consent, and I never did consent, and I never will consent to be lost in you. Swallow up everything else, and welcome. The peculiarity of my temper is, ma'am, that I won't be swallowed up alive.' [*LD* I 15] We are close here to thoughts of mother spiders that devour their young and bite off the genitalia of their male offspring; to Picasso's innumerable representations of women with serrated mouths and genitalia-like lobster claws, who could not kiss or copulate with a man without mutilating him. These come to mind in Mrs Clennam's dark room as we watch her toying with her morning tray of oysters and reading aloud from the more blood-curdling passages of the Scriptures.

In the expression of his own mother-hate, Dickens began with the fluttery, silly figure of Mrs Nickleby. In *Little Dorrit*, however, he reached the depths of the truth. And in 1857, when he had reached that truth, he realized that Arthur Clennam – that is, himself – needed a companion to rescue him from his mother. Kate Dickens was actually his wife, but having borne ten children, lost her looks and become a fat wretch of misery worn down by his bullying; she had taken the place, in his imaginative life, of the mother he could not forgive for her treatment of him in childhood. She had become a hate object. The only way of escape was to find a nymph-dream, a little girl-woman who could never turn out to be his mutilant-abusive mother in disguise. A Little Dorrit. He needed Nelly, had invented her, even before he met her in Manchester during *The Frozen Deep*.

'Do you happen to know, Mrs Clennam, where she lives?'

'No.'

'Would you, now, would you like to know?'

'If I cared to know, I should know already.'

[*LD* I 15]

Mrs Clennam here deflects the questioners of the nineteenth century of whom she knew nothing, but whom her intelligence can intuitively sense lurking in the shadows, waiting, like Jeremiah Flintwinch, to pounce. Herr Marx is waiting to tell her that her accumulation of wealth is ill-gotten gains, and Herr Doktor Freud is trying to tell her what she has done to Arthur. The point is only further emphasized when we realize that she is not, actually, Arthur's mother at all. The two 'truths' that these powerful, intellectual German-speaking sages would so earnestly and so destructively profess to unearth – namely, that the whole capitalist dream was based on exploitation, and that at the heart of supposedly blissful family life there lay a core not of love, but of hate and power-games – these were things which, if Mrs Clennam cared to know, she should know already. How is life tolerable in such a society? By pursuing the art of 'How Not to Do It', and by taking the view that the misery of things is 'Nobody's Fault'. If these demons were unearthed and confronted, they would devour us, and so, like Flintwinch, we do not let them. Yet, as in Affery's dreams, the novel tells us that one of these days the whole edifice – of respectability, and family structure, and capitalism – is going to come tumbling down. Dickens achieved few more brilliant things than *Little Dorrit*.

And the fact that he was writing *Little Dorrit* in the period immediately before the *coup de foudre* that was his encounter with Nelly says much. Panto or burlesque could no longer provide the consolations they had been offering since childhood. Dickens was never again going to be able to produce sunlit figures like Pickwick or Micawber. Even dramatics themselves were not going to be effective in holding reality at bay, or transforming it. When she became deeply involved with Dickens, Nelly herself would give up the stage. He, for his part, would continue to perform, but, more and more, in the solo role of himself, enacting scenes from the novels in his public readings. Yet, as we shall see, the more he involved himself in these enactments, and the more his later fiction darkened and enveloped him, the less clear it became whether they were his creation or whether he had become the prisoner of his own inventions.

Amateur novelists, those who believe that everyone somehow has 'a novel in them', tend, when they write their one or two novels, to put down their own experiences, or what they artlessly believe to have been their experiences, and simply change the names of characters, making the figure who represents themselves rather more clever, attractive or adventurous than was the case in real life; or, for ironists, more accident-prone, more foolish and so on. Habitual novelists, however – especially those who take the novel to the height of an artform – are in a very different situation. They might very often 'use' real life. Tolstoy's Bald Hills is indistinguishable from the house where he grew up, and all the characters in the opening chapters of *War and Peace* were drawn directly from life, though as the novel progresses, this was less and less the case and they developed that mysterious 'life of their own' which seems to be the alchemical effect of all great imagination.

Tolstoy, however, came to hate the art of fiction, perhaps for the very simple reason that he could observe the process at work which we observe in, for example, Dickens. The habit of mind that allows a great imagination to transform experience into a novel, the mimetic arts that it exercises, the processes of make-believe that it requires, are often stronger than the parts of the writer's personality that are exercised in their everyday lives, their relationships with their families, and so forth. One of the most conspicuously hilarious examples of this was given in Evelyn Waugh's *The Ordeal of Gilbert Pinfold*, in which the novelist, for the time being, driven insane by a mistaken admixture of a sleeping draught and copious quantities of alcohol, is imprisoned in his own creative self. He is a caricature. His face has become an irremovable carapace.

Dickens, as an actor and as a novelist, and as a man, was a man of masks, who probably never revealed himself to anyone; quite conceivably, he did not reveal himself to himself. As time went by, and in particular as he became caught up not merely in writing, but in performing his novels in public readings, he was, in effect, as much a fictional character as Bill Sikes or Mrs Gamp.

'From these garish lights, I now vanish for evermore,' Dickens had said at what was to be his last public reading from his novels. In the nineteenth-century theatre the footlights were garish indeed, a row of smoking oil – later gas – lamps, melting the greasepaint of the players on the one side, half blinding those in the front rows of the audience on the other.

Dickens wanted to live on both sides of this garish, overheated row. He had grown up stage-struck. When he was seven, his mother and father took him up to London to see the Christmas pantomime, and he had been entranced by the make-up of the clowns, their thick white face-paint, and their appetite for sausages. Harlequin and Pantaloon held him in raptures, and he 'thought that to marry a Columbine would be to attain the highest pitch of all human felicity!' A little later, a troupe of them had visited Chatham, where his improvident father was working as a naval clerk, and the child had stared with wonder at the little boys 'with frills as white as they could be washed', smelling of sawdust and orange peel, and accompanied by 'a crafty magician holding a young lady in bondage'. Even after he had begun to enjoy great success as a writer, after the publication of *Pickwick*, and in the middle of writing *Oliver Twist*, Dickens, at a publisher's request, took on the task of revising a clumsily written biography of the great clown Grimaldi, whom he had seen perform at the Theatre Royal, Chatham. Dickens, very appropriately, dictated his revisions to his father, out of charity – for John Dickens was everlastingly on the point of tumbling into debt. Dickens wrote to his friend John Forster, 'Seventeen hundred Grimaldis have already been sold, and the demand increases daily!!!!!!!!!!!!!!!!!!!!!!'

In addition to pantomime and burlesque, Dickens had also seen mainstream, serious theatre as a child, and was among those lucky enough to have witnessed Edmund Kean and Charles Mathews's interpretations of the great Shakespearean roles. As a schoolboy in London, and as an aspirant journalist, he devoted every available evening to attending the theatre. In those days only theatres with a licence could produce spoken drama, but there were many who added songs to the performance, and cobbled together 'burlettas'. He also haunted 'private theatres' where amateurs performed. Mr Wopsle's Hamlet was no fantasy.

In *Sketches by Boz*, Dickens tells how 'dirty boys, low copying-clerks, in attorney's offices' and 'capacious-headed youths from city-counting-houses' trod the boards under stage names – 'Belville, Melville, Treville, Berkeley, Randolph, Byron, St Clair'. [*SB* 13, 'Private Theatres']

The fascination of being somebody else: that was what the theatre offered, whether you were a 'low clerk' pretending to be Macbeth or a professional actor such as Mr Vincent Crummles, or whether you were sitting in the audience night after night. It was only by the time of his marriage, when he needed the regular income which writing had begun to provide, that Dickens appears finally to have given up the hope of an actual career on the stage. And the desire to write, and perform in, plays never left him. In the year he was writing *Pickwick*, he was offered £30 for a farce in two acts called *The Strange Gentleman*, which was a stage adaptation of one of the *Sketches by Boz* called 'The Great Winglebury Duel'. It was produced at St James's Theatre. A year or so later he wrote *The Lamplighter*, which he hoped would be acted by William Macready, though nothing came of this. As soon as he found himself with surplus cash, having moved into 48 Doughty Street – just north of Gray's Inn – with his wife and burgeoning family, Dickens had begun to donate to theatrical charities – the Theatrical Fund, the Artists' Benevolent Fund and the Drury Lane Theatre Fund – and, of course, as well as writing for the theatre, attending the theatre and supporting the impoverished members of the acting profession, he was himself an enthusiastic actor.

However busy he was meeting deadlines as a novelist or a journalist, Dickens nearly always had some theatrical project on the go. In 1845, for example, he hired a private theatre in Dean Street, Soho, where Frances Kelly, a retired actress, ran a theatre school. Here he, his future biographer John Forster, Mark Lemon, the editor of *Punch*, and other friends enacted Ben Jonson's *Every Man in His Humour*. Dickens commissioned the scene painting and oversaw the making of the costumes, which were based on seventeenth-century pictures. 'I am half dead with managerial work – and with actual work in shirt sleeves; with a dirty face, a hammer and a bag of nails.' They assembled an impressive audience – Tennyson, the Duke of Devonshire, Count d'Orsay, Macready. Not everyone was impressed – Carlyle wrote of 'poor little Dickens, all painted in black and red, and affecting the voice of a man of six feet'. But others were less scornful. One guest remembered, 'He literally floated in braggadocio. His air of supreme conceit and frothy pomp in the earlier scenes came out with prodigious force in contrast with the subsequent humiliation.' (Dickens was playing Bobadil.)

Another production at Miss Kelly's theatre was *The Merry Wives of Windsor* with George Lewes,

Augustus Egg and George Cruikshank in the cast. (Carlyle was more impressed by this performance – 'Plaudite, Plaudite!') Queen Victoria and Prince Albert themselves saw Dickens's benefit repeat performance of *Every Man in His Humour*. They also attended a performance of his own comedy *Not So Bad as We Seem*, some three weeks before the opening of the Great Exhibition in 1851.

By 1857, when the Dickens family were enduring a painfully long visit from Hans Christian Andersen, Dickens put on the play on which he had collaborated with Wilkie Collins, *The Frozen Deep*. When it was staged in London, it drew perhaps the most star-studded of all Dickens's audiences, with the Duke of Somerset supplying hothouse flowers. The Queen not only enjoyed the melodrama, but also stayed behind to see the farce that was enacted after the interval, and sent to Dickens that she wanted to meet him. He declined, saying that he could not be presented to his sovereign in the costume of a farceur. She replied saying that the costume could not be 'as ridiculous as that', but he still declined.

Such was the success of *The Frozen Deep* before privately invited audiences in London that it was decided to take it to a commercial theatre in the provinces. They took the Free Trade Hall in Manchester towards the end of August 1857, and had audiences of more than 3,000. Speaking of Dickens's performance in Manchester, Wilkie Collins recorded, 'The trite phrase is the true phrase to describe that magnificent piece of acting. He literally electrified the audience.' Dickens himself spoke of 'rending the very heart out of my body' as he enacted the main role.

The move from an amateur to a professional stage had required an adjustment to the cast. His daughters Mamie and Katey, and the other female members of the cast, had to be replaced with professional actresses. Thus it came about that the Ternans entered Dickens's life.

It is impossible to say on which side of the garish lights the thunderclap took place, but this production of *The Frozen Deep* was to change Charles Dickens's life. The melodrama of existence was to soar into a new act. 'If you make believe very much, it's quite nice,' the Marchioness said to Dick Swiveller, telling him that if he put pieces of orange peel into cold water he could make-believe it was wine. [*OCS* 64] Make-believe becomes its own redemptive Marriage Feast at Cana.

Dickens had been, up to this point in his life, an artist without parallel in the history of literature, a modernistic novelist who took the novel into the direction of burlesque and pantomime. Like Ben Jonson (as formative a role model, really, for Dickens, as Shakespeare), his technique was to crowd his stage with 'characters'. His own life-story had been plundered freely – more, perhaps, than we shall ever know, because (as in the case of Ruth Richardson recently discovering that the

45

infant Dickens grew up almost next door to the Cleveland Street Workhouse) new biographical research is always uncovering the ways in which 'real life' fed into the fiction, the ways in which he hopped to and fro from either side of the footlights. But these wonderful Sketches and Episodes, sewn together haphazardly as serial novels, had lacked an underlying unity. Then in 1849, when he was thirty-seven, had come *David Copperfield*, a sort of spoof autobiography, which had knit together experience. There had followed three novels of overpowering greatness, *Bleak House*, *Hard Times* and *Little Dorrit*. As we have suggested, in *Little Dorrit* Dickens had revisited painful areas of his childhood experience, and his consciousness of family-membership. Micawber cannot be crushed. He bobs up like a cork whenever the waves engulf him, and in the end he is transported – one might almost say translated – to Australia where, against all probability, he becomes a successful colonial administrator. After the experience of watching his father die in the 'slaughterhouse' of Keppel Street, Dickens could not project his experiences in anything like so sunny a way. Dorrit is a much crueller portrait of his father than Micawber. Dorrit is selfish, manipulative, pretentious and, much of the time, odious. But unlike the uncrushable Micawber, he is defeated. Even if eventually, in obedience to the requirements of the creaking plot, he is found not to be a debtor after all, and is released in style from the

Marshalsea, Mr Dorrit is a broken man. Dickens saw the debtor as Pushkin saw the little man crushed by the Bronze Horseman, the vast statue of Peter the Great against whom the 'little man' does not stand a chance: a figure who could never be strong enough against the system.

Dickens himself was the passionate champion of the small person against the system, both in his fiction and in his various charitable endeavours. He had ceased to be a small person. He was a man of consequence. The man who was now laid out, gasping, on the carpet of the dining room at Gad's Hill was one of the great men of the age, his company sought out by the Queen herself, his name familiar in everyone's mouth as a Household Word indeed.

That was not how it felt inside. His childhood self was his secret sharer, his hidden stowaway, his constant companion throughout the triumphs of his adult existence.

Mr Dorrit, when he became confused at the public dinner in Italy, began to blurt out his unmentionable past, and to speak as if he were still in the Marshalsea Prison. This is one of the most excruciating scenes in literature, and the creation of a man who, figuratively, was in constant danger of exposing his weaknesses. Hence the need, in the truly great artist, to guard his divided self, or selves. The healthy soul is integrated, at one. He has no need for subterfuge or pretence. He is Joe Gargery, able, with such devastating truthfulness, to explain to Pip why they will no longer be suitable companions in the future: "'Pip", said Joe, appearing a little hurried and troubled, "there has been larks. And, dear sir, what have been betwixt us – have been.'" [*GE* 57]

Dickens was many personae, wore many masks and was a divided, sick soul, as far from Joe Gargery as it was possible to be. Those who lead the divided life find comfort in formalizing these divisions. Hence the relationship with Nelly. She left no record of it, or of how it felt to be his secret, though she did murmur in later life that she had 'often' been to Gad's Hill, and it may be that they were together much more than has sometimes been supposed.

There is a danger, among those who interest themselves in Dickens's 'secret' or 'private' life, that one is doing no more than engaging in tittle-tattle. That a Victorian man in his forties took a mistress, and kept her existence a secret from the world, is surely neither here nor there.

But Dickens was more than just a Victorian man. He was one of the greatest artists who ever chose to write in the English language. And central to that art, pivotal, is the division of self. It was a divided self who created the alternative comic universe that is 'The Dickens World'. Only a sick soul, or a divided self – however one describes it – could have created these books. Dickens the human being, like many in an unhappy relationship, looked for another person to provide him with love. Dickens the artist, a magpie beadily seizing on a trinket that caught the sunlight, needed something in his life that would formalize the division of his imaginative existence. His daughter Katey – as we shall see – looked back, horrified at the behaviour of herself and her siblings in allowing Dickens to smash up the family and send his wife into exile. He 'didn't give a damn about any of us'. This is true, but his was more than the simple, selfish old story of someone committing adultery, and more than the cliché of the bored man having a middle-aged crisis and taking up with a much younger woman, though it is obviously both those things. It is also the story of an artist whose art depended on having a divided self, depended on having a double life.

Acting, the theatre, burlesque, pantomime, they were all of vital importance to Dickens's art, but his art was not here. It was in the novel that he soared to his great heights, in the novel that he touched millions of human hearts. In the alternative-universe autobiography *David Copperfield*, he offered readers what was clearly meant as a piece of his own, real autobiography, and was also in the nature of a novelist's manifesto. The context is this. David has lost his mother's love to her new husband, Mr Murdstone, who is cruel and unfeeling. As he felt 'more and more shut out and alienated from my mother' [*DC* 4], he retreated into reading fiction and then – hence the novel we find in our hands as we read about it – into the writing of it.

When he came to write novels, there is one aspect of Dickens's genius that must trouble even his most ardent admirers: namely, his depiction of women, and his imaginative need to desex them, to eviscerate them sexually, emotionally, imaginatively.

The supposed reason for British Victorian novels being sex-free zones is that middle-class fathers and mothers liked to read them aloud in the bosom of their family, and it was clearly undesirable for graphic depictions of sexual love, such as you might find in Balzac, to corrupt the innocent young hearers. This might or might not have been the case, but it does not really address what for some readers is the problem of Dickens and the women. His great contemporary, Thackeray, for example, wrote his masterpiece *Vanity Fair* with a woman, Becky Sharp, as the most lively and beguilingly wicked central intelligence. Dickens, it could be answered, narrated half of one of his masterpieces, *Bleak House*, in the voice of Esther Summerson, but this only highlights what for some readers is the problem. Esther is only a half-presence on the page. Her virtues of submissiveness and forbearance are frankly tedious, and very often her 'voice', which is a simpering one, is mercifully replaced by Dickens's own, when he forgets to 'be' Esther. As for Victorian novels not dealing with real-life women,

50

or with sexual matters, this is simply not true. Consider the novels of George Eliot, where, for example, the disastrous marriage of Dorothea Brooke to Mr Casaubon in *Middlemarch*, while not being physically graphic in the manner of, say, D. H. Lawrence, is realistically analysed, as are the marriages of the other pairs in the book. Anthony Trollope, in every way a lesser novelist than George Eliot or Dickens or Thackeray, nevertheless has women who are recognizably people with sexual feelings and independence of mind.

Dickens's novels pulsate with sexual feeling – we shall be discussing this later – but it is the feelings of the author, rather than the feelings of, say, Kate Nickleby, Dora Copperfield, Agnes Wickfield, Esther Summerson and the gallery of submissive, sexless-seeming wifelets and nymphs and half-child-brides, who tiptoe through his pages.

The generalization needs to checked. It is only in a respectable middle-class setting that the women are so wet. We do find women with profound sexual feelings in Dickens's pages: Nancy, the prostitute in *Oliver Twist*; Miss Wade, the overpowering lesbian in *Little Dorrit*, who elopes with 'Tattycoram'; Bella Wilfer, in *Our Mutual Friend*. For the most part, however, when we are aware of women as sexual beings, it is in their sense of emotional frustration – Edith Dombey, or Mrs Joe Gargery, who, one assumes, is both frustrated in her relationship with the child-like blacksmith and is undergoing the menopause.

I write 'one assumes', but what one is less sure of – and *this* is the problem of Dickens, for some readers – is that we cannot be sure that Dickens himself understands these things, or, if he understood them, whether he found them even remotely sympathetic. Whereas Joe grows in the course of the book and becomes a character we truly admire, Mrs Joe remains a joke harridan, a furious pantomime dame wielding the cane with which she intends to berate her younger brother.

Katey Collins said her father did not understand women – whatever that means. The fiction is full of women, many of whom are realistically observed, sometimes with sympathy, sometimes not. What we scarcely find in the novels is either the depiction of a successful, fulfilled relationship between the sexes or, with the possible exception of the empathy between the 'china doll' and Mr Crisparkle in *The Mystery of Edwin Drood*, an entirely satisfactory relationship between a mother and a son.

This must be admitted, even by the most ardent Dickensian, as a fault in our hero. One of his finest, cruellest comic creations is Mrs Skewton in *Dombey and Son*, the seventy-year-old who dresses as if she is twenty-seven. 'It was a tremendous sight to see this old woman in her finery leering and mincing at Death, and playing off her youthful tricks upon him.' [*DS* 37] Dickens calls her Cleopatra, a good joke, but one that, by reminding us of the Cleopatra in Shakespeare, only recalls the absence in these novels of any woman of the depth, range and realism of the Shakespearean Egyptian queen. And where in Dickens is a Rosalind, or a Juliet, or a Hermione, or a Portia, or a Beatrice, or even, to choose a play in which Dickens himself acted, a Mistress Page and Mistress Ford? There are some memorable harridan mothers – such as Mrs Clennam – to set beside Volumnia, but they are drawn with infinitely less sympathy. And what animates them is the relationship of their male victims to the female caricature.

One thinks of this when one contemplates the wonderful gallery of Dickensian 'characters'. In the Dickens Museum at 48 Doughty Street – the novelist's marital home in earlier days – one can see the famous unfinished watercolour by Robert William Buss – *Dickens's Dream*. It depicts Dickens in his study at Gad's Hill, his eyes closed, a cigar in his hand, slippers on his feet, and the characters of his fiction dancing about him, not unlike the fairies in *A Midsummer Night's Dream* gambolling around the head of Bottom. Buss – whose greatest distinction was fathering Frances, pioneer of female education and founding headmistress of Camden School for Girls – died before he could finish this charming, if saccharine, work. (He had, in his youth, been taken on by the publishers Chapman and Hall as a potential illustrator for *The Pickwick Papers* when the original illustrator committed suicide, but Buss's work was, rightly, deemed to be unsatisfactory.)

Presumably the picture was in part prompted by Dickens's suggestive phrase, in his 1867 Preface to *David Copperfield*, in which he wrote of how 'the Author feels as if he were dismissing some portion of himself into the shadowy world, when a crowd of creatures of his brain are going from him for ever'.

The *Dickens's Dream* version of the novelist and his achievement is one that explains, for many, the nature of his appeal. Here they all are: Little Nell, and Mr Pickwick, and Peggotty and Oliver Twist and Fagin – Characters with a capital 'C', so many of them deriving, as we have acknowledged in this chapter, from the traditions of pantomime.

No one would deny that an abundance of varied characters did indeed emanate from Dickens's fertile imagination; and that this is one of the reasons for the abiding popularity of his fiction. This also explains why so many actors have enjoyed playing the 'characters' and why there are so many films, plays and TV adaptations of the novels.

Dickens's achievement, however, was so much deeper, so much more sophisticated and so much more complex than the simplistic *Dickens's Dream* implies. One of the oblique tributes to him that has spoken most vividly occurred almost as a throwaway moment in a late novel by Elizabeth Bowen, *Eva Trout*. One of the characters, a highly intelligent retired schoolmistress, is translating a fresh French evaluation of Dickens, *Le Grand Histrionique*. She visits the house, now a museum, at Broadstairs, Kent, which was called Fort House, now named Bleak House. It was where much of *David Copperfield* was written and *Bleak House* gestated. Immersing herself in Dickens, his letters and his novels, Iseult asks herself, 'What, now one came to think of it, *had* James, that Dickens really had not? Or if he had, what did it amount to?'

It was a conversion moment, for me, reading that scene in the Bowen novel when it was published in 1969. Still in my teens, I had supposed that Henry James, the great psychological realist, was in every way a more 'interesting', more sophisticated, deeper artist than Charles Dickens, even though, since my childhood, I had read and reread Dickens with obsessive rapture, beginning in a childhood of abject misery when his books, more than anything in the Bible or anything said by a living person, offered me what felt like salvation.

No writer, not even Shakespeare, can visit or inhabit every emotion, every human experience. Dickens's novels do, however, contain so much more than a series of comic episodes and exaggerated caricatures. They are records of experience, and he would not have been able to write them had he not undergone the particular experiences that he underwent. This is an obvious thing to say, but it is worth underlining. It is not that biography, or tittle-tattle, can take the place of intelligent appreciation of the novels as they stand. But it is to say that his experience of life between 1812 and 1870 was something that, like pantomime in his essay, contributed to 'the general enjoyment which an audience of vulnerable spectators, liable to pain and sorrow, find in this class of entertainment'.

The vast, smoky, cruel, boundlessly energetic, steel-hearted nineteenth century was Dickens's canvas, and his subject. It was the century in which economic liberalism, global capitalism, trans-formed the world, leading to the enrichment of Britain beyond any historical parallel, enrichment bought at great cost by the poor of the cities. It was the century in which religion was seen by many intellectuals to be disproved by science, in which materialism triumphed over faith; and Dickens reacted to this not by asserting the old doctrines, but by insisting that the essence of Christianity was in its injunction to be kind. Cruel and complicated as Dickens was, kindliness – and its necessity – was the one value that he held dearest of all others, and it was the value that explains his enduring popularity.

What had James that Dickens, really, had not? Iseult, who asked the question in the Elizabeth Bowen novel, is a former school teacher, as I am, and it is probably the sort of question that teachers, more than other readers, like to ask. What it implies, however, is that Dickens's 'take' on experi-ence is one of the deepest and widest, which can help us, as great art always can, to make sense of our own experiences of childhood, loss, fear, love.

It is the reason that when the exhausted, tiny, over-sexed, whiskery body at Gad's Hill exhaled its last breath, the world itself felt bereft. Few deaths in the entire nineteenth century were so mourned.

They were mourning a great, a unique, artist. It is not sentimental, it is merely accurate, to say that of all the great artists, however, Dickens was most mourned by the unsophisticated and the poor, as well as by the book-buying, literate classes. He had begun the journey just before the end of the Napoleonic Wars, in the year that Moscow was besieged. He ended it in the year that Prussia conquered France and set the seal for all the subsequent horror story of European history. Personalized, pantomimic and unpretentious as Dickens's version of the century was, he had palpably – much more obviously than any of his contemporaries – been on the same journey as the mass of Victorian men, women and children, the ones who lived on the precipice of risk: the ones who feared the workhouse and the debtors' gaol, the ones who never owned property and whose lives were nastier, more brutal and shorter than the contemporaries of Thomas Hobbes who had first coined that phrase. The death of Dickens in 1870 took them back to the infancy of their complicated, soot-grimy, violent century. And as he lay there on the carpet at Gad's Hill, with his sister-in-law holding his hand, the consciousness or soul of Dickens – the imaginative self whose

57

immortality had found its place in the books, more than in a specifically religious hope for a future disembodied life – drifted back in memory and time, through the thirteen years with Nelly, back through the good and bad times of his marriage to Kate Hogarth, to his burgeoning manhood and his effervescent apprenticeship as a writer, to the core of it all, the buried childhood.

Anyone who dies with a secret on their conscience must wonder at what juncture, if any, it will come to light. Dickens had hidden his secrets in the most cunning of places – in the novels, where anyone with an eye could read about them, while supposing they were all inventions. But death has a way of bringing to light hidden things, which the dying one wished never to be disclosed. Could it be, as his eyelids flickered and he prepared for the ultimate mystery, that the curtain was not going to come down, but up; that the garish lights of the theatre were to be turned up, and the actors found unprepared upon the stage?

'Clear the stage,' cries the manager, hastily packing every member of the company into the little space there is between the wings and the wall, and one wing and another. 'Places, places. Now then, Witches – Duncan – Malcolm – bleeding officer – where's the bleeding officer?' – 'Here!' replies the officer, who has been rose-pinking for the character. 'Get ready, then; now,

White, ring the second music-bell.' The actors who are to be discovered, are hastily arranged, and the actors who are not to be discovered, place themselves, in their anxiety to peep at the house, just where the audience can see them. The bell rings, and the orchestra, in acknowledgement of the call, play three distinct chords. The bell rings – the tragedy (!) opens . . . [*SB* 13]

CHAPTER 2

THE MYSTERY OF HIS CHILDHOOD

But who's this hairy youth? She said;
He much resembles thee:
The bear devour'd my youngest son,
Or sure that son were he.

Percy's *Reliques*

Christmas games played a large part in the annual celebrations of the Dickens family at Gad's Hill. His enjoyment of charades and memory games owed much to the fact that he was good at them, and could always win. In the game where one player went out of the room and the others chose an object, he always managed to work out what the object was, by a ruthless series of Socratic questions, however obscure the answer might be. He especially liked the memory game, in which each player had to remember a list of phrases, objects, stray words or objects, before adding an item of their own. Henry Fielding Dickens remembered the last Gad's Hill Christmas – 1869 – when his father had been suffering from pain in his left arm and left leg and was too unwell to come downstairs until the evening. When he had done so, Dickens wanted them to play the memory game.

'My father, after many turns, had successfully gone through the long string of words, and finished up with his own contribution, "Warren's Blacking, 30, Strand!" He gave this', Henry remembered, 'with an odd twinkle in his eye and a strange inflection in his voice, which at once forcibly arrested my attention and left a vivid impression on my mind for some time afterwards'.

Dickens's past, which had been fictionalized and rearranged so often in the course of his life, was safely hidden, never shown or shared. Gad's Hill and, indeed, all the houses in which Dickens raised and housed his children were the houses of gentlefolk. The Dickens family who assembled to play the Christmas games at Gad's belonged to the safe class, of carriage-folk and professional people, for whom workhouses and prisons and burglars and prostitutes on the run from the police were things you read about or, in the case of their father, wrote about, in books. We emphasized in the last chapter that Dickens, alone of all the great figures of the Victorian public scene, alone of all their great imaginative or intellectual giants, had known what it was to have fallen into the abyss. Whereas Henry Dickens, who remembered this Christmas game, was a scholar of Trinity College, Cambridge, growing up to become the well-clad clubman, the lawyer who rose to be a judge, the sort of man who, when he wanted a glass of brandy and water, would ring for a servant to fetch it for him, Charles Dickens was the grandson of domestic servants. He could remember his grandmother, a former housekeeper, and her various relations, dotted about them when they lived in Marylebone, working in undistinguished jobs. Above all, he could remember his parents, and all they had and had not done for him during the grotesquely sad galanty show of his childhood, the constant nightmare of money worries, the darting from lodging to lodging to avoid the debt-collector and the rent-collector, such as Pancks in *Little Dorrit*:

> Throughout the remainder of the day, Bleeding Heart Yard was in consternation, as the grim Pancks cruised in it; haranguing the inhabitants on their backslidings in respect of payment, demanding his bond, breathing notices to quit and executions, running down defaulters, sending a swell of terror on before him, and leaving it in his wake. [*LD* I 23]

Dickens's children had never known this. But for Dickens and his siblings, it was the atmosphere that had coloured every month of their youth.

'Jesus turned this water into wine,' Dickens told his own children in his *Life of Our Lord*, 'by only lifting up his hand; and all who were there, drank of it. For God had given Jesus Christ the power to do such wonders; and he did them, that people might know he was not a common man.' [*LOL* 2]

The blacking factory was not only his apprenticeship as a novelist. It cut loose the childhood into two sections as neat as the chapters of a book. Before the Dickens family came to London, they had lived in Kent, and this was the idyllic world of Chatham and Rochester. The Medway ran through this glorious world like the four rivers flowing around the Garden of Eden in the Bible. The innocent, pure Medway sparkled in sunlight and sang songs of innocence. The murky, corpse-floating, ordure-stinking, corrupt Thames flowed through unhappy London and sang songs of experience.

> Bright and pleasant was the sky, balmy the air, and beautiful the appearance of every object around, as Mr Pickwick leaned over the balustrades of Rochester Bridge, contemplating nature, and waiting for breakfast. The scene was indeed one which might well have charmed a far less reflective mind . . . On either side, the banks of the Medway, covered in cornfields and pastures, with here and there a windmill, or a distant church, stretched away as far as the eye could see. [*PP* 5]

Dickens's first full-length fiction began in the prelapsarian world of his childhood. In *Pickwick*, Rochester and its environs were bathed in light. By the time Dickens had reworked his version of his own history many times, and confronted the imperfections of his own nature in *Great Expectations*, the marshes were places of menace, and Rochester – home to Estella and Miss Havisham – was a place where he was compelled to confront his snobbery, his vanity, his failure in love, his shame and resentment of his family. The novelist, in making this confrontation with the brutally ambitious, callous figure he had been and was, creates a version of autobiography in which he is entirely alone, being brought up by his elder sister, Mrs Joe Gargery, and her amiable blacksmith husband. The deplorable family are all safely buried. 'It is a most miserable thing to feel ashamed of home.' [*GE* 14] And when he wrote that sentence, Charles Dickens might have been summoning up the corrupt, complicated muses who inspired him. He carried shame of home to gloriously comedic, poignantly tragic, imaginative heights. And in the capitalist world that makes 'social mobility' one of its central creeds – a desirable end, rather than a shaming, cruel aspiration; cruel because it encourages shame of home – he spoke for millions. Whether you label it the American Dream, or Social Mobility, or Providing Opportunities, the thought that we should all, from infancy, be trained to have a 'higher' or 'better' level of income or education than our mother and father is an open invitation to be ashamed of them. 'There may be black ingratitude in the thing, and the punishment may be retributive and well deserved; but that it is a miserable thing, I can testify.' [*GE* 14] The class system is designed to make most of the people miserable most of the time, either because they are ashamed of their origins or wish they could overcome them. Those born above the Plimsoll line, the upper class, and those who cheerfully remain in the working class are alone immune from this particular form of inbuilt and systematic insecurity, which persists in Britain to this day but in the nineteenth century was so much stronger; was, indeed, the *raison d'être* of the entire Victorian social system.

In the unfinished novel upon which he was engaged, as a dying man, Dickens once more returned to Kent, to the Rochester of Miss Havisham and the marshes of Magwitch and the escaped criminals; only now, the sunlit cathedral town on the banks of the pure Medway had become an autumnal, brooding place, and the bright waters threatened menace and death.

The very house in which he lay dying, Gad's Hill Place, was part of the prelapsarian childhood story. As a small boy in the company of his father, Dickens would cross that very Rochester Bridge where Mr Pickwick had leaned on the balustrade, and would walk up the two-mile slope towards

Gad's Hill. There stood the Georgian house, red-brick with a small white bell turret surmounting its gambrel roof: a gentleman's house. Oh, to be a gentleman! John Dickens would tell the little boy that, if he worked hard, he might one day live there or 'in some such house'. Only, it was not some *such* house, it was *that* house; it was the very house his father had pointed out to him. Dickens lived in many houses, but it was in this house that he had aspired to live – in his own version of his life at least – since those early days beside the banks of the unpolluted, innocent Medway. It was in this house that he would die, and where he could, at least, estimate how far he had come and whether the journey, and all its pain and scramble, had been worth the agony.

Once he had acquired Gad's Hill, the emblematic division of Dickens's life into two – the innocent childhood, sunlit world of Kent, and the grimy world of money-making London – was fixed, and, just as he made an almost weekly journey between the two, so his imagination sang its divided songs of innocence and experience. Early in *Barnaby Rudge*, Dickens mentions the story of Valentine and Orson ('Ursine' in the version in which he read it – Percy's *Reliques of English Poetry*). It was a ballad that haunted his boyhood reading and defined his analysed, projected adult divided self. The ballad tells of twin brothers, Valentine and Orson, who are lost in the woods moments after their birth. Valentine was found by King Pepin and grew up in the royal court. He was upright, gentle and controlled. The other twin, Orson (Ursine, or Bear's son, from the Latin *ursinus*), was reared as a savage boy by bears in the forest. He was covered in fur. He drinks the blood of men and terrorizes the neighbouring countryside. Sir Valentine comes to save the terrified population, by confronting the club-wielding savage who has been 'reared by ruthless beares'. He overcomes the wild brother and brings him back to court, where he tames him, makes him civilized. In the most popular of Dickens's moral fables, *A Christmas Carol*, mention is made once more of Valentine and Orson when, in Stave Two, Scrooge discovers his childhood self reading, 'one solitary child', about Ali Baba and 'Valentine and his wild brother Orson'.

Dickens's novels tell the story over and over again of his divided self. The villainous characters so often, down to the tiniest and most apparently trivial detail, have characteristics that were peculiarly his. That habit, of *not* telling us something, with a strange twinkle in his eye, of calling out 'Warren's Blacking' to an audience who do not know what secret he was conveying, is one of the everlasting threads in the tapestry.

A conspicuous example occurs when Nicholas Nickleby is sent off to teach in the hideous Dotheboys Hall and his mother exclaims:

'Poor dear boy – going away without his breakfast, too, because he feared to distress us!'

'Mighty fine certainly,' said Ralph, with great testiness. 'When I first went to business, ma'am, I took a penny loaf and a ha'porth of milk for my breakfast as I walked to the city every morning; what do you say to that? Breakfast! Pshaw!' [*NN* 5]

This is almost word for word the same as his reminiscence in the Autobiographical Fragment: 'My own exclusive breakfast, of a penny cottage loaf, and a pennyworth of milk, I provided for myself.' No reader of *Nicholas Nickleby* could possibly have known, when they read the exchange, what Dickens was doing – transposing his innocent childhood self into the heartless soul of a novel's villain. It is the same phenomenon of the final Christmas memory game at Gad's. It is all of a piece with those moments in the fiction where he holds before us linguistic sexual references, which the 'innocent' selves of narrator or reader cannot allow themselves to recognize. The companion of the Artful Dodger, boy procurer for the manifestly paedophile Fagin, is called Master Bates. 'With this irrepressible ebullition of mirth, Master Bates laid himself flat on the floor: and kicked convulsively for five minutes in an ecstasy . . . At the sight of the dismayed look

68

with which Oliver regarded his tormentors . . . Master Bates fell into another ecstasy.' [*OT* 16] And so forth.

'The Dodger made no reply; but, putting his hat on again, and gathering the skirts of his long-tailed coat under his arm, thrust his tongue into his cheek, slapped the bridge of his nose some half-dozen times in a familiar and expressive manner, and, turning on his heel, slunk down the court. Master Bates followed, with a thoughtful countenance.' [*OT* 12] This is not so much a smutty joke, shared between an adult Dickens and his more knowing readers, as it is of a part with his constant habit of concealing things by placing them on the surface of conversation or narrative. The secrets are on the surface. The true histories, mythologized, lie beneath.

This is the reason that, if we look for the biographies of many of Dickens's contemporaries, we look in their letters and diaries and in the reminiscences; but if we try to do the same for Dickens, we are always led back to the novels. His letters, and the one remaining engagement diary, give us only hints. The full story is what he wrote out for us himself. And the novels come out of the warfare, or companionship, or both, of the two brothers: Valentine, the privileged prince from the court of King Pepin, trying to civilize the bear-child covered in hair; the man of peace and the hairy savage wielding a club.

'My parents, at the best, were of that sort whose care soon ends, and whose duty is soon done; who cast their offspring loose, early, as birds do theirs, and, if they do well, claim the merit, and if ill, the pity.' [*HM* 1]

John Dickens, who was twenty-six years old when his son Charles was born, was a clerk in the Navy Pay Office. It was an exciting time to be playing a small, bureaucratic part in that most vital of national roles, financing the Royal Navy. Seven years before Dickens was born, Nelson had been shot dead by a French sniper, but not before guaranteeing victory at the Battle of Trafalgar and thereby checking the power of Napoleon. The war continued until Dickens was three years old. The Hundred Days – the dramatic period after Napoleon left Elba and gathered about him his scattered armies, marching northwards through France, filled the whole of Europe with alarm. 'BONEY BROKE LOOSE' was the title of one cartoon by George Cruikshank, displayed in the print-shop windows of London.

By then the Dickenses had begun a three-year stint living in the capital, where John was working as a clerk at Somerset House. They took lodgings in a house belonging to a cheesemonger named John Dodd. The family consisted of John and Elizabeth Dickens, their firstborn Fanny (b. 1810), Charles (b. 1812) and little Alfred, who was born in London and would die in infancy. From the windows of 10 Norfolk Street three-year-old Charles was held up to see candles lit in every household in celebration of the defeat of Napoleon at Waterloo.

Norfolk Street – part of present-day Cleveland Street, leading down to Charles Street, present-day Mortimer Street – was chosen because of the proximity of John Dickens's mother, who had retired as a domestic servant and was living in Marylebone. Both John and Elizabeth had family nearby. John's brother William ran a coffee shop on the south side of Oxford Street. A cousin had a draper's shop directly opposite, No. 35. One of Elizabeth Dickens's brothers, Mr Barrow, lived in Berners Street, and in the same street her great-aunt Charlton kept a boarding house.

John Dickens was the child of domestic servants. His father – dead by the time Charles was born – had been steward at Crewe Hall, in Cheshire. His mother had been a housekeeper there: the model, presumably, for old Mrs Rouncewell in *Bleak House*. (Before her marriage she had been a servant in the house of the Marquess of Blandford in Grosvenor Square.) The servants of the upper classes were witnesses to the unbridged gulf between the upper class of that century and the rest of the world. Living in their country seats and their vast London houses, they never consorted with the middle classes. Their servants, too, existed in this bubble, detached from the world where people went to offices or factories to earn money, travelled on the newly invented trains or on horse-drawn omnibuses and lived in over-crowded rented rooms, with shared outdoor lavatories and very little running water, even for the more genteel types of folk. The servants of the upper class were often confused into supposing that they too were gentlefolk, or if not actual gentlefolk, more like them than they were like the majority of their fellow citizens, who were seen from carriage windows or glimpsed in the street, but never known. John Dickens would grow up into a delightful fantasist, who conceived of himself as a gentleman. He spoke with a rarefied genteel voice and, fatefully, always lived beyond his very modest means. William Dickens, the novelist's grandfather, had died in 1785, and the Crewes had taken a kindly interest in the welfare of his surviving sons. Lord Crewe, who at the time was MP for Chester, persuaded his friend George Canning, then Treasurer of the Navy, to give the nineteen-year-old John Dickens a post at Somerset House in London, as a clerk in the Navy Pay Office.

A clerk in the same office was Thomas Culliford Barrow, the son of a musical instrument-maker. John Dickens and Barrow became friends, and on 13 June 1809, in the church nearest to their office, St Mary-le-Strand, John married Barrow's sixteen-year-old sister, a small, pretty, comical figure named Elizabeth. The following year Elizabeth's father ran away with over £5,000 of embezzled cash. Not long after the marriage, John Dickens went to Portsmouth Dockyard as a pay clerk, and it was near there, at 387 Mile End Terrace, on 7 February 1812, that Charles Dickens was born.

The task of paying the officers and men of the Royal Navy was vital work, in which John Dickens the clerk played his tiny role. His wages were never very high. When he was moved from Portsea to London, his pay did not match the increased costs of living in the capital, and the lodgings in the cheesemonger's house were modest. The family were probably squeezed into four rooms at the top of Mr Dodd's house. This was the house where they lived for a couple of years, before John was sent back to work in Sheerness, Kent, in Chatham dockyards.

Ruth Richardson, in *Dickens and the Workhouse*, a brilliant piece of literary detective work (from which all the information in the previous paragraphs is culled), has established not only that Mr Dodd's house and shop are still standing in Marylebone, but that, in the Dickenses' day, they were a few doors down from the Cleveland Street Workhouse. Between the ages of three and five, Charles would scarcely have been able to form a judgement of this institution, but his family could scarcely have been unaware of it.

The Barrows, Elizabeth's family, were lowly enough; the Dickenses were servants who had been wholly dependent on the benevolence of their employers. They were, in short, nobodies, and those were perilous times in which to be a nobody. The Royal Navy did not merely seal the fate of Napoleon and guarantee an eventual victory by the Allied Powers, Russia, Prussia and Britain. It also protected and guaranteed the spread of British trade in the post-war years and protected the belligerent success of the new capitalist order – the order that had been brought to birth by the Industrial Revolution.

This revolution – originating with the personal ingenuity of eighteenth-century technocrats, scientists and entrepreneurs such as Josiah Wedgwood, Matthew Boulton and James Watt – had led to an increase in the capacity of manufacture and trade of which previous generations could not have dreamed. The agricultural economy was to be transformed, in a few generations, into an urban, industrialized economy. The rural population flocked to the towns for work. The huge cities – London the hugest – that form the backdrop of all Dickens's greatest works were the monstrous, cruel, vibrant, life-pulsating, filth- and plague-infested death-factories that generated the wealth of the Empire. Mills, factories, canals, machines, works, chimneys, belching and polluting smoke and a leap in the population were not accompanied by a steady upward curve of economic growth. On the contrary. The first fifteen or twenty years of Dickens's life saw the greatest turmoil yet known in European economic history. This was capitalism without any of the safety nets deemed essential by the post-Weimar, post-Soviet world. Banks went to the wall with no protection from a non-existent World Bank or International Monetary Fund. The fate of the two most famous British novelists in the early nineteenth century – Charles Dickens and Sir Walter Scott – should not so much make us suppose they were notably improvident (though they were); their experience could have been replicated in the lives of the nation's butchers, bakers and candlestick-makers. Sir Walter, the richest and most successful author of his day, was himself, following the crash of the London banks in 1826 and the subsequent ruin of the printers and publishers whom he had underwritten, ruined; Charles Dickens, at the other end of the social and economic scale, experienced the imprisonment of his father for debt.

Capital, which Karl Marx saw as a monster devouring the human race, institutionalized the penalties for the victims it was ready to devour: at the bottom end of the scale, the workhouse was deliberately designed to be a place of dread for the 'undeserving poor'. Meanwhile, for those aspirant strugglers whose income could not match their expenses, there loomed the prospect of the debtors' gaol. Dickens grew up, quite literally, in the shadow of both these institutions. As a young child, he was breathing the stench of the Cleveland Street Workhouse. Its insanitary conditions caused the stink. The air around it was filled with clouds of dust as the inmates were set to their tasks – carpet-beating in the yards, or stone-breaking, particles of which flew out into the street.

The novel, perhaps more than any other literary form, celebrates the distinctiveness of self, of character, whereas institutions, especially punitive ones such as workhouses, boarding schools and prisons, did the opposite, attempting to reduce human beings to mere numbers, statistics.

What an excellent example of the power of dress, young Oliver Twist was! Wrapped in the blanket which had hitherto formed his only covering, he might have been the child of a nobleman or a beggar; it would have been hard for the haughtiest stranger to have assigned him his proper station in society. But now that he was enveloped in the old calico robes which had grown yellow in the same service, he was badged and ticketed, and fell into his place at once – a parish child – the orphan of a workhouse – the humble, half-starved drudge – to be cuffed and buffeted through the world – despised by all, and pitied by none. [*OT* 1]

Dickens carried inside him the everlasting consciousness that poverty could lead you inescapably to this dreadful institution. His first truly finished work of art, *Oliver Twist*, concerned the *accouchement* in a workhouse of a woman with pretensions to gentility. The child, Oliver, is a victim – not just of the bullying workhouse beadle, Mr Bumble, not just of the criminal gang, run by Fagin, who kidnap him, but a victim as Dickens himself was, and so many million others were, of having been born in England in the nineteenth century. The sheer heartlessness of its laws and institutions was a given.

Dickens reckoned himself a radical, though he was by no stretch of the modern usage left-wing. He dreaded institutions. Humphry House, a sensible twentieth-century don (who wrote one of the very best studies of the novelist – *The Dickens World*), mocked Betty Higden's stupidity (in *Our Mutual Friend*) for preferring to die on the street, with money for her funeral sewn into her clothing, rather than be trapped behind the doors of a workhouse. Dickens did not mock her. Whether he is contemplating the petty corruption and cruelty of Mr Bumble in Oliver Twist's workhouse, or the pointless charitable endeavours of Mrs Jellyby in *Bleak House*, or the clumsy noisy philanthropy of Honeythunder in *The Mystery of Edwin Drood*, he hated – while endeavouring to engage in it himself – systems of organized charity, and he certainly distrusted the state, at national or local level, trying to better the lives of the poor. The sheer nastiness of the England into which he had been born: that is what he confronted in *Oliver Twist*. Oliver, and Little Jo in *Bleak House*, and all the other strays and starvelings who drift across Dickens's pages, are to be saved not by a Circumlocution Office or a Parish Board, but by kindness. The novels endure, through all the changes in British political history, and make their appeal throughout the world in whatever form of society they are translated and read precisely because of their anti-institutionalism, their appeal to each of us to try to be a bit kinder. It is Mr Brownlow who saves Oliver Twist, not the Poor Laws, with their hateful workhouses and their beadles and boards.

An example of the institutional heartlessness which the child Dickens could see on his doorstep was the stipulation of the Poor Laws that individuals must apply to their own parish for assistance. This meant that paupers from neighbouring parishes, or people taken suddenly ill, such as Oliver Twist's mother, did not have to be admitted either to hospitals or workhouses. The Middlesex Hospital, next door during Charles's first spell of living in London, regularly turned away destitute patients who might, in modern parlance, have been 'bed-blockers', had they been admitted. The Cleveland Street Workhouse was actually meant to serve the parish of St Paul's, Covent Garden. St Paul's was nearly a mile to the south, so if you were a destitute person in Cleveland Street, you might not be able to receive assistance either from the hospital or the workhouse. A news report of 1810 stated:

A scene, most shocking to humanity, was witnessed on Wednesday evening near Fitzroy Square. A poor woman, actually in labour, and attended by her midwife, was delivered of a child at the door of a poor-house, to which she in vain requested admittance. A crowd was naturally collected, and the utmost indignation was expressed at the brutal indifference shown by the officers of the poor-house, for while the poor creature was labouring in agony, they remained inexorable. The infant perished during this inhuman scene. At length the people broke open the doors of the house and carried the unhappy mother into one of the wards.

Streets on which scenes could take place, streets full of smells and fear and pickpockets, were alarming. When John Dickens was posted back to Kent, the family felt themselves transported into happiness. For a short time they were in the naval town of Sheerness on the Isle of Sheppey, in a house that abutted a theatre. They could hear laughter and applause coming through the walls, and used to join in the singing of the national anthem at the end of each show.

Then they were moved to Chatham dockyards, where they lived until 1822. All biographers agree these were Dickens's happy years. You could not escape the humiliations of the class system, even in Chatham. As Mr Jingle reminded the Pickwick

Club, 'queer place – dockyard people of upper rank don't know dockyard people of lower rank – dockyard people of lower rank don't know small gentry – small gentry don't know tradespeople – commissioner don't know anybody'. [*PP* 2]

This was the Garden of Eden before Dickens had realised he hated his mother. Elizabeth Dickens was his first teacher. She taught him to read, and she even taught him a little Latin – probably the only Latin he knew. When he was old enough, she sent him to a dame's school in Rome (pronounced Room) Lane, Rochester. The point of such schools was not especially to educate the children as to demonstrate the gentility of the parents. John Dickens, who was so far from being a gentleman, was always at pains to stress that this was what he was. He described himself on his marriage licence, at St Mary-le-Strand in London, as a 'gentleman', which he most certainly was not.

Unlike his wife's father, John Dickens was not an embezzler, but he found it just as difficult to keep afloat. By the time he was transferred from Chatham back to London, there were seven children – Fanny, Charles, Letitia (b. 1816), Harriet (b. 1818), Frederick (b. 1820), Alfred Lamert (b. 1822, the first Alfred having died in infancy) and Augustus (b. 1827). Plenty of siblings here to eat the parents out of house and home (literally), and for Charles to be ashamed of. They moved, not back to Marylebone, but to the cheaper district of Camden Town. Into the tiny terraced house they also crammed a lodger, James Lamert, who was hoping to be able to buy himself a commission in the army; and a maid, the Orfling, a girl fished out of the Chatham workhouse. Lamert was a connection by marriage. Mrs Dickens's Aunt Fanny had married an army surgeon, Dr Matthew Lamert, quartered at the Ordnance Hospital at Chatham, and James was his son by a previous marriage.

'I want to escape from myself – my blankness is inconceivable – indescribable, my misery – amazing,' Dickens once confided in Wilkie Collins. A novelist's way of 'escaping' differs, perhaps, from those of another person. One thinks of Evelyn Waugh, who could not escape the persona he had half invented for himself to hide behind. The mask had stuck. Just as Evelyn Waugh would die of being Waugh, Dickens was dying of being Dickens. Because Dickens was the most novelistic of all novelists, the condition was especially acute. Over and over again he had made experience into fiction, to the point where he was no longer able to distinguish what he had undergone and what he had invented.

In his fictionalized boyhood, *David Copperfield* (his own initials reversed, CD/DC), he described how, made wretched by his mother's remarriage to the sadist Mr Murdstone, he would retreat into novel-reading.

My father had left a small collection of books in a little room upstairs, to which I had access (for it adjoined my own) and which nobody else in the house ever troubled. From that blessed little room, Roderick Random, Peregrine Pickle, Humphrey Clinker, Tom Jones, the Vicar of Wakefield, Don Quixote, Gil Blas, and Robinson Crusoe came out, a glorious host, to keep me company. They kept alive my fancy, and my hope of something beyond that place and time . . . It is curious to me how I could ever have consoled myself under my small troubles (which were great troubles to me), by impersonating my favourite characters in them – as I did – and by putting Mr and Miss Murdstone into all the bad ones – which I did too . . . This was my only and my constant comfort. [*DC* 4]

Far from the reading of fiction being a purely passive act – allowing it, so to say, to wash over him, or distract him – Dickens here speaks of choosing to enact it; to inhabit the novels he enjoyed, and to make of them a reality more potent than the experiences he was actually undergoing. That this is true, to a greater or lesser degree, for everyone who enjoys novels – how much more so, drama and film, in the case of most people – explains the potency of the unreal. It is the ultimate reason why Plato, a purist contemplating an Absolute Good and an Absolute Reality of which this world is but a shadow, banished Homer and the Poets from his ideal Republic. Nineteenth-century industrialized Britain was a place so brutal, so ugly, so destructive of spiritual calm that Plato himself, had he been born in it, might have felt tempted to retreat into the cave and enjoy the illusive shadows cast by the fire, rather than venture out to the supposed reality of the sun, which had itself, more than 2,400 years after the Athenian philosopher, become scarcely visible through the polluted smogs and smokes of the smutty, coke-flecked cities.

Dickens was an unashamed advocate of the illusory as a way of finding another reality, the reality that is contained within the covers of a novel. He found the exercise so easy, so beguiling, and ultimately so dangerous, because from an early age he had seen the act of reading as an escape from the lesser reality of being; the act of imagination as an escape from the world of work, earning, suffering and boredom. The most potent of maestros, Dickens could summon up an alternative world, recognizably that of the Victorians, and of all of us, yet comedic. Where our tears are of sorrow, the tears he drew forth were ones of pathos and sentiment. The grotesquerie and horror of unhappy workplaces, squalid living conditions and exploitative or cruel family life weigh upon those who suffer them, yet in the pages of Dickens they

83

are transformed into pantomimic comedy and tear-jerking melodrama. Only by self-transformation, self-deception and the acting of parts could the fiction come into being, the carapaces he adopted as self-protection being a puppet show for all.

He had revealed his nightmare past again and again in his art, but the family, and presumably all his friends and acquaintances (except his wife Kate – was that another reason he felt compelled to get rid of her?), knew nothing of this. As far as they were concerned, Dickens was the sensationally successful author, the public figure who, in his velvet coats and with his well-brushed whiskers, was constantly asked to address banquets and dinners in London. They had no idea that the workhouse urchins, the imprisoned debtors, the vaudevillized bankrupts, the wretchedly unhappy little waifs picking their way, terrified, through the Victorian urban jungle and into his pages, were all projected from memories. 'Warren's Blacking, 30, Strand!' was nothing to them. Could anything demonstrate more vividly than that moment during the last Christmas games the extent to which Dickens kept his mystery hidden from those who believed themselves to know him best? And he had kept it hidden all those years in the most ingenious manner possible: by displaying it. With an 'odd twinkle in his eye and a strange inflection in his voice', he had told the story over and over again.

Childhood, and the childhood self, the

mysteriousness of being and consciousness, were as vividly explored by Dickens, in his fashion, as by Proust in the first volume of *À la recherche du temps perdu*. And so much of the memory-tapestry was interwoven with Kent, and the country within a twenty-mile tramp of where he now, on 9 June 1870, lay dying on his dining-room floor, with his sister-in-law Georgina Hogarth holding his head, while the children – those of whom were still in England – were hurrying to railway stations and clambering into cabs, in the hope of reaching Gad's Hill to see him alive. Meanwhile, the mind that had contained Charles Dickens's past, and formed his fictions, was now in suspense.

The layers of truth – as human beings unpeel the past – grow, unfold, change. Psychoanalysis is one method, since the beginning of the twentieth century, by which bruised individuals have recovered or changed their past. Writing and reading fiction is another. Dickens's version of his childhood, and, by extension, his relationship with his mother and father, lay hidden. He had flashed it out during those last Christmas games, played with his sons and daughters, and they did not even know he had done it. Just a twinkle in the eye hinted at the past they would never see, and probably never understand. By not talking about it, and by fictionalizing it, Dickens had made the past his own possession. Only after he was dead, when his children read John Forster's *Life of Charles*

Dickens, did they realize the little game their father had played. They had thought it was a memory game, but it had actually been a forgetting game, or a concealing game. He had called out the scene of his childhood humiliation and trauma. No one in the room during the Christmas party, except Dickens himself, knew the significance of the address 'Warren's Blacking, 30, Strand!' Forster himself, who was privileged to know much more of his friend's secret life than any of the novelist's children, but who never came within a mile of understanding his old friend, only came to learn the story in a roundabout way.

Forster had asked Dickens if he were acquainted with Charles Wentworth Dilke, a friend of Keats, who went on to be the editor of *The Athenaeum*. Dickens acknowledged that he knew Dilke, who had been a clerk in Somerset House at the same time as his father. He told Forster that he remembered Dilke visiting him as a child when he lodged in the house of an uncle in Gerrard Street. 'Never at any other time.' The memory, of course, was a false one, and the notion that a gentleman such as Dilke was on visiting terms with one of Dickens's uncles was simply a smokescreen. The Dilkes were upper middle class, the Dickenses were out-and-out nobodies. Dickens's mother, father, uncles and cousins, with their unconvincing aspirations to gentility and their ludicrously implausible pretensions, were not Dilke's friends, though it was possible that, as a senior clerk in Somerset

House, Dilke had noticed John Dickens, a clerk in the humblest way, when, with a pay cut from his earlier work in the pay office at Portsmouth, he had been moved to do his pen-pushing, for a short and disastrous period, in London.

Forster told Dickens that he had heard otherwise. No memories of calling cards or Gerrard Street. Heard that Dilke had visited a certain warehouse near the Strand, a short walk from Somerset House, having seen the child Dickens through the window, engaged in sticking labels on the jars of boot-blacking. Heard that Dilke had gone in to give the little boy half a crown. (Why would he do that, unless someone had tipped him off to do so?) Heard that the boy had given Dilke a deep bow. The boy was a very different Dickens from the celebrated adult Forster had known, and whose life he tried to recover in biography. Sickly, timid, thin-skinned, this was the Dickens who had been sent by his mother and father to work among workhouse children in a squalid little factory. Had John Dickens, sometime colleague of Dilke and everlasting scrounger, shamelessly admitted to Dilke that his boy was in the labels line at Warren's Blacking, and suggested that half a crown would not go amiss? It is just the sort of embarrassing thing he *would* have done! Who will ever forget the squirm-making scene when Arthur Clennam follows Little Dorrit to the Marshalsea Prison, the debtors' gaol, and is presented to her father

– 'The Father of the Marshalsea' – who loses no time in 'touching' Clennam for a 'testimonial'? ('Sometimes,' he went on in a low, soft voice, agitated, and clearing his throat every now and then, 'sometimes – hem – it takes one shape and sometimes another; but it is generally – ha – Money.' [*LD* I 8]) Who, in Somerset House where John Dickens and Charles Dilke briefly coincided, would be likely to forget that Charles Barrow, John Dickens's future father-in-law, had held the responsible position of 'Chief Conductor of Moneys in Town', until it was discovered that he had conducted the moneys – £5,689, three shillings and threepence between 1803 and 1810 – into his own bank account? He had pleaded mitigating circumstances, ten children (one of them Dickens's mother, Elizabeth) before skedaddling to France, leaving the Revenue to seize and sell his paltry household possessions? Just as the relentlessness of the system forced the poor, 'deserving' and the opposite, to struggle at all costs against the humiliation and pain of being incarcerated in the workhouse, so those who were a little higher than this in the category of things were forced by the dread of debt to excesses of work and worry. As Pancks the rent-collector says:

Here am I . . . What else do you suppose
I think I am made for? Nothing. Rattle me
out of bed early, set me going, give me as

short a time as you like to bolt my meals in, and keep me at it. Keep me always at it, I'll keep you alw ays at it, you keep somebody else always at it. There you are with the Whole Duty of Man in a commercial country. [*LD* I 13]

Part of the tragicomedy, the horror and the farce, of the position in which Dickens's parents found themselves is that, compared with many of their contemporaries, they were in a good position to 'better' themselves. When he first married, John Dickens had been on a salary of £200 per annum. By 1822 in Chatham, when Charles was ten, his father was on an annual salary of £441, but he was living beyond his means even then, and when he got posted back to London, at a cruelly reduced pay of £350, the trouble started, and the Micawberish discrepancy between money earned and money owed threatened all their security. (They owed a staggering £40, one-tenth of their annual income at the best of times, to the baker in Camden Town.)

Dickens, by melodramatizing and mythologizing his own circumstances so blatantly in the novels, paradoxically drew attention away from himself, for the simple reason that almost everyone in that relentlessly commercial country could see themselves in his pages. He was writing down their great experience: the commercial success story that made Britain the richest imperial power in the world's history, the commercial failures that created the Oliver Twists and the Amy Dorrits. The many paradoxes of Dickens's mystery included the fact that his entire oeuvre is a cry of satirical rage, a whoop of contemptuous laughter, against the earnest, utilitarian Benthamite creed that Pancks enunciated: yet there was no one, probably, in the kingdom, after the success of *The Pickwick Papers*, who 'kept at it' more relentlessly than the workaholic Dickens. His Blakean Muse hymned the pleasure of laughter, the merriment of inns and theatres, the happiness of children at play. The machine of his capitalist conscience, of his dread of ever returning to the circumstances that had led him to Warren's Blacking, 30, Strand, kept him everlastingly, suicidally, 'at it'. Fecklessness, idleness, the ability to put pleasure before work are often, in his novels, attractive qualities, as exemplified by Dick Swiveller or Mr Jingle or Mr Micawber. In the case of his parents, however, things were very different.

So the Dickens that Forster was for the first time resurrecting, when he remembered the half-crown and the handshake, and the excruciating bow in the blacking warehouse back in the reign of George IV, was a very different figure from the 'Boz' who had burst on the world ready-made as the brilliant writer, wit and diner-out a year before the reign of Queen Victoria, a little woman with whom, to amuse the company, the young Dickens pretended to be in love. The Dickens They All Knew, and

90

who had – to use a brilliant phrase of Kitty Muggeridge applied to a twentieth-century celebrity – 'risen without trace', was a very different figure from that waif in the warehouse, so inconveniently recalled by Charles Dilke. This was the Dickens, born into a family that had invented its own claims to gentility, but which in reality belonged to the servant class, being hurled back, through his parents' heedlessness, to the bottom of the heap. Moreover, it was especially painful because the little Charles, of all the Dickens children, had been singled out for this uncongenial role. The other members of his family were not put out to work in this way. Dickens was one of eight children: there was his elder sister Fanny, who won a scholarship to the Royal Academy of Music, and who was a professional musician; there was little Alfred, who died in infancy in 1814; and there were Letitia, Harriet, Frederick, Alfred Lamert and Augustus. We notice that in the fictionalized version of his autobiography, *David Copperfield*, Dickens/David was an orphan and an only child. The imagination that created The Rookery, and Peggotty, and the doll-like, pretty widowed mother of Copperfield, had cut out Dickens's appalling family altogether, allowing only the father a quasi-farcical supporting role as the Clown of the story, the loveable spendthrift Mr Micawber.

In *Great Expectations*, where the autobiography was rewritten in a much less sparing and more merciless mode, Dickens, as it were, killed off all his siblings, imagining them to be the babies in the graves on the edge of the marshes at Cooling, on the Hoo Peninsula near Rochester: 'I found out for certain that this bleak place overgrown with nettles was the churchyard; and that Philip Pirrip, late of this parish, and also Georgiana, wife of the above, were dead and buried; and that Alexander, Bartholomew, Abraham, Tobias, and Roger, infant children of the aforesaid, were also dead and buried.' [*GE* 1]

Now, through the chance of his mentioning Dilke and the half-crown, Forster had ripped off the outer carapace, released the infant Dickens – the real, as opposed to the fictionalized infant – to confront his adult self.

Whereas Dickens had transmogrified his experience into art, so that it was probably no longer entirely feasible to separate what he had imagined and what he had experienced, Forster's revelation to him threatened the unravelling of the tapestry, by opening up the philistine game of matching 'real' and 'imagined' life. With deeper energy, more tearful and hilarious passion than any other writer I know of, Dickens had put himself, and his experience, into the novels. Great artist as he was, however, the process made it not so much difficult, as unnecessary, to distinguish between experiences he had actually undergone and ones that he had refashioned as story. Now, however, the conscious self was

compelled to release the unconscious; the successful mid-Victorian gentleman was forced to look
at a sickly little waif, the 'strange little apparition'
from the reign of George IV.

> I was such a strange little fellow, with my
> poor white hat, little jacket, and corduroy
> trowsers, that frequently, when I went into
> the bar of a strange public house for a glass
> of ale or porter to wash down the saveloy
> and the loaf I had eaten in the street, they
> didn't like to give it me.

Forster's hearsay released Dickens's reticence.
Once unmasked, it was inevitable that Dickens
should have felt compelled to set down the non-
fictional account. In a sense, however, there was
a danger that, having transformed experience into
art, he was going to tempt readers of his biography
to perform the superfluous philistine exercise of
translating the art back into an account of what
'really' happened.

In another sense, the encounter between the
adult Dickens and that funny little Georgian waif,
making his terrified way through the alleys and
streets of the Artful Dodger's London, reminds us
of the centrality of the art of fiction to that
particular generation. Those of us who have lived
through the twentieth or twenty-first centuries
have enjoyed the fiction of our contemporaries,
but for an account of what has happened to us

since the Second World War we have tended to go to historians, journalists, social commentators. Only, perhaps, the Russians discovered, through reading the supposed fiction of Alexander Solzhenitsyn, an account of what they had been through that was more realistic and more accurate than the official histories and propaganda journalism fed to them by authority.

For the Dickens generation, the generation of Balzac and Tolstoy, things were otherwise. After the Napoleonic Wars, Europe passed through incomprehensible convulsions. Economists, social commentators and journalists tried to explain what had happened, and what was happening, which is why men and women turned the pages of Taine, de Tocqueville, Marx, Carlyle, Bentham, Mill. In a mysterious way, however, all these commentators, however astute, left something out. Balzac anatomized the convulsions in the class system, the money dramas, the sexual politics of his generation more accurately than any journalist or historian. Tolstoy told Russians the history of their patriotic war, the conditions in which they now lived, the spiritual crises of their Church and political classes more vividly than anyone.

Dickens's anatomy of British society was no less powerful. Whereas Balzac and Tolstoy, in their relentless realism, were really taking the art of fiction into the realm of history and political analysis, Dickens was doing something very different – much more radical and 'modernist'. No doubt on some levels he would always have defended his art as completely realistic, but we can see that this is not really the case. On the one hand, he was translating the nineteenth-century experience into vaudeville and pantomime and fairy tale. On the other hand, he was going much deeper than any surface account of mere 'events'. 'No other ghost has haunted the boy's room, my friends, since I have occupied it, than the ghost of my own childhood, the ghost of my own innocence, the ghost of my own airy belief,' he wrote in *The Haunted House*. [CS 1859] By prompting memory of the blacking factory, Forster had prised open the lid, and for a moment we look inside the treasure chest of the greatest imagination of the British nineteenth century. We see not merely his secret childhood, but the alchemy by which, in transforming it into fiction, he was able to hold up a mirror to the Victorians and explain them to themselves. If the Liberal Party or the Radicals, or the Charitable Institutions or the Workhouse Boards, or the Army Board or the Houses of Parliament or the Church of England or the Women's Suffrage Movement had been able to sweep away all that was painful in that experience, then we should indeed be living in paradise and the novels of Dickens would be redundant. He always distrusted institutions, found them indeed to be ridiculous, and those who open his pages today find the stories of the damaged child and wonder whether all the reforms, changes and improvements to life attempted in institutional form in East and West have changed the pain of being born, the bewilderment of being a child, or the powerful compulsions of so many malformed grown-ups to torment and ruin the infancy of their children.

Jonathan Warren claimed to have invented a particular recipe for blacking boots, but after a family row, the business ran into financial difficulty. It was sold to one George Lamert, who employed his cousin (and brother-in-law) James Lamert, the Dickenses' lodger who was a relative by marriage of Elizabeth Dickens. Warren's (Blacking Factory and Warehouse) was sold to Lamert:

> in an evil hour for me, as I often bitterly thought. Its chief manager, James Lamert, the relative who had lived with us in Bayham-street, seeing how I was employed from day to day, and knowing what our domestic circumstances then were, proposed that I should go into the blacking warehouse to be as useful as I could, at a salary, I think, of six shillings a week. I am not clear whether it was six or seven. I am inclined to believe, from my uncertainty on this head, that it was six at first and seven afterwards. At any rate the offer was accepted very willingly by my father

and mother, and on a Monday morning I went down to the blacking warehouse to begin my business life.

It is wonderful to me how I could have been so easily cast away at such an age . . . No one had compassion enough on me – a child of singular abilities, quick, eager, delicate, and soon hurt, bodily or mentally – to suggest that something might have been spared, as certainly it might have been, to place me at any common school. Our friends, I take it, were tired out [does he mean 'tried'?]. No one made any sign. My father and mother were quite satisfied. They could hardly have been more so, if I had been twenty years of age, distinguished at a grammar-school and going to Cambridge.

At ten years old, his novelistic apprenticeship began. Warren's Blacking warehouse saved Dickens the novelist, just as a grammar school and Cambridge would have destroyed him. It is difficult to imagine a richer gift to a novelist than this gift of Lamert's: Dickens, the pert, talented child, one of a large, improvident, fanciful family, was singled out for the drudgery of the blacking warehouse. Had the family been prosperous, had they not teetered uncertainly between the hopes of prosperity and the abyss of bankruptcy, had there not hovered behind them the spectre of the class system, Dickens might have been as 'successful' as Dilke – first a clerk in Somerset House, and then the editor of a stodgy periodical.

The enacting of the fiction on the podium in the public readings only increased the confusion, and the carefully carapaced self, the good humour, the witty speeches, the constant acting, the hiding away of Dickens's sexual and romantic attachment, his complete rewriting of and concealment of his actual family background. These habits too took their toll. He was as much a creation as Pickwick or Mrs Gamp. He had made into 'The Novel' – his habit of fictionalizing – something that he thought he had been running away from, or running home to, all his life: a prison.

This was true even in the sunny novels. *The Pickwick Papers* begins as a burlesque, picaresque novel; it ends as a novel about a man finding salvation – through prison. It is positively Dostoevskyan. Of his fifteen major works, ten involve prison. *Oliver Twist* starts in the semi-prison of the workhouse and ends in Newgate Gaol, with Fagin about to be hanged. *Barnaby Rudge* reverts to prison and the most vivid scenes are those in which the mob storms Newgate and the other prisons. *A Tale of Two Cities* has a man, Dr Manette, a jailbird from the Bastille, who, like Mr Dorrit in his delusional moments, and like Dickens himself, was not quite sure whether he was in prison or not. *Great Expectations* reveals Pip to be the heir not of the genteel Miss Havisham, the jilted bride who has made a prison for herself of her own house where the wedding breakfast has never been dismantled, but rather of Magwitch the convict – who has won his liberty from the prison-ships by being rescued by little Pip – who stole from his brother-in-law's blacksmith's forge a file to escape his leg-irons, and purloined from his tyrannical sister's larder a slaveringly appetising meat pie. Prison doors clang in the majority of the novels, and we feel the cell doors clink behind us as we enter Dickens's world. Fiction had been his escape route from the prison of childhood and had turned out to be another prison. Was Dickens a free man, with his frenzied public performances, or was he acting out lines not so much written by himself as mouthing words dictated by his inner psychological destiny?

Likewise, when not in prison, his characters find themselves trapped in other ways – in nightmare marriages or non-marriages they had never intended. Again, even the merry *Pickwick Papers* carries this theme at its heart, with Pickwick sued for breach of promise, and threatened with prison in consequence of not wanting to marry Mrs Bardell. (Or, indeed, never having had any intention of doing so.) Of *course* it is comic, or supposedly comic, but what were all the music-hall jokes about shrewish wives, nagging mothers-in-law, timorous or philandering husbands – but the unhappiness of home translated into necessary humour? The Meagles, the doting parents of an only daughter who jokingly refer to themselves as jailbirds at the beginning of *Little Dorrit*, when they are temporarily in quarantine in Marseilles, create a domestic prison for the charity girl, Tatty-coram, whom they adopt into their smotheringly sentimental domestic gaol. Of warmth, cosiness and control.

Little Dorrit is one of the finest, and the most vividly realized, of the prison novels. George Bernard Shaw saw that '*Little Dorrit* is a more seditious book than *Das Kapital*. All over Europe men and women are in prison for pamphlets and speeches which are to *Little Dorrit* as red pepper to dynamite. Fortunately for social evolution, Governments never know where to strike. Barnacle and Stiltstalking were far too conceited to recognize their own portraits.' Shaw was saying that Dickens's novel is seditious because of the farcical representation of British government and administration in the Circumlocution Office. But the truly seditious thing about the novel is not its mockery of Tite Barnacle, it is its hideous determinism – we can none of us escape the prison of self. One of the truly disturbing things about the novel is that, when the Dorrits have left the Marshalsea, we feel bereft. We miss the prison. Like Little Dorrit herself, we have been born there and never knew anything else.

It is the positioning of the first paragraph of the sixth chapter of *Little Dorrit* that is so shocking. If it had been at the very beginning of Chapter 1 we should have known where we were. But by now we have started in the prison in Marseilles; we have endured the would-be prison of quarantine in which the genial Mr Meagles refers to himself and his fellow quarantines as jailbirds; we have been to the House of Clennam, where Mrs Clennam speaks of herself as a prisoner and Little Dorrit flits through the shadows with her sewing and her trays . . . And then, of a sudden, after the sheer fancifulness of the writing, the searing sun of Marseilles, the night-terrors of Affery's dreams, we have a straightforward pair of sentences which Dickens has been waiting nearly seventy pages to write – seventy pages and, we suspect, about forty years:

> Thirty years ago, there stood, a few doors short of the church of Saint George, in the Borough of Southwark, on the left-hand side of the way going southward, the Marshalsea Prison. It had stood there many years before, and it remained there some years afterwards; but it is gone now, and the world is none the worse without it. [*LD* I 6]

Balzac's biographer Graham Robb, commenting on that great masterpiece *Splendeurs et misères des courtisanes*, says that for Balzac, prison had always been the 'home of the creative mind'. Dickens

101

took it further, however, which is why Shaw was right to think *Little Dorrit* more seditious than *Das Kapital*. In a passage that is actually highly reminiscent of the more descriptive passages of *Das Kapital*, Dickens sees the most horrible truth of all about the debtors' gaol: that in the competitive, thrusting Samuel-Smilesey go-getting world of nineteenth-century capitalism, prison is about the most restful place you can be:

> Elsewhere people are restless, worried, hurried about, anxious respecting one thing, anxious respecting another. Nothing of the kind here, sir. We have done all that – we know the worst of it; we have got to the bottom, we can't fall, and what have we found? Peace. [*LD* I 66]

So says the drunken old doctor whom Clennam meets in the Marshalsea. The Victorians had created for themselves such a hellish society that the place where you could most certainly be at peace was locked up in prison. The hundreds of prisoners and internees in Solzhenitsyn's work never express this view: everyone in the Soviet Union, even those who most fervently believed in Marxism, could see there was something fundamentally wrong with the system by the time Stalin exercised power, whereas, in the more bewildered world of Victorian England, they wanted to believe they were creating an earthly heaven, when

Britannia ruled the waves and it was merely the pace that exhausted some of them, the pace that was intolerable.

Dickens's mother always walked with a limp – the consequence, as a young woman, of falling through a trapdoor on the stage of the Soho Theatre. Though she never pursued a life in the theatre, this was clearly the direction she would have liked to have followed. Dickens disguised his feelings of bitter hatred for her by recognizing her essential comicality. He used to visit her when she suffered from premature senile decay.

> On one of these visits he noted that she was better, 'for,' said he, 'the instant she saw me, she plucked up a spirit and asked me for a pound!' Upon another occasion he observed: 'My mother, who was left to me when my father died (I never had anything left to me but relations) is in the strangest state of mind from senile decay: and the impossibility of getting her to understand what is the matter, combined with her desire to be got up in sables like a female Hamlet, illumines the dreary scene with a ghastly absurdity that is the chief relief I can find in it.'

We know about the cause of Mrs Dickens's limp from Mrs Davey, the wife of a Bloomsbury doctor who treated Dickens's father in 1850. She wrote in reaction against John Forster's account of Dickens's relationship with his parents. Forster knew Dickens well, Mrs Davey scarcely at all. Forster knew that Dickens hated his mother. Mrs Davey, unwilling to recognize what a high proportion of the human race – angry, perhaps, to have been born – hate their mothers, wanted to put the record straight by suggesting that 'a great deal of Dickens's genius was inherited from his mother. He possessed from her a keen appreciation of the droll and of the pathetic, as also considerable dramatic talent. Mrs Dickens has often sent my sisters and myself into uncontrollable fits of laughter by her funny sayings and inimitable mimicry.' That we can believe – that, and Mrs Davey's memory that Charles 'always treated her respectfully and kindly'. Less true is her assertion that he was decidedly fond of his mother.

In his personal recollections and anecdotes, he made his mother into a figure of farce. She is the ludicrously vain Mrs Nickleby, who overlooks the manifest lunacy of her next-door neighbour (his affection takes the form of hurling vegetables at her head and imagining she is the 'niece to the Commissioners of Paving and daughter-in-law to the Lord Mayor and Court of the Common Council'. When Kate Nickleby points out that her mother's admirer is obviously a madman, the mother protests, 'He may be a little odd and flighty, perhaps, many of us are that; but downright mad! and express himself as he does, respectfully, and in quite poetical language.' [*NN* 41]

The feckless father grew, in the fictions, into figures who could be seen as loveable – Micawber, even Dorrit sometimes, though Dorrit is a wretched creature. As for Mrs Dickens, her son's imagination turned her into a figure of farce, before disposing of her altogether. Mr Dorrit is a widower. By the time Dickens's greatest fiction came into being, his imagination had no need of the woman who had, in his recollection, been the cause of so much of the childhood trauma. He blamed her directly, personally, and without even the attempt to forgive or to understand, for the fact that, when his parents fell into debt, he was sent to work in Warren's Blacking factory.

Dickens's mother died on 13 September 1863. Did she notice, over the years, when or if she was reading her son's fiction, that it would be difficult to find a single happy child in all those thousands of pages? It is as difficult to find a happy child in his stories as it is to find an adequate mother. The good mothers are nearly always working class, or poverty-stricken lower middle class, like Mrs Cratchit, or Mrs Plornish, the plasterer's wife in *Little Dorrit,* or Kit Nubbles's mother in *The Old Curiosity Shop.* Did Elizabeth Dickens, as she read, notice the recurrent, obsessive theme of the mother who rejects her child? Edith Dombey, Louisa Gradgrind, Annie Strong – the ridiculous mothers who reject them. The entire plot of *Bleak House* revolves around the fact that Esther Summerson has been rejected by her mother, Lady Dedlock, as has Arthur Clennam who, it turns out, is not the son of the terrifying Mrs Clennam, but a child of sin whom she has elected to rear. The feckless mothers who are seen to neglect their children – Mrs Jellyby and Mrs Pocket – give birth to children who 'were not growing up or being brought up, but . . . tumbling up'. [*GE* 22]

But actually in Dickens's writing there is nothing so unsparing as the Autobiographical Fragment, when it comes to his exploring the extent to which his own mother rejected him. He softens the blow: was it because he could not bear to confront the truth, for most of the time, or was it out of consideration for, or fear of, the real mother? The bad mothers who are obviously more central to his exorcistic fictional processes, the mothers of the figures who in some way stand for himself, tend not to be the mothers but mother-substitutes. Pip's real mother – 'Also Georgiana, wife of the above' – is conveniently dead. It is his elder sister who behaves towards him like a rejecting mother.

'I have only been to the churchyard,' said I, from my stool, crying and rubbing myself.
'Churchyard!' repeated my sister. 'If it warn't for me you'd have been to the churchyard long ago, and stayed there. Who brought you up by hand?'

'You did,' said I.

'And why did I do it, I should like to know?' exclaimed my sister.

I whimpered, 'I don't know.'

'*I* don't!' said my sister. 'I'd never do it again! I know that. I may truly say I've never had this apron of mine off since born you were. It's bad enough to be a black-smith's wife (and him a Gargery) without being your mother.' [*GE* 2]

So she does speak as if she were Pip's mother. Likewise in the other alternative-autobiography, *David Copperfield*, the hero was able to absolve his foolish mother from neglect because she dies, and the cruelty perpetrated on him is inflicted by his stepfather and his sister – Miss Murdstone. It is they, the cruellest pair of human beings in Dickens's entire oeuvre, who send David to work in the Thameside warehouse, Murdstone & Grinby, which bears so close a resemblance to Warren's Blacking, 30, Strand.

We are now able to see what Dickens himself was probably unable to see: that his flawed relationship with his mother is the defining feature, of the man and of his art. We shall return to this in the next chapter when we enter the dark forest of his marriage and his relationship with Kate Hogarth. For the time being, we can be content to observe the appalling determinism of human psychology. Elizabeth Barrow had been born when her elder sister was twelve months old, and the next child appeared fourteen months later. She was just sixteen when she married John Dickens, and seventeen when her father's fraudulent activity at the Navy Pay Office caused him to bunk off abroad. It was scarcely a stable upbringing, and, when she watched her new husband getting them into financial difficulty, she must have sensed history repeating itself. Her pathetic and inadequate attempt to start a school, to make ends meet, when they had moved to London was, of course, laughable. It got no further than her taking the lease on 4 Gower Street North, from Michaelmas 1823, at an annual rent of £30, and appending a large brass plate – MRS DICKENS'S ESTABLISHMENT – to the front door. Dickens himself contemptuously remembered, 'Nobody ever came to the school, nor do I recollect that any ever proposed to come, or that the least preparation was ever made to receive anybody.' He wrote about 'recollecting' the event, but the reality was that at the time of her starting the school, or at least buying the brass plate, he was only eleven years old, and his parents would have been unlikely to keep him abreast of their grown-up plans, still less of the details of their financial worries.

On the surface of things, it is difficult to avoid the conclusion that both John and Elizabeth Dickens behaved appallingly to the twelve-year-old Dickens whom they cast out of their home and forced to go to work in a factory, at a wage of six or seven shillings a week. This was at a time, even during his imprisonment for debt, when John continued to earn £350 per annum as a clerk, and had also inherited £450 as a legacy from his mother. They were able to help Fanny, their first-born, apply for a scholarship and become a boarder at the Royal College of Music, and so begin a plausible and creative career.

We know that in that century when women usually lay up for days, sometimes for weeks, after childbirth, Elizabeth Dickens was dancing within a day of Charles's birth in 1812, and it is clear that in grown-up life his relationship with her was one of cold contempt. We can conclude that, for whatever reason, she had been simply incapable of giving him love.

In addition to the many inadequate mothers in Dickens's fiction, we must add the list of children who believe they should never have been born. Dickens was much impressed by Dr Johnson's *Life* of his friend Richard Savage. He urged his wife to read it, and he longed to have her reaction to it. Many people now question whether Savage had told Johnson the truth about his life, but that is not of importance here. Dickens responded with intensity to a story of an illegitimate child of the Countess of Macclesfield, who cast off her son to be brought up by a poor woman, Mrs Brett, forced into an apprenticeship to a poor shoemaker in Holborn, but triumphing over these appalling odds by making a name for himself as a writer.

For Dickens, it was a sort of parable: the unwanted child could be reborn as a published author.

Born so soon after his sister Fanny to a young pleasure-loving mother, Dickens felt unwanted long before she insisted upon him going out to work at the age of twelve. Long ago, the sage Hugh Kingsmill saw Dickens's short story 'George Silverman's Explanation', 'drenched in self-pity and self-abasement' as it is, as an allegory of the novelist's entire life. This is probably an exaggeration – the differences between Dickens and 'George Silverman', an elderly clergyman who had risen from extreme poverty through education and patronage, and who disgraces himself by performing the wedding ceremony for the daughter of his patroness and an unsuitable partner, are more obvious than the parallels. The centrality of the story, though, is that George cannot escape his poverty-stricken origins; he cannot escape the troubling but obvious fact that no one wanted him to be born in the first place. When he had finished the story, in 1868, Dickens wrote that 'I feel as if I had read something (by somebody else) which I shall never get out of my head.' The 'somebody else' was surely the unrecognized part of himself. Penned supposedly by the civilized self, Valentine, it is actually the story of Orson, 'a mangy young dog or wolf-cub' – 'a young vampire' is how he describes his working-class self before he rose through education and was sent to Cambridge. 'I pen it for the relief of my own mind,' 'George Silverman' wrote at the conclusion of the tale.

Dickens's oeuvre is dotted with unwanted children, from Trotty Veck in *The Chimes*, to Florence Dombey, to Esther in *Bleak House*. Child psychologist Bruno Bettelheim, pioneer in treating autism, discovered that many schizoid children had been born at a time of crisis in their parents' relationship, the birth only making a bad relationship worse, adding to the poverty or tensions of the household. Such patients, frequently criminal delinquents or sociopaths, believed they had no right to have been born, just as Trotty, in *The Chimes*, thinks the poor are 'born bad'. Trotty has to learn – hence the tears of all Dickens's friends, captured by Maclise as the novelist read them the Christmas story – that 'their Great Creator formed them to enjoy' [*TC* 4] a rightful share in man's inheritance. George Silverman accepts that he had no right to be born, he accepted his parents' low view of himself and, because innocent, acted as if he were guilty. There was, naturally, another course, the one followed by Dickens himself – instinctively rather than consciously – a course that was much more fruitful, though aggressive. That is, to divide the self into two.

It is a wonderful recipe for a great creative dramatist or novelist – whether it is Shakespeare in love with two loves, comfort and despair, a bright and a dark angel, or Dickens, with his good and evil selves, carefully compartmentalized and fictionalized.

However, woe betide the composed or integrated self who tries to form a relationship with such a person! That fate was handed out to Catherine Hogarth, the wife who was, as far as we can tell, the only person to whom Dickens ever told the truth about his childhood, before he wrote down the Autobiographical Fragment.

The words Dickens spoke about his mother to Forster are an indictment. 'I never afterwards forgot, I never shall forget, I never can forget.'

The concept of the 'False Self' was introduced to psychoanalysis by Donald Winnicott in 1960, but versions of it had been around before that. He believed that the happy baby, confident in its parents' love, learns the simple art of being – being itself – just by enjoying the dawning sensation of being alive, whereas the badly parented child has to develop a carapace, has to learn to be a False Self in order, usually unsuccessfully, to please its parents. Such False Selves often grow up to become manipulative, cruel and controlling people, incapable of making their own partners or children happy. Charles Dickens certainly would appear to be a textbook case of the False Self, and we can only be grateful that there was no Donald Winnicott in existence, as Dickens began to make sense of his experience in youth or young manhood, who would have been able to destroy his art by therapy.

Inside, there was the burning anger and resentment: 'I never shall forget, I never can forget.'

There was also, however, the never-so-aptly named False Self. Whereas the mother, frivolous, young, still little more than a teenager herself, and exhausted by the birth of Charles so soon after his elder sister, was simply not equipped to offer him love, the father urged him to perform, act and write. Dickens would be placed on the table, as on a stage, to entertain the guffawing aunts and cousins. He wrote a tragedy called *Misnar, the Sultan of India*, which his father urged him to put on for the entertainment of the larger family, and he wrote and performed sketches – in one he pretended to be a deaf old man, and in another he cruelly imitated the old woman who cooked their meals in Bayham Street, Camden Town. They could not give him the inward reassurance of knowing that he was loved, but they offered a knowledge that was much more seductive: the knowledge that he was entertaining.

CHAPTER 3

THE MYSTERY OF
THE CRUEL MARRIAGE

It was 8 June 1870, his last day of consciousness. With the help of the servants, Georgina Hogarth lifted Dickens from the floor and placed him on the sofa. One of the maids was sent to bring the local doctor, who recognized that Dickens had suffered a paralytic stroke. An effusion of blood on the brain made his imminent death inevitable. Georgina sent telegrams to his daughters Mary and Katey and to Dr Beard – Frank Beard, who had been Dickens's medical adviser for a number of years and was the brother of one of his very oldest friends, Thomas Beard, who had known Dickens before he wrote his novels and was rising to fame as 'Boz'. They arrived at Gad's Hill that night. Early the next morning, Charley, the only one of the children who had insisted that he should live with their mother after the parents separated, arrived with the London doctor. Charley had explained to his father, when he went to live with Kate Dickens, that he still loved him: he merely considered it his duty to look after his forsaken mother. He worked with

Dickens on *All the Year Round*, and he had been at Gad's for the last Christmas, the one when his father had blurted out, 'Warren's Blacking, 30, Strand!' during the memory game.

While Charley came down to Gad's Hill to see his dying father, his sister Katey Collins went in the opposite direction. She decided that she must return to London at once and tell the person whose absence from this scene was most conspicuous: Dickens's wife. Did she remember that bitter sentence in *Dombey and Son*, referring to 'Mr Punch, that model of connubial bliss'? [*DS* 31]

'Why did you get married?' said Scrooge.
'Because I fell in love.'
'Because you fell in love!' growled Scrooge, as if that were the only thing in the world more ridiculous than a merry Christmas. [*CC* Stave 1]

I am writing these words overlooking the garden of my neighbour, 70 Gloucester Crescent, Camden Town. For the last twenty-one years I have stared at this house, where Charles Dickens dumped his wife Kate after the fateful obsession with Nelly Ternan took over his existence. Before I became aware of this fact, I felt the place exuded an atmosphere of menace and melancholy. Since I discovered the Dickens connection, within a few weeks of moving in, I have often meditated upon the misery of it all. And now there has come to light the correspondence of one of Kate's neighbours, which discloses that, not content to humiliate her by a very public separation, Dickens also wanted to cast doubt on her sanity and have her locked away. Even if you do not buy the Winnicott notion of the False Self in all its details, you can't deny that no woman marrying Dickens could have avoided coming up against the consequences of the childhood demons. His controllingness (not trusting his wife to do the shopping, for example, and often accompanying her to butchers, fruiterers, fishmongers and the like), his obsession with mesmeric control – which will be explored later – his testiness, his obsessive neatness, later the violence of his language to her: all these would presumably have been directed against anyone who had the misfortune to marry him.

When it was all over, and the years had passed, and she was looking back on the ruins of their family past, Dickens's artist daughter Katey said she believed that whoever her father had married, it would have been a disaster. 'He did not understand women.'

The week before he died, Katey had come up to Gad's Hill from London. She had been worried about her father's health. He had been grey in the face, and looked far older than his years. During dinner, however, the greyness evaporated and 'it was a lively meal accompanied by merry laughter'. Father and daughter sat up talking until three in the morning. She talked about her painting – she was an artist, married to the painter Charles Collins (Wilkie's gay brother, painter of *Convent Thoughts*, one of the campest of all camp Pre-Raphaelite canvases) – and she discussed her ambition to go on the stage. It had probably been the ambition of Dickens's mother. His sister Fanny had been a professional musician. Dickens himself, as a youth and young man, had been to the theatre every night for three years and yearned to achieve fame on the boards. He and Fanny had even auditioned with his favourite actor, Charles Mathews, and the equally famous Charles Kemble, but nothing had come of the hope. Dickens understood the wish to act, but he told his daughter, 'You are pretty and no doubt would do well, but you are too sensitive a nature to bear the brunt of what you would encounter. Although there are nice people on the stage, there are some who would make your hair stand on end. You are clever enough to do something else.'

The conversation turned to other subjects, and it is obvious from what Katey later told her friend Gladys Storey that Dickens was led, by the lateness of the hour, and the warmth of a good dinner followed by brandy and cigars, to confide in his daughter. The seriousness with which he wanted to spare her the pains and humiliations of an actress's life inevitably led to the thought of the actress who had obsessed him for the last thirteen years, Nelly Ternan. He said he wished he had been 'a better father, a better man'. 'He talked and talked, *how* he talked, until three o'clock in the morning, when we parted for bed. I know things about my father's character . . . that no one else ever knew; he was not a good man, but he was not a fast man, he was wonderful! He fell in love with this girl, I did not blame *her* – it is never one person's fault.'

The next day she went to him in the Swiss chalet in the garden, where he wrote. Normally, when parting from his daughters, he would merely offer his cheek. On this occasion it was he who kissed Katey, very affectionately. There were two words he never liked to say – 'good bye'. It was the last time she saw him conscious.

And now, as he lay dying on the sofa, Katey, having made her last farewell to a father, returned to the railway station. She took the train to Charing Cross, and a cab conveyed her across London. In reverse, it followed the route that he would have taken every day during the dread years, as a boy, of his employment at Warren's Blacking, from Covent Garden northwards through Bloomsbury to Camden Town, to 70 Gloucester Crescent. These houses, which had been erected by specu-lative builders during and just after the coming of the railways, were grander than anything his parents had known, but they were scarcely mansions. They were for the middling sort. Number 70 was, however, the pleasantest in the crescent because it had almost an acre of garden surrounding it on three sides – albeit overlooked by the taller houses to the north-west in Regent's Park Terrace, in one of which I am sitting to write this page. I am looking into the drawing room where Katey broke the news.

After her parents separated, Katey's mother only spoke twice to her of Charles Dickens. Once, looking at his photograph in a gilt frame, which she kept in her drawing room, she asked, 'Do you think he is sorry for me?'

Years afterwards, nine years after Dickens had died, when Mrs Dickens was suffering from cancer, she asked Katey to go to her drawer and fetch her a bundle of letters, and a locket that contained a likeness of the novelist and a lock of his hair. 'With great earnestness', she said to her daughter, 'Give these to the British Museum – that the world may know that he loved me once.'

To her neighbours in Gloucester Crescent, Mrs Dickens had been less reticent. Edward Dutton Cook, a novelist and man of letters, and his young pianist wife Lynda befriended Mrs Dickens and her son Charley, who were living next door. She told Cook that, contrary to what Dickens put about, 'a great affection subsisted during a long course of years between' her and Dickens, but that when he decided to bring the marriage to an end, he pretended they had never been able to get along. She also told the Cooks that he had tried to persuade the doctor who attended her to

119

sanction an accusation of mental illness, which would permit him to have her confined to an asylum. Dickens had close friends in the medical profession. John Sutherland wrote, 'To be accused of "mental disorder" with Dr John Connolly and John Forster . . . hovering in the background was highly ominous. For a physician like Connolly, Mrs Dickens' alleged "languor" and her excitability about her husband's infidelity would have been quite sufficient for a certificate of "moral insanity" to be drawn up. He did it for [Dickens's friend] Lord Lytton, would he not do the same for his friend Mr Dickens?'

As she made her way to Gloucester Crescent to tell her mother that Dickens was dying, Katey was confronted with the essential mystery of the thing. This was not that two people had tried to get along together and failed: there is nothing mysterious about that. The mystery was: how could the apostle of kindliness, the novelist who, more than any other, extols the virtues of charity, who waged war on Scrooge, and Bumble and Bounderby, how could he, of all the people in the world, have been so furiously unkind, so vindictively, pointedly and quite unnecessarily cruel, to the woman who had borne his children, and whose faults, in so far as anyone has noted them, were trivial? Even if Dickens could not contain his marital hatred, how could he not have seen that by ending his marriage in the way he did, he was causing incalculable pain to the children? Such is the madness of marriage separation, of course, as all those who have been through it will most bitterly know. But even by the selfish standards of the divorcee, Dickens's behaviour was beyond easy explanation. Maybe the simple answer, when puzzling over this problem, is the same we should give when trying to explain his mother's neglect of him, and her insistence that he should return to Warren's Blacking, even after John Dickens was released from gaol: that in family relationships, sometimes bad behaviour is the only option. It is not to be excused, but it is a fact.

By many accounts, Kate could be petulant and moody. Compared with her favoured sister Georgina, she was a bad household manager. She was impractical. But were these reasons not merely for putting her away, but for doing so very publicly; for advertising her faults in his own periodical, *Household Words*, and also in *The Times*; for plotting with the doctors – though there is not the smallest evidence of Kate being insane – to have his wife incarcerated in a lunatic asylum? And, perhaps most extraordinary of all, for forbidding her children to see her? Further to this mystery is the mystery of Dickens's power: how and why he exercised his mesmeric power over those often strong-willed children.

'My father was like a madman when my mother left him,' daughter Katey recalled. 'This affair brought out all that was worst – all that was

121

weakest in him. He did not care a damn what happened to any of us.'

On another occasion, Katey said to Gladys Storey, 'We were all very wicked not to take her part; Harry does not take this view, but he was only a boy at the time, and does not realize the grief it was to our mother, after having all her children, to go away and leave us. My mother never rebuked me. I never saw her in a temper. We like to think of our geniuses as great characters – but we can't.' In her old age she would recall her first husband, Charles Collins, often begging her to go and see her mother, and that she had refused. She had the painful recollection of how, in their teens, she and her sister Mamie had taken music lessons in Gloucester Crescent in the house opposite their mother's. 'They would drive up and drive away, but never call to see their mother, who had either seen them arrive or depart, or had been told they had done so by one of her maidservants. Often had she waited in expectation of them coming – who could condemn the tears she shed in the desolation of her home – when after time they did not cross the road and ring her doorbell.'

Kate Dickens, born Catherine Hogarth, could have read, and probably did read, a very severe danger-signal two years before her husband even met Nelly Ternan. In 1855, three days after his forty-third birthday, Dickens was making arrangements to take the family to France for a while, to give him space to start a new novel – the book that would become *Little Dorrit*. When the post was brought into his study, there was a letter from the woman he had first loved as a youth: Maria Beadnell.

He replied to it. 'Three or four and twenty years vanished like a dream, and I opened it with the touch of my young friend David Copperfield when he was in love.'

He had first met Maria when he was nineteen. Her father, a City banker called George Beadnell, invited Dickens to dinner when he was working as a newspaper reporter for parliamentary debates. Maria was a year older than Dickens, tiny, 'a pocket Venus', and he first saw her sitting in a 'sort of raspberry-coloured dress' playing the harp. He was to fall deeply in love with her. Understandably enough, the Beadnells looked askance at an impoverished young journalist, who had no family and no apparent prospects. Dickens had made a success of the parliamentary reporting. The absurdities of the parliamentary system were never lost on him, but he did the work faithfully. So much so that the future prime minister Lord Derby, when still Mr Stanley, actually asked for the young reporter on the *Morning Chronicle* to come to his house in Carlton Terrace to take down the salient points of one of his speeches, because he had recognized Dickens (without knowing his name or what he would one day become) as the most accurate of the parliamentary reporters.

Dickens, from the first, had shown application, energy, all the qualities he would one day bring to his art. And when the work took him to report political meetings and elections in the furthest parts of the country, he had been capable of writing wherever and whenever necessity required: he later described himself as scribbling as they galloped 'through a wild country, and through the dead of night, at the then surprising rate of fifteen miles an hour'.

This small, ambitious, hyper-energetic young man, however, had scarcely been the sort of son-in-law sought by a successful City banker. 'I have never loved and I never can love any human creature breathing but yourself,' Dickens wrote to Maria. His infatuation with the Pocket Venus was, of necessity, without hope. Maria flirted with him, and was amused by his attentions, while clearly scorning him as a mere 'boy'. When Dickens reconstructed the painful relationship between Pip and Estella in *Great Expectations*, it would seem as if he were drawing on the excruciating memory of these humiliations. In class-ridden Britain there are few things that remind someone so acutely of their place in the hierarchy of things as falling in love with someone out of your class. Eventually, after eighteen months of torture, he could tolerate Maria's heartless displays of indifference no longer and broke off relations with her, in a tirade of hurt feelings – 'to you a matter of very little moment still I *have* feelings in common with other people'). She was careful enough to take a copy of the letter before she returned it to him.

And now, nearly a quarter of a century later, a novelist at the height of his powers, fame and success, Dickens received a letter from Maria out of the blue. He replied that he was about to go to Paris, but when he returned, his wife Kate would call on Maria to suggest a date for dinner. For, yes, Maria was married now – she was Mrs Winter, the mother of two young daughters. 'In the unsettled state of my thoughts, the existence of these dear children appeared such a prodigious phenomenon, that I was inclined to suspect myself as being out of my mind, until it occurred to me that perhaps I had nine children of my own! Then the three or four and twenty years began to arrange themselves in a long procession between me and the changeless Past.'

It was the middle-aged Maria Winter who had written to him, but in his fantasy, it was the youthful Pocket Venus with whom he was once again in love. Dickens was bored by his petulant, moody wife, and they were getting on badly. When he was in Paris, he was haunted by the thought of Maria. Was it really true, a friend asked him, that he had loved her so much? He replied, 'there was no woman in the world, and there were very few men, who could ever imagine how much'.

Both the forty-four-year-old Maria and the forty-three-year-old Dickens, before they actually met, were falling in love again on paper. She protested to him, in advance, that she was now old and fat and ugly, but he would not believe it. She must, from the tone of his letters (hers do not survive), have coquettishly suggested that, contrary to appearances, she had indeed loved him all those years ago and had been merely prevented from accepting his advances by the strictness of her family.

She suggested that they should meet *à deux* before the shared dinner with Dickens's wife and her husband; he told her to come to Tavistock House, where the Dickenses were then residing, and to ask for his wife. It is not completely clear where the meeting took place, but on Sunday 25 February 1855 they met.

The glorious creation that came out of their meeting is known to all the world as Flora Finching in *Little Dorrit*.

> Flora, whom he had left a lily, had become a peony; but that was not much. Flora, who had seemed enchanting in all she said and thought, was diffuse and silly . . . 'I am sure,' giggled Flora, tossing her head with a caricature of her girlish manner, such as a mummer might have presented at her own funeral, if she had lived and died in classical antiquity. 'I am ashamed to see Mr Clennam, I am a mere fright, I know he'll think me fearfully changed, I am

126

actually an old woman, it's shocking to be so found out so really shocking.' [*LD* I 13]

The meeting with his old love, like everything else in a novelist's heartless life, was grist to Dickens's mill. The pathos of it was retained, but coated in farce, like sea salt lending piquancy to vanilla ice cream. So many of the saddest things in Dickens's experience were transubstantiated into farce. As he planned the novel that grew out of his father's ruin and life in the Marshalsea, he would also draw on the humiliations visited upon him by the Beadnells, who had appeared to be somebody when he was a nobody, but were now seen as the banking nobodies who had cruelly rejected a genius. Maria's harmless prattle, her nervous inability to finish sentences, her gross size, her exhausting and embarrassing coquettishness all became the ludicrous and unforgettable Flora Finching. For good measure, he gave her the companionship, not of a dull husband, but of a dead husband's aunt, the furious old 'Mr F's aunt', whose surreal and inconsequential outbursts are among the funniest things he ever devised: "'When we lived at Henley, Barnes's gander was stole by tinkers.'" [*LD* I 13]

The disillusionment he felt with Maria was strong, but the dinner went ahead as planned on 7 March. Mr Winter was a bore. Mrs Winter, fat, simpering, silly, had a bad cold which Dickens (always prone to colds) caught. Her fate was sealed.

127

What the real Maria could not know – because, unlike Dickens and the 'characters' whom he had been dreaming up ever since boyhood, she was not a 'character' in a novel – was that she, Maria Beadnell, had ceased to exist. Flora Finching had come into being. Her attempts to get in touch with Dickens after this disastrous dinner were met with brush-offs. Her usefulness was now at an end.

Kate Dickens, who knew her susceptible husband all too well, could read his disillusionment very easily. Like his first love Maria, Kate Hogarth, having reached her forties and borne Dickens ten children, one of whom had died, was also fat and unappealing, with bad teeth and a red face. She was in no doubt that, in his heart, if not yet in his bedroom or his day-to-day existence, she had been demoted, and she must on some level have feared complete banishment.

After the disappointment of being snubbed by the Beadnell family, Dickens at twenty-one had been transmogrified into 'Boz'.

Having made a success as a reporter of parliamentary debates, and of political meetings around Great Britain, as far afield as Edinburgh, Dickens found that his witty iconoclastic accounts ('Lord Lincoln broke down and sat down') led to his being taken on, first as a regular on the *Monthly Magazine* and then on the *Morning Chronicle*. In addition, the *Monthly* had begun to publish semi-fictionalized 'sketches' of London life. When he was on board a ship taking him up to Edinburgh, Dickens had seen a commercial traveller laughing over his copy of the *Monthly* – which contained his sketch of 'The Bloomsbury Christening'. He wrote under the pen-name 'Boz'. It had been the nickname Dickens himself gave his younger brother Augustus, 'whom in honour of the *Vicar of Wakefield*, he had dubbed Moses'. The child's nasal mispronunciation of 'Boses' led to the shortening to 'Boz'.

The magpie adoption of a name that had belonged to another – his brother – and the transmogrification of experience into fiction: all this went hand-in-hand with the beginnings of Dickens's sucess. The world of the Fourth Estate was a peculiarly classless one, much more so than the law – had he chosen to become a law clerk. Social climbing was not his sole end, but it was a useful skill for an aspiring writer and one that was made possible because he had started to woo the daughter of a fellow journalist.

Dickens was a small, dandified, smooth-faced young man, with thick chestnut-coloured hair. He developed the capacity to strike out on his own, took chambers at Furnival's Inn (a legal Inn of Court), which he shared with his younger brother Frederick, while trying – out of his income as a journalist – to bail out his hopeless father from one financial scrape to another. John Dickens, having failed to make a living as a clerk, had himself drifted into journalism and had been given an opening, reporting on the arcane procedures of Doctors' Commons – that 'lazy old nook' – and it was here, too, that Charles Dickens found work, doing legal reports at Doctors' Commons: a branch of the ecclesiastical courts 'where they granted,' as he recalled, 'marriage licences to love-sick couples and divorces to unfaithful ones, registered the wills of people who have any property to leave, and punish hasty gentlemen who called ladies by unpleasant names'.

It was in Doctors' Commons that Tony Weller, father of Mr Pickwick's companion and servant Sam, went as a coachman and inadvertently found himself buying a marriage licence from two porters who were licence touts.

'Pray take a seat, vile I makes out the affidavit, Sir,' says the lawyer. – 'Thankee, Sir,' says my father, and down he sat, and stared vith all his eyes, and his mouth vide open, at the names on the boxes. 'What's your name, Sir?' says the lawyer – 'Tony Weller,' says my father. – 'Parish?' says the lawyer – 'Belle Savage,' says my father; for he stopped there ven he drove up, and he know'd nothing about parishes, he didn't. – 'And what's the lady's name?', says the lawyer. My father was struck all of a heap. 'Blessed if I know,' says he. – 'Not know!' says the lawyer. – 'No more nor you do,' says my father, 'can't I put that in arterwards?' [*PP* 10]

Weller was a name that haunted Dickens. Mary Weller had been his nurse in childhood in Chatham, a sort of Peggotty, but with horror stories with which to regale her charge – she had told him the tale of Captain Murderer, as he recollected in 'Nurse's Stories'. Her younger sister Anna married Dickens's brother Fred, a union no more successful than his own marriage to Kate. By contrast, long after he had written *Pickwick*, in Liverpool in 1844 he would meet a young pianist called Christiana Weller. He read 'An angel's message in her face . . . that smote me to the heart.'

For eighteen months after his childhood ended Dickens had worked as a legal clerk. But taking rooms in an Inn of Court did not suggest any ambition to pursue a career in the law. Like Thackeray's Pendennis:

> the man of letters can't but love the place which has been inhabited by so many of his brethren, or peopled by their creations, as real to us at this day as the authors whose children they were – and Sir Roger de Coverley walking in the Temple Garden, and discoursing with Mr Spectator about the beauties in hoops and patches who are sauntering over the grass, is just as lively a figure to me as old Samuel Johnson rolling through the fog with the Scotch gentleman at his heels on his way to Dr Goldsmith's

chambers in Brick Court; or Harry Fielding, with inked ruffles and a wet towel round his head, dashing off articles at midnight for the Covent Garden Journal, while the printer's boy is asleep in the passage.

Dickens's early forays into journalism brought him into contact with other writers, and he was befriended by William Harrison Ainsworth, seven years his senior, who was celebrated for his sub-Scott historical fiction. *Rookwood* was an exciting tale of Dick Turpin the Highwayman.

Dickens would not follow Ainsworth's manner when he turned to fiction, but he aped his dress sense, with velvet coats and embroidered waistcoats he could scarcely afford. The Victorian Age had not yet begun and, as far as clothes were in question, fashion still followed the tail end of the Regency. Mr Turveydrop, the dancing master and teacher of deportment in *Bleak House*, would have approved of them. It was looking velvety and colourful and heavily pomaded that Dickens first met his future father-in-law George Hogarth, who had been a Writer to the Signet (a lawyer) in Edinburgh, had known Sir Walter, and had come south to work as a music critic on the *Morning Chronicle*. Dickens would boast of 'My marriage with Miss Hogarth – the daughter of a gentleman who has recently distinguished himself by a celebrated work on Music, who was the most intimate friend and companion of Sir Walter Scott, and one of the most eminent among the Literati of Edinburgh.' Scott, by far the most famous writer in the English language before Dickens, and with a huge following in Europe as well as at home, had only died four years previously, in 1832.

At the age of fifty, Hogarth was made editor of the newly founded *Evening Chronicle* and Dickens became a regular visitor to his house in Chelsea, in those days still separated from the rest of London by green fields. Dickens gave shorthand lessons to Hogarth's son Robert, and flirted with the daughters, Mary, Georgina and Catherine.

Catherine Hogarth (Kate), inclined to plumpness even then, was a voluptuous, blue-eyed brunette – small, like Nelly, like Maria – with whom Dickens formed a quick bond; though, stung as he had been by the Maria Beadnell experience, he held back a little more of himself than he had done aged nineteen.

Anyhow, circumstances had now changed. The nineteen-year-old who had tried to woo Maria had been a penniless boy. It is not known how much the Beadnells knew about the penurious Dickens family, but they could have guessed that here was not a man of substance, even if the full truth – his grandparents in domestic service, his father an habitué of the Marshalsea – might have been tactfully hidden. The crimson-velveted 'Boz' had cut loose from reality altogether, and there was no need for him to spell out in too much detail to the Hogarths who he was or where he came from. They were all citizens together in the republic of London journalism. It was the world of Thackeray's *Pendennis*, and it was one that Dickens inhabited cheerfully all his life. He was, like Pendennis and his friend Warrington, 'of the Corporation of the Goosequill – of the Press, my boy . . . of the fourth estate'. Passing a newspaper building in the Strand at night, '"Look at that, Pen," Warrington said, "there she is – the great engine – she never sleeps. She has her ambassadors in every quarter of the world – her couriers upon every road. Her officers march with armies, and her envoys walk into statesman's cabinets. They are ubiquitous . . ."' To this great republic, which burgeoned so fully in the nineteenth century, Dickens belonged. He was indeed its creature: he always chose to publish in periodical, rather than in volume, form.

Prodigious as was his output as a novelist, and successful on every level as these novels were, Dickens never abandoned journalism. Scarcely a month of his life passed without his writing for one periodical or another, and he was the founder editor of two periodicals – *Daily News*, which he inaugurated in 1845, and *Household Words*, which started life in 1850 just as he was finishing *David Copperfield*. Even the fiction appeared periodically, as if it were journalism. Dickens loved and needed the tension of journalistic demands, the deadlines and the instant gratification of seeing work appear

134

speedily in print. He described how, in December 1835, he had dropped the first of his sketches – 'A Dinner at Poplar Walk' – through the door of the *Monthly Magazine* 'up a dark court in Fleet Street'. When the magazine appeared, he bought a copy in Hall's bookshop in the Strand and saw himself in print for the first time. He walked to Parliament to begin his evening stint of reporting, 'my eyes so dimmed with pride and joy that they could not bear the street, and were not fit to be seen'. He never lost this 'buzz', and for those who feel it, there are few stronger emotions, which is a poor lookout for those they marry.

He might have loved Catherine Hogarth at first, but he already loved Boz – or at least being Boz – more. *Sketches by Boz* was published on his twenty-fourth birthday, 7 February 1836. Thereafter, his career enjoyed meteoric success.

It was in Hall's bookshop that he had first seen his work in print. When Mr William Hall himself visited Dickens on 10 February 1836, it seemed like a good omen. Hall had gone into partnership with Edward Chapman, and Chapman and Hall intended to start a periodical called *The Library of Fiction*, published in monthly episodes from April 1836. They offered Dickens £14 per month to write for it. He was to provide 12,000 words per issue to accompany some comic illustrations by the melancholic artist Robert Seymour. These were sporting sketches of life in the country, and, while eagerly accepting the offer of well-paid work,

Dickens had felt bound to tell Chapman and Hall that he intended to interpret the brief fairly liberally, since he had no taste for country sports and had never been hunting, shooting or fishing in his life.

On 18 February, he wrote to Chapman and Hall the momentous words, 'Pickwick is at length begun in all his might and glory. The first chapter will be ready tomorrow.'

Dickens had not met Seymour, the illustrator, when he had the boldness to write to him, suggesting that he alter one of his etchings. By then – 14 April 1836 – *The Pickwick Papers* were under way, and Dickens was writing one of the many diversions – 'The Stroller's Tale'. He told Seymour the alterations he needed, adding, 'With this view, I have asked Chapman and Hall to take a glass of grog with me on Sunday evening (the only night I am disengaged) when I hope you will be able to look in.' It was the only time they met. Seymour provided illustrations for the first two issues of *The Posthumous Papers of the Pickwick Club*. His own illustrations were soon to be posthumous. A week after providing Dickens with a revised drawing, Seymour went into the summerhouse in his garden in Liverpool Road, Islington, and shot himself. A verdict of insanity was declared by the coroner. Dickens liked to tell the story that, a week before killing himself, Seymour had asked his wife to try on a widow's cap. Thomas Hardy would have liked that story.

Dickens was not to blame for the depressive Seymour's suicide. Nonetheless, there is a cruel aptness to it. What a horrible contrast between the young writer's fitness and success and the low-spirited artist's sense of abject failure. We sense the writer's superabundant love of life, and ability to bring forth life – his many children, as well as the work, which pulsates, roars, laughs aloud with life, like God on the final day of Creation considering His work very good, grinding down the artist's inability to face existence. He must increase and I must decrease. There was something relentless, callous, about Dickens's romping to glory. For *Pickwick* was to be a success such as had never really been witnessed in the history of English fiction.

Not that the Auguries appeared at all propitious. The first episode sold a mere 400 copies. Then, after Seymour committed suicide, a new illustrator, R. W. Buss, was engaged and he was no good. We'll meet him later. Having sacked Buss, the publishers looked about for another artist for the third issue. One idea was to engage William Makepeace Thackeray, an accomplished draughtsman and illustrator, who would illustrate his own work, such as *The Rose and the Ring*. In the end, however, Dickens lighted upon the twenty-one-year-old engraver employed in-house by Chapman and Hall, Hablot Knight Browne – who would be known to the world as 'Phiz'. Dickens, having been offered the 'Cockney humourist' pictures of Seymour, took them over, changed the story, made Pickwick, Tupman and Snodgrass into something Seymour had never intended, *sui generis*, unclassifiable figures, blundering from one incident – bizarre, hilarious, sometimes tear-jerking – to the next. By the time Pickwick meets Sam Weller in Chapter 10, Phiz was luckily in control, to illustrate one of the most enduring partnerships of literature.

The illustrations are an essential part of the experience when reading a novel by Charles Dickens. Q. D. Leavis, in her superb chapter on the Dickens illustrations, wrote that, 'If Dickens never read Blake, then it is an extraordinary coincidence how wonderfully his novels incarnate *Songs of Innocence and Experience*; he is indeed the Blake as well as the Shakespeare of the novel.'

They remind us that when we open these pages, we are entering an alternative universe, a version of the nineteenth century, but not a photographic version. Dickens was no Zola, he made no attempts at *cinéma vérité*. The reader, like all his intimates, his friends, his children, his wife, accepted the world on his terms or not at all. No one looking at the Phiz illustrations before reading could suppose they were going to read realistic accounts of the world. Yet no one who has absorbed either Phiz or Dickens in the system will ever quite lose the habit of seeing the world through their spectacles, recognizing people in 'real life' as highly 'Dickensian', and imagining how they would appear when drawn by Phiz, or Cruikshank.

At about the time that Boz was entertaining an increasingly rapturous public with the Pickwick Breach of Promise case, Dickens had become a married man. He and Kate were married in the Hogarths' parish church, St Luke's, Chelsea, on 2 April 1836. Like Dickens's own mother, Kate was marrying very young, at just twenty. Because she was not yet of age, they had to obtain a special licence from the Archbishop of Canterbury. To get this, Dickens had to revisit the arcane old haunts of Doctors' Commons, which gave him the idea for the fourth episode of *Pickwick*, when the fraudulent actor Mr Jingle obtains a parchment from the Archbishop via Doctors' Commons, addressed to his 'trusty and well-beloved Alfred Jingle and Rachael Wardle'. [*PP* 10]

Charles and Kate had a brief honeymoon in Kent, the land of innocence, in the village of Chalk, near his childhood home in Rochester, and, all too soon for Kate's liking, she was taken back to share his set of rooms in Furnival's Inn with her sister Mary and his brother Frederick. It was there, in the first month of their marriage, that Dickens entertained Seymour, Chapman and Hall to that glass of grog, twelve days after their wedding and a week before Seymour's suicide. It was there that Kate realized that, although she was to share his bed, and – when he had the time or inclination – his leisure hours, for the most part she was to be alone, while he gave himself up to frantic activity.

Kate became pregnant almost at once, their first child, Charley (Charles Culliford Boz Dickens), being born on 6 January 1837. In that time, while Dickens praised her neatness and said she was 'a capital housekeeper', and wrote and spoke to her in baby language, begging her not to be 'coss' at his neglect of her, he had thrown himself into polemical journalism, theatricals and fiction-writing. He had, moreover, become famous. The amusing young Boz, who had been in the nature of a Hogarth-family discovery, was no longer Kate's property: she found herself married to someone prodigiously successful and celebrated. By the time of their first wedding anniversary, *Pickwick* was selling 6,000 copies per month, and on 8 April 1837, Chapman and Hall gave him a cheque for £500 and a dinner to celebrate his ever-growing success. The Dickenses left the cramped quarters of Furnival's Inn and moved into 48 Doughty Street, a substantial terraced house near Gray's Inn.

By now he was on to *Oliver Twist*. The past never stays still. It changes, which is why the task of the historian changes with each generation. Those taught as students that the British Empire was their country's moral, as well as political, apogee lived to see the absolutely opposite viewpoint become the orthodoxy. In personal narratives, this phenomenon is observable in almost every human life. In the life of one of the greatest creative geniuses, it is inevitable that his narrative of his own marriage should be presented with especial forcefulness; with such a pungent strength that biographers of Dickens have inevitably divided between those who sided with his version of the marriage and those who have subsequently found it dismaying.

John Forster, a young journalist and aspirant writer, two months the novelist's junior, met Dickens in the year of his marriage. He was destined to be not merely one of Dickens's closest friends and allies, but also his biographer. Forster's is not one of the very greatest literary biographies. It is not in the league of Boswell's Johnson, Froude's Carlyle or Eckermann's *Conversations with Goethe*, but it is a wonderful book, and everyone who tries to become acquainted with the life of Dickens is in his debt. Whereas Carlyle specifically entrusted Froude with the task of telling the full truth about his less-than-happy marriage, Forster felt constrained by his close friendship with Dickens, and his own personal antipathy to Mrs Dickens. He made as little as possible of the marriage, mentioning Dickens's wife only when strictly necessary. In some senses, Forster and his version of history are set up by the biography as Kate Dickens's rival. For example, he claimed to be the only person to whom Dickens had imparted the secret of his working at Warren's Blacking. One of Kate's only comments about the biography, when it appeared, was that she had known of, and read, the Autobiographical Fragment in which Dickens revealed his secret childhood misery. Our first impressions of Mrs Dickens, if we rely on Forster, are therefore likely to be skewed; but not so skewed as if we merely read Dickens's self-justificatory accounts of the marriage when it was over.

On 9 May 1858, he would write to Miss Angela Burdett-Coutts, the devoutly Christian philanthropist with whom he did so much charitable work:

> We have been virtually separated for a long time. We must put a wider space between us now, than can be found in one house. If the children had loved her, or ever loved her, this severance would have been a far easier thing than it is. But she has never attached one of them to herself, never played with them in their infancy, never attracted their confidence as they have grown older, never presented herself before them in the aspect of a mother. I have seen them all fall off from her in a natural – not *un*natural – progress of estrangement, and at this moment Mary and Katey (whose dispositions are of the gentlest and most affectionate conceivable) harden into stone

figures of girls when they can be got to go near her, and have their hearts shut up in her presence as if they were closed by some horrid spring.

No one can understand this but Georgina, who has seen it grow from year to year, and who is the best, the most unselfish, and most devoted of human Creatures. Her sister Mary, who died suddenly and who lived with us before her, understood it as well in the first months of our marriage. It is her misery to live in some fatal atmosphere which slays every one to whom she should be dearest. It is my misery that no one can ever understand the truth in its full force, or know what a blighted and wasted life my married life has been.

Forster, by contrast, recorded many moments in the marriage when it was clear that there were years in which Dickens enjoyed happiness in Kate's company. During Dickens's first tour of America in 1842, he could write:

Kate . . . you recollect her propensity? She falls into, or out of, every coach or boat we enter; scrapes the shins off her legs; brings great sores and swellings on her feet; chips large fragments out of her ankle-bones; and makes herself blue with bruises. She really has, however, since we got over the first trial of being among circumstances so new and so fatiguing, made a *most admirable* traveller in every respect. She has never screamed or expressed alarm under any circumstances that would have fully justified her in doing so, even in my eyes.

This letter recognized that Dickens did have a tendency to find her annoying, that he did think she was unnecessarily querulous, as well as clumsy; but that nevertheless, he was happy in her company. A Bostonian lady recalled after this trip:

There was no sign then of any disagreement or incompatibility between husband and wife . . . After their return to England I saw several amusing and familiar letters written by Dickens to his Boston friends – letters in which repeated and affectionate allusions were made to 'Kate' – and it struck me with the greatest surprise when several years afterwards I learned that conjugal difficulties in the Dickens household had led to estrangement and separation.

Similar words could be written about the two protagonists in any failed marriage. Had Dickens and his wife struggled on bravely together to the end, had he been able to subdue the irritation she awoke in him, and had he never become infatuated with Nelly Ternan, the discontents and quarrels in the marriage would not necessarily have loomed large, when the story of his life came to be told.

That said, we can see cracks appearing in the marriage, even if we do not accept Dickens's completely negative version of events, after it had fallen apart.

In the autumn of 1856, for example, we find a passage in the diary of Nathaniel Hawthorne:

> Speaking of Dickens last evening, Mrs [Monckton] Milnes mentioned his domestic tastes, how he preferred home-enjoyments to all others and did not willingly go much into society. Mrs Bennoch, too, the other day, told us how careful he was of his wife, taking on himself all possible trouble as regards his domestic affairs, making bargains at butchers and bakers, and doing, as far as he could, whatever duty pertains to an English wife.

January 1857 found him writing to Wills, sub-editor on *Household Words*, that 'I am going to Newgate Market with Mrs Dickens after breakfast to shew her where to buy fowls.' The fact that he took her shopping can be read either as over-controlling – he did not trust Kate to buy the fowl herself – or affectionately uxorious. It shows that, despite what he later liked to claim, it was not always her sister Georgina who ran the household, and Kate did cater for at least some of the meals.

The tenth and last child, Edward Bulwer Lytton Dickens, was born on 13 March 1852. By the time he was born, Kate had given birth nine times, and she had suffered a number of miscarriages. She was only thirty-five years old and she was not in a robust state of health, physically or mentally.

He decided to take her to Malvern for the celebrated water cure. It was while she was there that Dickens hurried back to London and witnessed the gruesome death of his father, which was described in our first chapter. It was also at this time that their eight-month-old baby Dora, being tended at home in London – they were living in Devonshire Terrace, Regent's Park – died. With so much else going on, Dickens was also rehearsing a play for a Royal Command Performance: it had the all-too-appropriate title of *Not So Bad as We Seem*. Douglas Jerrold, again all too appropriately, added, 'But a great deal worse than we ought to be'. In the event, Kate had been so distraught that Dickens was obliged to postpone the performance, while he took his wife to Fort House in Broadstairs. They sublet the house in Devonshire Terrace until September. After only a few weeks beside the sea, Dickens breezily wrote, 'I am quite happy again, but I have undergone a great deal.' His wife's happiness had been cracked, destroyed, by the loss;

its commonness – the death of babies – in that era making it no less heartbreaking.

Some – a very few – of Dickens's stories end with a happy marriage, but most do not. Three years after Dickens met Nelly Ternan, readers of the 8 September 1860 edition of *All the Year Round* had been treated to a fiction entitled 'Nurse's Stories', an expanded version of the tale told to him as a child by his nurse, Mary Weller, in Chatham. Her story told of a Captain Murderer whose 'mission was matrimony, and the gratification of a cannibal appetite with tender brides'. ['Nurse's Stories', *UT* 15] At a certain stage of the courtship of his victims, the Captain would ask if they could make pie crust. 'And if she couldn't by nature or education, she was taught.' There is something on the verge of pornographic about that slavering sentence.

Having been forced to roll out an enormous piece of pastry, the 'lovely bride' would ask, 'what pie is this to be?'

> He replied, 'A meat pie.' Then said the lovely bride, 'Dear Captain Murderer, I see no meat.' The Captain humorously retorted, 'Look in the glass.' She looked in the glass, but still she saw no meat, and then the Captain roared with laughter, and suddenly frowning and drawing his sword, bade her roll out the crust. So she rolled out the crust, dropping large tears

upon it all the time because he was so cross, and when she had lined the dish with crust and had cut the crust all ready to fit the top, the Captain called out, '*I* see the meat in the glass!' And the bride looked up at the glass just in time to see the Captain cutting her head off; and he chopped her in pieces, and peppered her, and salted her, and put her in the pie, and sent it to the baker's, and ate it all, and picked the bones. ['Nurse's Stories, *UT* 15]

Through all the decades of public and parliamentary debate about marriage, decades in which the disastrous royal marriages were oft-repeated public jokes, and the few divorce cases were eagerly devoured newspaper scandals, Dickens was writing his novels. Almost every one deals, directly or tangentially, with the theme of marital disintegration. Even in the early novel *Oliver Twist*, written in the first year of his marriage, a book that appears, at first, to be the melodrama of a child lost in the terrifying streets of criminal London, the theme of marital misery surfaces. Monks, the villain who turns out to be Oliver's half-brother, is the child of an unhappy marriage; and old Mr Brownlow, who has loved Oliver's mother and who rescues him from Fagin and the criminals, confesses, '"I also know . . . the misery, the slow torture, the protracted anguish of that ill-assorted union. I know how listlessly and wearily each of that wretched pair dragged on their heavy chain through a world that was poisoned to them both. I know how cold formalities were succeeded by open taunts.'" [*OT* 49]

'Captain Murderer' is one of the many instances in Dickens where we read, not merely totally unsympathetic accounts of marital incompatibility, but quasi-comic glorifications of monster husbands. Jerry Cruncher comes to mind, grave-robber and wife-beater, in *A Tale of Two Cities*. True, by the end of the novel he has undergone a slightly improbable change of heart and even allows, nay, encourages, his wife's habit of prayer, which in the earlier chapters he has so vigorously opposed: '"Saying your prayers! You're a nice woman! What do you mean by flopping yourself down and praying agin me?"' [*ATTC* II 1] When she tries to say grace before the meal he exclaims, 'Aggerawayter! What are you up to? At it agin? . . . I won't have my wittles blest off my table.' [*ATTC* II 1] Cruncher – pre-conversion – is not presented as loveable exactly, but he is drawn with relish.

'Perfectly goblin-like', the archetypical monster husband Quilp dominates *The Old Curiosity Shop*. Tiny, malign, he is a demonic projection of Dickens himself, and genuinely frightening. His mother-in-law, Mrs Jiniwin, did not exaggerate when she told her gaggle of female friends, '"He is the greatest tyrant that ever lived, she daren't call her soul her own, he makes her tremble with a word and even with a look, he frightens her to death.'" [*OCS* 4] "'He's a Salamander you know, that's what he is,'" says Dick Swiveller of Quilp to Frederick Trent, who does not stop to enquire "'whether a fire-proof man was as a matter of course trustworthy'". [*OCS* 23]

One of the high points of the Dickenses' visit to the Kingdom of Naples in 1845 was to climb the still-fuming Mount Vesuvius. It was February, and the six of them – Kate, Georgina, Dickens and three others – were accompanied by twenty-two guides and saw it in the severest weather conditions. One side of the mountain was 'glazed from one smooth sheet of ice from the top of the cone to the bottom'.

The more the other travellers flagged, and the more frightened they were, the more Dickens revelled in the adventure. He insisted on them all slithering and staggering onwards and upwards towards the volcano's crater.

> You may form some notion of what was going on inside it, when I tell you that it is a hundred feet higher than it was six weeks ago. The sensation of struggling up it, choked with the fire and smoke, and feeling at every step as if the crust of the ground between one's feet and the gulf of fire would crumble in and swallow one up (which is a real danger), I shall remember

for some little time, I think. But we did it. We looked down into the flaming bowels of the mountain and came back again, alight in half a dozen places, and burnt from head to foot. You never saw such devils. And I never saw anything so awful and terrible.

Quilp's name is a shortening of Quill-pen, or the Writer. One remembers him pouring a glass of liquor and adding hot water as he smoked his noxious pipe, and proffering it to Dick Swiveller.

> 'Is it good? . . . Is it strong and fiery? Does it make you wink, and choke, and your eyes water, and your breath come short – does it?'
> 'Does it?' cried Dick, throwing away part of the contents of his glass, and filling it up with water, 'why, man, you don't mean to tell me that you drink such fire as this?'
> [*OCS* 21]

In the last two years of the marriage, Dickens's ex-publisher, Frederick Evans, and his near-worshipper (when in all-male company) W. H. Wills, who was managing editor of *Household Words*, declined to go to Gad's Hill 'because they "could not stand his cruelty to his wife"'. When asked by a friend what he meant, Evans explained, '"Swearing at her in the presence of guests, children and servants" – swearing often and fiercely. He is downright "ferocious" now, and has quarrelled with almost every friend he ever had. Next to him, Forster behaved worst – aggravating his discontent with his wife, who is "not the sort of woman they say", Mr E declares. Dickens had terrified and depressed her into a dull condition, and she never *was* very clever.' Thus wrote Harriet Martineau.

While Dickens himself became ever more energetic, and filled his life with more and more – journalism, theatricals, dinners, as well as writing fiction – Kate sank into 'indescribable lassitude'. There was a sort of inevitability that one day he would meet a young woman and discard his wife. He denied Kate's competence as a mother, but this had, nonetheless, been her function for the last twenty years and inevitably, as she became more and more of a mother, less and less of a lover, he should punish her as he needed to punish his own mother.

Some months after he had met Nelly, he wrote to Kate's maid, Anne Cornelius, at their London house, from Gad's:

My dear Anne,
I want some little changes made in the arrangement of my dressing room and the Bathroom. And as I would rather not have them talked about by comparative strangers, I shall be much obliged to you,

my old friend, if you will see them completed before you leave Tavistock House.

I wish to make the Bath-room my washing room also. It will be therefore necessary to carry into the Bath room, to remain there, the two washing-stands from my Dressing-Room. Then to get rid altogether, of the chest of drawers in the Dressing-Room, I want the recess of the doorway between the Dressing-Room and Mrs Dickens's room, fitted with plain white deal shelves, and closed in with a plain light deal door, painted white. Rudkin can do this – or Lillie [Benjamin Lillie, a plumber and painter] being in the house, can do it if he likes. The sooner it is done, the better.

Without consulting his wife, Dickens was literally building a barrier between them. It is especially chilling that he asserts his old friendship with the maid in his pincer-movement, within the household, to force everyone – servants as well as children – onto his side, in the warfare that, in October 1857, he was now planning.

He and Nelly were not yet lovers. One inclines to agree with all the biographers and commentators who imagine that she took a long time to yield to his fervent wooing, and must, however flattering it was, have been frightened by it, its fervour, its Quilpian heat, its basic insanity. By May 1858 Dickens had decided that it was impossible for him and Kate to continue together in the same house. In his letter of 9 May he told a shocked Angela Burdett-Coutts, 'I believe my marriage has been for years and years as miserable a one as ever was made. I believe that no two people were ever created, with such an impossibility of interest, sympathy, confidence, sentiment, tender union of any kind between them, as there is between my wife and me.' He concluded his letter accusing Kate of 'the most miserable weaknesses and jealousies . . . Her mind has, at times, been certainly confused besides.' We are in *Gaslight* territory.

He was more than a little in awe of Miss Burdett-Coutts, who tried to urge a reconciliation. He only came clean to her about the separation when it was all about to come to light in the most public manner possible.

We have reached the period during which, in his daughter Katey's view, Dickens was 'like a madman'. He was on the point of beginning the paid public readings that tightened the bond with his adoring public. While these began, lawyers were preparing a formal separation. Rumours flew about London's drawing rooms and clubs. There was a story that Dickens had bought a bracelet for Nelly and it had been wrongly delivered to Mrs Dickens, with the inevitable ensuing row. One afternoon, Katey passed the open door of her mother's bedroom in Tavistock House and heard sobs. Her mother was sitting at her dressing table in a bonnet, with the *New York Tribune* and tears

154

cascading. Dickens had insisted that she visit Nelly to apologize for the appalling insinuation that her jealous rage implied.

'Your father has asked me to go and see Ellen Ternan.'

'You shall not go!' Katey remonstrated, 'angrily stamping her foot'.

Kate's parents, the old Hogarths, were staying in Tavistock House, and both they and their daughter Helen made it clear that they thought Nelly was his mistress. Unable to 'bear the contemplation of their imbecility any more', Dickens stormed out and walked to Gad's Hill through the night, a distance of thirty miles.

Thackeray had heard the rumour – and repeated it in the Garrick Club – that Dickens was the lover of Georgina. Another friendship bit the dust. And then came Dickens's decision to publish the so-called Violated Letter. He insisted that Helen Hogarth and her mother should sign it, and vowed that he would never forgive them, 'living or dead', if they persisted in accusing Ellen Ternan of adultery. He asked his good friend Mark Lemon, the editor of *Punch*, to publish the Violated Letter and he refused. Another friendship destroyed.

Dickens himself, who was now appearing in public for the readings to audiences agog to see the central figure in this excruciatingly embarrassing drama, showed the Violated Letter to Arthur Smith, who was organizing the public readings, authorizing him to show it to any who believed the rumours put about by 'two wicked persons' – Mrs Hogarth and Kate's sister Helen, presumably. On 29 May they signed the retraction that he had demanded.

The Violated Letter appeared in the *New York Tribune* and was subsequently reprinted in the English papers. Dickens, very naïvely, was surprised – or said he was surprised – that the journalists had got hold of it, but it was, by now, scarcely a secret. In June, he published it himself, in *Household Words* and in *The Times*; it was, as Edgar Johnson said in his biography, 'the maddest step he had yet made in his unhappy and hysterical state'.

The Violated Letter is a repetition of what he had told Miss Burdett-Coutts: that he and his wife had been unhappy for years. The separation was entirely on the grounds of incompatibility. It was, moreover, a tribute to Georgina.

> Nothing has, on many occasions, stood between us and a separation but Mrs Dickens's sister, Georgina Hogarth. From the age of fifteen, she has devoted herself to our home and our children. She has been their playmate, nurse, instructress, friend, protectress, adviser and companion. In the manly consideration toward Mrs Dickens which I owe to my wife, I will merely remark of her that the peculiarity of her character has thrown all the children on someone else. I do not know – I cannot

by any stretch of fancy imagine – what would have become of them but for this aunt, who has grown up with them, to whom they are devoted, and who has sacrificed the best part of her youth and life to them.

In his Will, Dickens would describe Georgy as 'the best and truest friend man ever had', and this is probably simply factual. While he set out on the first of the big public reading tours, Georgy left her family behind in Tavistock House and settled in Gad's Hill, where she would spend the last twelve years of Dickens's life as his companion, housekeeper and helpmeet. She became Nelly's friend, spent a week with her, after she had married, at Margate, and even went to the school run by Nelly's husband, to give out the prizes.

It is obvious that she and Dickens were not lovers. All the evidence points to her having been a decent, level-headed person. Most of those who contemplate the Dickens marriage have rushed to judgement, and even the most ardent Dickensians find little to defend in his conduct during 1857–8. Georgy's loyalty to him should be weighed in the balance against his cruelty to her sister. That he was cruel can't be denied. Georgina is a witness, too, however, to something mysteriously missing about Catherine, some incurable personal defect. Hans Christian Andersen, when he grossly outstayed his welcome in the Dickens household in

1857, saw Georgina as 'piquante, lively and gifted, but not kind'. Nevertheless, might Georgy herself not have been right when she told Maria Winter that, 'by some constitutional misfortune, my sister always, from their infancy, threw her children upon other people, consequently as they grew up, there was not the usual strong tie between them and her – in short, for many years, although we have put a good face on it, we have been very miserable at home'.

Georgina saw it as her duty to protect Dickens, first of all from his wife's unhappy hostility, and next from the drain on his energy and resources by the grown-up children. She was all that a wife should be, apart from sharing his bed, and when he was dead, she was the fiercest guardian of the shrine. There will always be those who feel it is a duty, when miserable at home, simply to endure, for fear of cruelly inflicting more misery. The truth was, however, that in the practical, ever-changing and not especially religious Victorian world, there was no need to make an ideal of an everlasting marriage. Indeed, their very cult of marriage made it inevitable that the Victorians would introduce divorce. In the days of Chaucer, not only was life-expectancy lower – so that a life-vow was unlikely to be endured for more than a couple of decades – but the marriage bond and the love code were quite separate. In the days of Dickens, things were different. Their novels and poems all told them that a man and a woman should be lovers, companions, best friends, all in one. The 'Angel in the House' was not, as is sometimes supposed, the woman. The Angel was the spirit of love that fills the marital home. No wonder, when the Angel had fled, or was found never to have been there in the first instance, it seemed like time to call the marriage to an end.

English divorce is an essentially Victorian invention. The Victorians liked to think of themselves as domestic beings, defenders of the home and of marital respectability. Three years after Coventry Patmore's verse-novel *The Angel in the House* – the most saccharine, though brilliantly versified expression of the happy marriage – was published, the Matrimonial Causes Act of 1857 made divorce a possibility for most married people for the first time in English history.

Henry VIII, often spoken of as having divorced Katherine of Aragon, was actually never divorced in his life. His Archbishop of Canterbury, Thomas Cranmer, declared that marriage to be annulled. The second, with Anne Boleyn, ended, as did the fifth, with the axe on Tower Hill. Jane Seymour, the third wife, died a natural death. The 'marriage' with Anne of Cleves was contracted but never consummated. After Henry's death, no person, royal or otherwise, obtained a divorce in England for 130 years. The first person to do so, in 1670, was John Manners, Lord Roos, future Earl (later

Duke) of Rutland. The divorce was granted on the grounds of his wife's adultery.

For the next 180 years divorce was still highly unusual, and could only be obtained, in each case, by a special Act of Parliament. Even after the 1857 Act, it remained extremely difficult for a woman to obtain a divorce, since she had to prove not merely adultery, but adultery aggravated by incest, bigamy, rape, sodomy, bestiality, cruelty or desertion for more than two years.

The story of the 'road to divorce' (the title of a groundbreaking study of the subject by Lawrence Stone in 1990) coincides with the rise of the novel – a fact of clear relevance to Dickens's own marital history, and to the way in which he wrote about marital failure in his books. The two facts – the growth of the novel, and the exposition of particular types of marital misery and failure – are directly connected. Kelly Hager, a scholar who has written well on this subject, was correct when she wrote, 'the law is a set of social conventions, and it thus makes different sorts of plots available'.

Some of the novel-plots most familiar to us from these drew directly from public divorce cases. Wilkie Collins's *The Woman in White*, about a young woman forced into an illegal wedding against her will, drew on the real-life case of Maurice Méjan and Mme de Douhault, for his story of the perfidious Sir Percival Glyde forging legal documents to make it appear that his parents had married more than twenty years before they actually did. Legislation since the Marriage Act of 1753 aimed to prevent clandestine marriages and enforced marriages by nullifying all marriages that had not been recorded in parish registries, and which did not have the parental consent of the bride's family. Wife-sales, such as those that take place at the beginning of Thomas Hardy's *The Mayor of Casterbridge*, were real.

Dickens, when he was a reporter for the *Morning Chronicle*, wrote up the notorious case of 1836, when George Norton brought a suit for 'criminal conversation' (that is, adultery) against none other than the man who would become Queen Victoria's beloved first prime minister, Lord Melbourne. In *Pickwick*, this became fictionalized. As well as the case brought by Mrs Bardell against Pickwick, the novel has two interpolated stories of failed marriages – 'The Stroller's Tale', in which a dying alcoholic husband confesses to sustained and persistent marital cruelty, and 'The Convict's Return', in which a woman stays loyal to a drunken bully.

As far as the Norton case was concerned, it was really a clumsy attempt to blackmail Lord Melbourne, which led Norton to demand £10,000 from the Whig prime minister.

Although, or perhaps because, Norton was a barrister, the jury threw out his claims and he lost the case. His wife Caroline, a granddaughter of the Irish playwright Richard Brinsley Sheridan, was herself a novelist, author of *The Sorrows of Rosalie*, and a person of courage. Norton, as the law stood, had the power to prevent her, when she left him, from seeing her three sons. Nevertheless, Caroline Norton was a heroine in the story of 'the road to divorce'. When Parliament was discussing the matter in 1855, prior to the 1857 Act, she was brave enough to disclose to MPs details of her own miserable marriage to a bully. She could remind them, in a written statement, of the current state of the law.

An English wife may not leave her husband's house. Not only can he sue her for restitution of 'conjugal rights,' but he has a right to enter the house of any friend or relation with whom she may take refuge . . . and carry her away by force . . .

If her husband take proceedings for a divorce, she is not, in the first instance, allowed to defend herself . . . She is not represented by attorney, nor permitted to be considered a party to the suit between him and her supposed lover, for 'damages' . . .

If an English wife be guilty of infidelity, her husband can divorce her so as to marry again; but she cannot divorce the husband, *a vinculo*, however profligate he may be . . .

Those dear children, the loss of whose pattering steps and sweet occasional voices made the silence of [my] new home intolerable as the anguish of death . . . what I suffered respecting those children, God

162

knows . . . under the evil law which suffered any man, for vengeance or for interest, to take baby children from the mother.

Caroline Norton's open letter to the Queen made an enormous impression.

Despite her devotion to Prince Albert, Victoria's views on marriage were trenchant. 'All marriage is such a lottery – the happiness is always an exchange – though it may be a very happy one – still the poor woman is bodily and morally the husband's slave. That always sticks in my throat.' So wrote the Queen to her firstborn, the Princess Royal. And as Dickens was growing up, the narratives of royal marriages and their failures contributed to the hoard of stories from which fiction could be drawn. One thinks most notably of George IV's clandestine marriage to Mrs Fitzherbert, and his public disavowal of Queen Caroline, which were notorious features of the English scene during Dickens's boyhood (he was eight when George became king; eighteen when he died, to be succeeded by William IV, who had fathered ten children, the Fitzclarences, by the celebrated actress Mrs Jordan). One also thinks of the notorious marriage of Prince Albert's parents, which ended in a sordid divorce, and the fact that his father's mistress – 'La Belle Grecque' – wrote about the scandalous state of royal marriages in a bestseller that was very popular in England.

★　★　★

England, then, was ready for new divorce laws, before they eventually arrived in 1857. In that very year in which the Divorce Bill received Royal Assent, not only Charles Dickens, but also his brothers Frederick and Augustus, ended their marriages. (Augustus's wife was blind, and he left her for a younger woman and went to America.) Within the same calendar year, Marian Evans – known to us as George Eliot – moved in with George Lewes, a married man. George Meredith, poet and novelist, had to endure the agony of knowing that his wife was holidaying in Wales with her lover Henry Wallis, the painter of *The Death of Chatterton*, by whom she bore a son.

Given the way that Dickens wrote his novels, burrowing deeper and deeper into his psychological history, and reworking experience as his fiction became ever richer and darker, you can see that the writing of *Little Dorrit* in 1857 probably had as devastating an effect on his marriage as the meeting with Nelly Ternan. Creatively speaking, his relationship with his parents was of far greater moment than that with his wife, mistress or children. In *Little Dorrit* he had re-entered the shades of the prison house. He had seen and satirized his own early love(s). He had watched a little child-bride flit in and out of the shadows, unaware of the fact that, months after he finished dreaming about her, he would find her, materialized and realized, in a little actress in Manchester. Above all, he had imagined the destruction of his hated mother – a death-blow that his wife could only have realized, had she been psychologically aware, was a devastating step to have taken. For now, in the pursuit of his art, the reworking and rebuilding of experience in fictive form, nothing was going to be spared.

'My mother hated me, even before I was born,' Balzac told his mistress Mme Hanska. Dickens could have said the same, and it would have been as true of him as of Balzac – in the view of another of his mistresses – that he was 'an eagle hatched by geese'. When the mother gives birth to a poet in Baudelaire's poem 'Bénédiction', she rails against God:

> Ah! que n'ai-je mis bas tout un noeud de
>   vipères
> Plutôt que de nourrir cette dérision!

But the boy is free. While she tries to rip out his heart and feed it to the dogs, he has made a discovery that leaves him invulnerable – that suffering is a unique gift for the artist, a form of *noblesse*. The 'worse' that the husband, and son Dickens became in the twelve years left to him on earth, the greater his art became. The books that followed his separation from Kate – *A Tale of Two Cities, Great Expectations, Our Mutual Friend* – were getting better all the time in a progressive curve. Then came the final one, the one that killed him, *The Mystery of Edwin Drood,* the book where – into the idyllic world of boyhood Rochester – he allowed to intrude a confrontation of his own lust for mesmeric power over others.

CHAPTER 4

THE MYSTERY OF THE CHARITY
OF CHARLES DICKENS

When he was in the middle of writing *A Tale of Two Cities*, Dickens wrote to Wilkie Collins from the office of *All the Year Round* (16 August 1859) how 'I want very much to come to Old Broadstairs for a day, but cannot see my way there yet: having to pick up the story, and to blaze away with an eye to October. But I don't give it up; far from it. I really do hope to come for a day before your time is up. Perhaps a tumble into the sea might – but I suppose there is no nitrate of Silver in the Ocean?' The helpful footnote in the Pilgrim edition of *The Letters of Charles Dickens* reminds us that silver nitrate was 'used for cauterising warts and the treatment of ulcers'. It was also a regular remedy against gonorrhoea. This is the only reference to the possibility of Dickens having a sexually transmitted disease.

Four years earlier, however, in 1856, he had told Collins in a letter:

On Saturday night I paid three francs at the door of that place where we saw the wrestling, and went in, at 11 o'clock, to a Ball. Much the same as our own National Argyll Rooms. Some pretty faces – but all of two classes – wicked and coldly calculating, or haggard and wretched in their worn beauty. Among the latter was a woman of thirty or so, in an Indian shawl, who never stirred from a seat in a corner all the time I was there. Handsome, regardless, brooding, and yet with some nobler qualities in her forehead. I mean to walk about tonight and look for her.

If Dickens did have the clap, for however short a period, after the breakdown of his marriage, it would obviously have complicated his hopes for a relationship with Nelly. It would also have made a difference to how he felt about Urania Cottage, the establishment he had set up with Miss Burdett-Coutts in the 1840s for the rescuing of 'fallen women'.

Dickens's philanthropic work was continuous throughout his life, whether he was putting on theatrical performances for charity, speechifying for hospitals or impoverished actors, prison-visiting, campaigning for the establishment of schools for the poor or indulging in innumerable acts of private kindness and generosity. The doctrine of Christmas, and Kindliness, was central not merely to his work, but to his life. He always regarded himself as a Christian, impatient of doctrinal or liturgical nicety, but committed to the saying that insomuch as we have done acts of charity to the sick, the imprisoned, the poor, the vulnerable, we have done it to Christ. During his years of active involvement with the women's refuge known as Urania Cottage, 1846–58, aged between thirty-four and forty-six, he was kept busy by many other charitable concerns. The number of his children rose from six to nine. He founded, edited and ran *Household Words*. In addition to many articles and short stories, he wrote five great novels: *Dombey and Son, David Copperfield, Bleak House, Hard Times* and *Little Dorrit*. Humphry House wrote: 'This grind of charitable business would be astounding in any man: it is scarcely credible in the greatest English creative genius of his time.'

To this should be added that there was no disparity in Dickens between his own works of philanthropy, public and secret, and the frequent denunciations – in his fiction and in his journalism and speeches – of charitable institutions, professional do-gooders, Benthamite social reformers, Pardiggles, Jellybys and Honey-thunders. Unlike those who advertise their benevolence, for example, Dickens kept his connection with the House of Fallen Women a secret throughout his life. His article about it in *Household Words* was anonymous, its location and the name of its philanthropic backer, Miss Burdett-Coutts, suppressed.

Angela Burdett-Coutts (1814–1906), daughter of Sir Francis Burdett, a radical politician, and granddaughter of the celebrated banker Thomas Coutts, had known Dickens slightly before she came to inherit her substantial share of the banking fortune. Her father had a salon in St James's Square, where Bulwer-Lytton, Disraeli, Dickens, Thomas Moore and Samuel Rogers had all been habitués.

The money came to her via her stepmother who, after the death of banker Coutts, had become, *en secondes noces*, the Duchess of St Albans. Having considered the characters of her first husband's grandchildren, she selected Angela to be the residuary legatee of her estate, which amounted to £1.8 million in 1837 – billions in today's money.

After inheriting this gigantic sum, Angela Burdett added the Coutts to her name, moved into a large house in Stratton Street, Mayfair (just off Piccadilly), with her former governess Hannah Meredith, a fervent evangelical Christian who exerted a strong influence on the young woman. After 1849 they moved to Holly Lodge, Highgate. As one of the richest women in Britain, and as someone whose word was taken seriously at the family bank, she was able to offer financial assistance to the Queen herself in the early, impecunious years of her reign – before revenues from the Duchy of Lancaster made Queen Victoria the richest woman in her own kingdom – just as later she would lend money personally to Princess Mary of

Teck, mother of the future Queen Mary. (She was also godmother to Queen Mary's brother, Prince Francis of Teck.)

The greater part of Burdett-Coutts's fortune, however, was devoted to more obviously worthy objects of charity. Dickens regarded himself as her 'almoner', guiding her in how she should dispose of her abundance. He regarded her as 'the noblest spirit we can ever know'. Burdett-Coutts, as a token of her gratitude to Dickens, paid for his son Charley to go to Eton. The two remained friends until Dickens's death, but there was a cooling – perhaps this was one of the reasons for Dickens having become less involved at Urania Cottage – after the failure of his marriage: Burdett-Coutts was disapproving, as most people were, both of the separation and of its mode.

In 1846, Dickens had accompanied Burdett-Coutts to Limehouse in the East London Docks to see the ragged schools that had been established there, in disused coach factories, granaries, distilleries and warehouses, for 'the sweepings of the street'. Burdett-Coutts had lately provided £90,000 to build the Westminster church of St Stephen's Rochester Row, as a memorial to her father, and she wanted to establish a parish school alongside it.

So they looked at the schools, and then they parted. Burdett-Coutts (unlike Dickens, a fervent churchwoman) went off and started her parish school. Dickens, who had recently confronted the failure of his newspaper the *Daily News*, and was on the verge of travelling to Switzerland with the family to get out of England for a few months, wrote his friend one of the longest letters of his life.

In it, he proposed the establishment of a refuge for women, with a view to their eventually being sent to Australia 'for marriage, with the greatest hope for their future families, and with the greatest service to the existing male population, whether expatriated from Britain or born there'. This was a full four years before *David Copperfield*, in which David's childhood sweetheart, Little Em'ly, would be seduced by his schoolboy hero, Steerforth. When they were playing together on the beach at Yarmouth in Chapter 3, Little Em'ly, prancing on the wooden sea-barrier, with the waves crashing beneath her, very nearly fell into the sea. David reached out a hand and rescued her. David and Dickens know what her fate is going to be, though as yet the reader does not. David and Dickens know that Em'ly will lose her virtue to the caddish Steerforth. By reaching forth his hand, young David saved the child Em'ly from drowning, but:

> There has been a time since when I have wondered whether, if the life before her could have been revealed to me at a glance, and so revealed as that a child could fully comprehend it, and if her preservation could have depended on a motion of my

hand, I ought to have held it up to save her. There has been a time since – I do not say it lasted long, but it has been – when I have asked myself the question, would it have been better for little Em'ly to have had the waters close above her head that morning in my sight; and when I have answered Yes, it would have been. [*DC* 3]

It is difficult not to associate this passage with Dickens's later obsession with the murder of the prostitute Nancy in *Oliver Twist*, and his frequent enactments of the murder, not only on the stage, but in the privacy of his own garden. For David Copperfield, Em'ly, having lost her 'purity', would be better dead. Those who would like to believe that this habit of mind belongs exclusively to the creepier margins of the Victorian psyche have only to dwell on the innumerable cases, in our own day, of the murders of sexual victims, the killers unable to bear the loss of innocence which their own predatory behaviour has inflicted upon the child or young adult. It is, of course, *their own* loss of innocence they are wishing to eradicate, but this is not obvious to those who are plunged into the quagmire of sexual guilt and resentment. If, as hinted in that 1859 nitrate of silver, Dickens himself had 'fallen', and if he was among the very many Victorian men who frequented prostitutes, this was all the more reason for his wanting to help the young women of Urania Cottage.

Jenny Hartley, author of *Charles Dickens and the House of Fallen Women*, makes the telling point that, in his manifesto-letter, outlining to Burdett-Coutts his plan for the refuge, the whole scheme appeared to leap from his brain ready-forged. 'Like the *Daily News*, which he had been planning to edit (an ill-conceived notion, and the main reason for his flight to Switzerland), like the amateur dramatics he put on and persuaded his friends to act in with him – and even more like his novels and stories, this home for fallen women would be another total world for him to control.' That perception, both of the integral character of the plan, and of it being a vehicle for Dickens's *control*, are points very well made. Hartley's book (2008) is one of the finest recent works on Dickens's philanthropic work. As she reminds us, the scheme for Urania Cottage and the trajectory plotted for Little Em'ly in *David Copperfield* are all but identical. Em'ly 'falls', and then is 'rescued' and taken to Australia by her uncle Daniel Peggotty, Mrs Gummidge and Martha Endell. 'Theer's mighty countries, fur from heer. Our future life lays over the sea . . . No one can't reproach my darling in Australia.' [*DC* 51]

Dickens's manifesto, spelt out in the May 1846 letter, was that the more enlightened prison governors, such as Captain G. L. Chesterton of the Middlesex House of Correction, and Lieutenant Tracy of Cold Bath Fields, would recommend young women who showed signs of repentance and a desire for a new life. The proposed household would have only a dozen or so inmates at any one time. 'Order, punctuality, cleanliness, the whole routine of household duties – as washing, mending, cooking – the establishment itself would supply the means of teaching practically, to every one.' When they were ready, the young women would be shipped out to the colonies or dominions where, Little Em'ly-like, they could begin life afresh: 'No one can't reproach my darling in Australia.'

Burdett-Coutts provided the money – £1,000 in the first instance; when Urania Cottage was up and running, she was spending £72,000 a year on it. Every year, Dickens would go through the figures with her and account for the uttermost farthing. When he and his family returned to England in 1847, after a pretty painful time abroad (see Chapter 6), he found the house: Urania Cottage in Shepherd's Bush. It was a villa that could accommodate thirteen young women, and which was surrounded in those days by fields, and with outbuildings that he could envisage being converted into a wash-house.

A matron and a second-in-command were engaged. Mrs Holdsworth, the first matron, was forbidden, on the pain of dismissal, to discuss the young women's past lives. 'Dealing gently' should be the rule. 'These unfortunate creatures are to be tempted to virtue.' Dickens took charge of all the household practicalities. It was he who talked to the builders about alterations. It was he who went shopping for the furniture, the bookcases, the books. It was he who bought the household linen, the carpets and curtains; he who chose the women's clothes. From the first moment of their arrival, they were to be clad in new clothes. 'I have made them as cheerful in appearance as they reasonably could be – at the same time very neat and modest.' This was in marked contrast to their prison uniforms or the shaven heads and penitential garments of contemporary asylums of 'Magdalens'.

Some of the young women who came to be part of the Urania Cottage experiment were able to turn their lives around. Others were incorrigible, and would be sent away for stealing, or would simply abscond. They were by no means all prostitutes, nor had all of them been in prison, but they had all, one way or another, fallen foul of the system, and Dickens, Burdett-Coutts and the matrons of the institution were patently doing their best to help, though sometimes with what would seem to the twenty-first-century sensibility 'a tough love'.

Visitors would be allowed, but restricted. Parents could come once a month, other visitors every three months. Inmates would be assessed each week for good behaviour. There was a points system, which enabled inmates to 'bank' points so that when they left, they did so with money saved. The virtues looked for were 'Truthfulness,

Industry, Temper, Propriety of Conduct and Conversation, Temperance, Order, Punctuality, Economy and Cleanliness'. Dickens's near-mania for tidiness and cleanliness was observed by his daughter Mamie. At home, 'he made a point of visiting every room in the house once each morning and if a chair was out of its place, or a blind not quite straight, or a crumb left on the floor, woe betide the offender!'

The distinction between a desire to control and a desire to benefit the young women roped into the Dickens/Burdett-Coutts scheme is not easily drawn. In *All the Year Round*, Dickens wrote about how shocked he had been, when he took a house on the edge of Regent's Park, to realize that one often met with loud braying and coarse language, within the earshot of his children and their nurse. The Police Act made swearing in public a criminal offence. Dickens deliberately set out to the park to find someone in breach of this regulation and was satisfied to find a girl of seventeen or thereabouts, surrounded by a 'suitable attendance' of blackguard youths, in whose presence she let forth a stream of blasphemies and obscenities. Dickens followed them for a mile or so, while they abused him, until he met a policeman. The youths at this point melted away and Dickens apprehended the young woman.

He asked the policeman if he knew who he was. The constable did. Rather than explaining to the policeman that he was a man whose own publisher had stopped visiting his house because he could not stand the way the novelist constantly swore at his wife, Dickens asked the officer to arrest the girl for using foul language. The copper had never heard of such an offence, and hesitated to do so. Dickens then ran home to get his copy of the Police Act. It is surely very revealing that he possessed a copy! He appeared at the police station, where the girl was being held, and said he wished to press charges. Next morning, in the court, the magistrate dismissed Dickens's charge as frivolous. As Dickens told the story, very tellingly, he reduced the episode to one of fairy-tale pantomime. The girl, he said, had got herself up to resemble 'an elder sister of Red Riding Hood', leaving him with the only option, to resemble the Wolf. ['The Ruffian', *UT* 30] Surely, Mr Dickens, the magistrate asked, you do not want the girl to be sent to prison on such a charge? Yes, I do, answered Dickens, or I would not have come here. It was not the only occasion when he appeared in a magistrate's court to bring charges: in 1844 he had done so to prosecute a man who had sent him a begging letter. ['The Begging-Letter Writer', *RP*]

He commended private citizens intervening when they witnessed minor crimes; suggested that at all times they should summon the police, but when a constable was not on hand, we could all do our duty with 'our own riding-whips and walking-sticks'. The Ruffian, Dickens believed, was 'the common enemy to be punished and exterminated'. ['The Ruffian', *UT* 30] He once told Lord Brougham that he would like to have been a police magistrate, and in his frequent walks through the capital he envisaged himself as 'a higher sort of police constable doing duty' on his beat. ['On an Amateur Beat', *UT* 35]

This was the man who set out to rescue the young women who were invited to go to Urania Cottage. Nevertheless – and here is the mystery or paradox of the charity of Charles Dickens – there was a mercy in his heart, though it is difficult to know whether the truer metaphor would be that he was a divided self: one half the nice cop, the other the nasty cop; or whether the two cops were in some strange way commingled. As a schoolboy at Wellington House Academy he had impersonated street urchins and beggars, more conscious than his amused classmates of how recently and how nearly he had been a factory boy at work among workhouse boys. In the young women of Urania Cottage he could see people who were only a little different, in their misfortunes, from the scrapes into which his own flesh and blood had fallen. Above a certain level in society, among the decently educated, the propertied or professional or landed classes, there was the possibility of life going wrong, but not so catastrophically wrong as when you had no schooling, no status, no class, no property – nuffink. All the great writers among Dickens's contemporaries, even the poverty-stricken Carlyle (for he had been through the Scottish educational system and was a graduate of Edinburgh, married to a middle-class doctor's daughter), were on the comfortable side of this dividing line: Tennyson, Browning, Mill, Ruskin, the Rossettis, Trollope, George Eliot, the Newman brothers. They might sink into shabby-genteel poverty (the Newmans' father was an alcoholic publican who went bankrupt) but they could never be nobodies with nuffink. Dickens alone had not merely looked over into the abyss. He had lived in it.

Jenny Hartley makes the very convincing case that it was in hearing the life-stories of the young women that Dickens decided that he – who had once been a street boy on the edge of destitution – in 1849 or thereabouts would write out the Autobiographical Fragment, which he would later show to John Forster. He also freely plundered the experiences of the young women for his fiction.

Rhena Pollard was a case in point. Daughter of a farm worker near Petworth in West Sussex, she was the youngest of four. When she was nine years old, her mother was sentenced to fourteen days' hard labour for stealing a dress worth four shillings. From the local workhouse, Thakewell Union, Rhena was apprehended for petty larceny and graduated to Petworth Prison, of which the Duke of Richmond was a governor. Having heard about Urania Cottage, the Duchess of Richmond recommended Rhena to Angela Burdett-Coutts.

Shortly after Rhena joined the Cottage, there was a breakout and one of the young women ran away wearing her Sunday best – she jumped over the garden wall. Dickens was always especially angered when the young women escaped on a Sunday, wearing their more expensive clothes. Rhena, who had a fiery temper and was not settling in, threatened to do the same. Dickens was at first in favour of letting her go, but the matron, by then a Mrs Morson, pleaded for her. Dickens summoned Rhena before the committee. It was a freezing day in January. He had just been in Birmingham doing the first of his public readings from *A Christmas Carol*. To and about Rhena, he was relentless. If Rhena, in one of her tantrums, had said she wanted to leave Urania Cottage, then she should be put out into the frosty streets.

He knew – Jenny Hartley tells us, and I think we must believe her – that Rhena would scream, howl and plead with Mrs Morson. Then he knew that she would break down 'before all the rest'. He wanted her to be humiliated, and to beg to be allowed to stay. Eventually this was to happen. Dickens got two supreme rewards from the episode. On the one hand, he had found the character of Tattycoram:

A sullen, passionate girl! Her rich black hair was all about her face, her face was flushed and hot, and as she sobbed and raged, she plucked at her lips with an unsparing hand.

'Selfish brutes!' said the girl, sobbing and heaving between whiles. 'Not caring what becomes of me!' [*LD* I 2]

But Hartley convinces me that Dickens also knew that, having received her shock treatment, Rhena/Tattycoram would come right. Tattycoram, in *Little Dorrit*, elopes with Miss Wade – the only lesbian, as far as I have noticed, in the Dickens oeuvre. Rhena stayed the course at Urania Cottage, to the point where she was thought capable of living a decent life. She emigrated to Canada, married, put down her roots in Ontario. Hartley tells us, 'Otis and his family were Wesleyan Methodists. Rhena, to be different, joined the Salvation Army.' She died aged sixty-three, has many descendants living today and, satisfactorily, we have her wedding photograph.

Mrs Morson had appealed to the Christmas Spirit to persuade Dickens to be lenient, with the case coming up for consideration at the 'great forgiving Christmas time', something that she could do with some confidence, Dickens having just witnessed the response of enormous Birmingham audiences to the *Carol*.

Boz, in one of his very earliest excursions into print, had asserted:

There seems a magic in the very name of Christmas. Petty jealousies and discords are forgotten; social feelings are awakened, in bosoms to which they have long been strangers; father and son, or brother and sister, who have met and passed with averted gaze, or a look of cold recognition, for months before, proffer and return the cordial embrace, and bury their past animosities in their present happiness. Kindly hearts that have yearned towards each other, but have been withheld by false notions of pride and self-dignity, are again reunited, and all is kindness and benevolence! Would that Christmas lasted the whole year through (as it ought), and that the prejudices and passions which deform our better nature, were never called into action among those to whom they should ever be strangers! [*SB* 2]

A Christmas Carol changed not only Dickens's life, but the Western world. It invented the modern Christmas. By February 1844 at least three theatrical productions based on the book were being performed in London alone. In the years that followed, he would publish further Christmas stories, including *The Chimes* (1844), *The Cricket on the Hearth* (1845) and *The Battle of Life* (1846). As far as he was concerned, Christmas had become the busiest time of year and one of the most lucrative – especially after 1853, when he had begun a series of public readings of *A Christmas Carol*. The Christmas edition of *All the Year Round* was something he spent six months planning. For it was always the *Carol*, of all his stories for Christmas, that captured the imagination of readers. Before the *Carol* was published, Christmas Day was not a public holiday in Britain. By 1846 the newspapers were reporting that 'Experienced salesmen at Leadenhall-market state that the demand for Christmas geese this year exceeded that of any previous season, and that the establishment of clubs has, within the last few days, brought upwards of 20,000 geese into the market. In some parts of the metropolis, "plum pudding clubs" have been established.'

Three years after *A Christmas Carol* was published, the *Hereford Times* reported, 'We notice that at Ross and other towns, Saturday next, as it intervenes between Christmas-day and Sunday, will be observed as a holiday; and a declaration to that effect is now being generally subscribed to by the respectable tradesmen of this city, who have agreed to suspend business on that day.'

As Dickens-descended Lucinda Hawksley said in her charming book *Dickens and Christmas*, 'No one, it seems, wanted to be compared to Bob Cratchit's employer.' The Victorians, who were discarding the formality of theological faith in increasing numbers, reinvented Christmas. Dickens was not alone in encouraging them to do so.

His religious outlook, like much in his life, was divided. In 1850, at the Royal Academy Summer Exhibition, he saw John Everett Millais's *Christ in the House of His Parents*. He was not alone in hating the picture, which caused a storm of protest. *The Times* warned its readers, 'Mr Millais's principal picture is to speak plainly revolting. The attempt to associate the holy family with the meanest details of a carpenter's shop, with no conceivable omission of misery, of dirt, even of disease, all finished with the same loathsome meticulousness, is disgusting.' Far from thinking this was the voice of Pecksniff, Dickens entirely agreed, stating in *Household Words* that the picture was 'mean, odious, and repulsive'. Even some years later, when he had made friends with Millais, he felt the need to write to the painter to make plain, 'My opinion of that point is not in the least changed.'

One wonders whether Dickens, with his mania for neatness, was chiefly offended by the fact that the carpenter's workshop in Nazareth is depicted as having wood shavings untidily littering the floor, as a beautiful Virgin Mary kneels to be kissed by a beautiful, very English little Jesus.

Although his *Life of Our Lord*, written for his children, professes to believe in the miracles and the Resurrection, his definition of what it means to be a Christian makes no allusion to any of the theological reasons given in the New Testament – namely, a belief that Christ's death is a sin-offering which saves the believer from personal guilt, that Calvary washes away the believer's sin. 'It is Christianity to be gentle, merciful, and forgiving, and to keep those qualities quiet in our own hearts, and never make a boast of them, or of our prayers or of our love of God, but always to show that we love Him by humbly trying to do right in everything.' [*LOL* 11] That was how he ended *The Life of Our Lord*. For four years of Dickens's life, he joined the Unitarians, who specifically deny Christ's divinity. He wrote to a friend that they 'would do something for human improvement if they could', and they 'practise Charity and Toleration'. This was at a time when the Church of England was torn, especially in Oxford, by esoteric rows about the rival claims of the Church of Rome and Anglicanism, with reference to the 1,500-years-old – 1,500 years dead, as Dickens would have thought it – early councils and doctrinal disputes of the Mediterranean Church. The Oxford dons who led the country into this obsession themselves hankered after the church of our ancestors. Dickens, when he came into possession of Gad's Hill, decorated the false-spines of books on his library door. One set of volumes was entitled 'The Wisdom of Our Ancestors – I. Ignorance. II. Superstition. III. The Block. IV. The Stake. V. The Rack. VI. Dirt. VII. Disease'. He would have no time at all for the historicism or nostalgia of the Oxford Movement.

His cult of Christmas, in which he led his contemporaries, was a cult not of old superstition but of kindness and generosity. The better Victorians realized – as they looked about at their rural communities, impoverished by tariffs on imported corn; at the wretchedness of Irish peasants, soon to be starved in their millions; at the cities into which rural workers had fled, to be overworked, from childhood onwards, down mines, in mills and factories and refineries – that their beliefs in Free Trade and Industry and Progress had brought into being a nightmare. Their cult of Christmas was part of their attempt to fight back in the name of decency.

Henry Cole, one of the masterminds of the Great Exhibition of 1851, invented Christmas cards. The Queen and Prince Albert, in their German enthusiasm for Christmas trees, helped to popularize what now seems central, not merely to the decoration of Christmas households and townscapes, but to the meaning of the festival itself. But there can be no doubt that Dickens's *A Christmas Carol*, in capturing the Christmas 'mood', also helped to drive it forward.

The Great Forgiving Christmas Time was central to Dickens's view of life, just as his most enduringly famous story, *A Christmas Carol*, is central, really, to his oeuvre. Dickens was sometimes spoken of in his lifetime as a great social reformer, and his novels as exposés of great social evils. This

187

is to overlook the templates both for his fiction and for his life-view and life, namely fairy stories and pantomime. In protesting against the plight of illiterate street urchins or 'fallen' women, or in giving speeches in favour of better sanitation, Dickens might have seemed to be aligning himself with the worthier social radicals and liberals of the day, figures such as John Stuart Mill, perhaps. George Bernard Shaw, a Fabian socialist who sat for years on St Pancras Council and was a profoundly political man, spoke of *Little Dorrit* as more revolutionary than *Das Kapital* and by implication, therefore, a document of the Left. Its radicalism, which was indeed profound, was, however, of quite a different order from that of Marx, Mill or even his friend (with whom it had most in common, ultimately) Carlyle. These are all grown-ups attempting to change and improve the grown-up world in grown-up ways. Dickens's philanthropy was undertaken with a view to Cinders being allowed to go to the ball. Dickens was the figure of Buttons, who persuaded the audience she would be able to do so, if only they hallooed loud enough, or repeated the same silly jingles that he had taught them, and booed and hissed when the demon king or the Ugly Sisters stepped out of the wings.

In his magnificent critique of *Hard Times*, F. R. Leavis entered into the question of Dickens in relation to the two British institutions that, collectively, were making an attempt to address the social wrongs which he himself was trying to put right: namely, the Chapel and the Trade Union Movement. It is only here that I would wish to part company with Dr Leavis, even though one sees where he himself was coming from (his was the generation that fought in the First World War; retrospect made them see the virtues of the British nonconformist tradition, and its contribution to the betterment of working-class life through organized labour). He wrote:

> Just as Dickens has no glimpse of the part to be played by Trade Unionism in bettering the conditions he deplores, so, though he sees there are many places of worship in Coketown, of various kinds of ugliness, he has no notion of the part played by the chapel in the life of nineteenth-century industrial England. The kind of self-respecting steadiness and conscientious restraint that he represents in Stephen did certainly exist on a large scale among the working-classes and this is an important historical fact.

That this may have been a case in historical fact does not make it a fact that could easily be absorbed into Dickens's imaginative world-view, either as a philanthropist or as a novelist, or – to use Leavis's in a way better perception – as a poetic dramatist. Leavis took Dickens to task for regarding Parliament as the 'national dust-yard' [*HT* II 9] where the 'national dustmen' entertain one another 'with a great many noisy little fights among themselves' [*HT* II 12] and appoint commissions that fill blue-books with dreary facts and futile statistics – of the kind that helped Gradgrind prove that the Good Samaritan was a bad economist, and which Marx liked to pore over, for evidence in *Das Kapital* about the miserable conditions in which men and women worked. There are other readers of Dickens who would remember that his earliest writings – alas, we possess almost none of them – were reports of debates in the House of Commons. The Canadian mage Northrop Frye made the point that 'For him the structures of society, as structures, belong almost entirely to the absurd, obsessed, sinister aspect of it, the aspect that is overcome or evaded by the comic action.'

Dickens's burlesque manner of describing men of affairs – whether the politicians standing for election at Eatanswill in *The Pickwick Papers*, or the activities or, rather, non-activities, of Tite Barnacle and the Circumlocution Office in *Little Dorrit* – might be borrowed from pantomime and political cartoons. The reality he described seems to many readers, more cynical than Dr Leavis, to be palpably and obviously accurate.

In a similar way, Dickens's hatred of the Chapel went very deep, and it is a tragicomic fact that, had he ever returned to earth to read Dr Leavis or to hear him lecture, he would indubitably have seen in him a secular equivalent of Chadband or of the Reverend Melchisidech Howler. Much as Dickens mocked and disliked priestcraft, Catholicism and 'Puseyism', he reserved his most sustained and repeated invective and satire, as far as Christianity was concerned, for the chapel ranters. Again and again, with hammer blows, in his journalism and in his fiction, he returned to the attack. In Coketown, the sensible workers avoid worshipping at all eighteen chapels that have been erected for their edification. The cruel Murdstones in *David Copperfield* were evangelicals, as was Mrs Clennam with her great Bible full of murderous and misanthropic thoughts. In *American Notes*, Dickens summarized American evangelicalism: 'Wherever religion is resorted to, as a strong drink, and as an escape from the dull monotonous round of home, those of its ministers who pepper the highest will be surest to please. They who strew the Eternal Path with the greatest amount of brimstone, and who most ruthlessly tread down the flowers and leaves that grow by the wayside, will be voted the most righteous.' [*AN* 3] Even the fact that the American evangelicals were foremost in the anti-slavery movement did not prompt Dickens to speak in their praise – fervent as his hatred of slavery always was. In one of the many speeches made by Dickens at official dinners and charitable functions, he alluded to

Lord Shaftesbury's 'courage to face the worst and commonest of all cants; that is to say, the cant about the cant of philanthropy and benevolence'.

This speech was delivered to the Metropolitan Sanitary Association only a week or so after the opening of the Great Exhibition of 1851, and less than a year after one of the worst outbreaks of cholera in London. Dickens said that:

> Searching Sanitary Reform must precede all other social remedies [*cheers*], and that even Education and Religion can do nothing where they are most needed, until the way is paved for their ministrations by Cleanliness and Decency. [*Hear, hear*] . . . What avails it to send a Missionary to me, a miserable man or woman living in a foetid Court where every sense bestowed upon me for my delight becomes a torment, and every minute of my life is new mire added to the heap under which I lie degraded . . . I am so surrounded by material filth that my Soul cannot rise to the contemplation of an immaterial existence! Or if I be a miserable child, born and nurtured in the same wretched place, and tempted, in these better times, to the Ragged School, what can the few hours' teaching I get there do for me against the noxious, constant, ever-renewed lesson of my whole existence. [*Hear, hear*] But give me my first glimpse

of Heaven through a little of its light and air – give me water – help me to be clean – lighten this heavy atmosphere in which my spirit droops and I become an indifferent and callous creature that you see me – gently and kindly take the body of my dead relation out of the small room, where I grow to be so familiar with the awful change that even *its* sanctity is lost to me – and, Teacher, then I'll hear, you know how willingly, of Him whose thoughts were so much with the Poor, and who had compassion for all Human Sorrow. *[Applause]*

While himself keenly involved with a number of philanthropic schemes, Dickens was distrustful of philanthropy, and in his novels the do-gooders are generally seen as absurd, if not positively malign – Mrs Jellyby comes to mind, neglecting her own children in favour of supposed philanthropic interest in far-away Africa; while in the last novel, *The Mystery of Edwin Drood*, the loud-voiced philanthropist Honeythunder is a figure from whom the beneficiaries of his charity cannot get away too soon.

Philanthropists who added religion to the mixture were especially uncongenial. He despised the fancy dress of the Anglo-Catholics working in docklands in the 1850s. Equally, the mouthy interferences of the evangelicals into the harmless lives of the rest of us were objects of some of his best satire. 'The Great Baby', an article that appeared in *Household Words*, was by way of being a manifesto.

When Dickens began work as a parliamentary reporter in 1832, he would have noted that a Committee was set up in July of that year, issuing a report a month later on 'the Laws and Practices relating to the Observance of the Lord's Day'. The 300 pages of evidence assembled by this parliamentary report showed 'a systematic and widely-spread violation of the Lord's Day'. Nineteen out of the thirty members of the Committee were evangelicals. Their aim was to suppress Sunday trading, travelling and recreation, including the opening of public houses and tea gardens. The evangelical lobby was a powerful one. When the Queen and her family travelled south from Scotland on a Sunday train in 1848, they slipped out of Euston Station as unobtrusively as they could, aware of what damage it would do them in the eyes of many opinion-formers if they were seen desecrating the Lord's Day. For the rest of his life, Dickens never missed an opportunity to attack the Lord's Day Observance Society and the po-faced, self-advertising Christians who saw it as their function in society to prevent other people enjoying themselves. He supported the National Sunday League, a largely working-class movement started in the 1830s by radicals to permit, for example, the opening of the British

Museum on a Sunday, or the performance of Sunday open-air concerts. Arthur Clennam, returning from twenty years as a merchant in China, sits in a coffee shop and hears the bells of London's churches calling the faithful to worship. '"Heaven forgive me", said he, "and those who trained me. How I have hated this day!"' [*LD* I3]

Boz had opined in 'London Recreations', 'Whatever be the class, or whatever the recreation, so long as it does not render a man absurd himself, or offensive to others, we hope it will never be interfered with, either by a misdirected feeling of propriety on the one hand, or detestable cant on the other.' (This quotation appears in the original *Evening Chronicle* 'London Recreations', 17 March 1835, but was omitted from the later *Sketches by Boz* version.) One of the most magnificent of these attacks was 'The Great Baby'.

Norris Pope makes the valid point that Dickens, always animated with contempt for Select Committees in the House of Commons, had not bothered, before he wrote 'The Great Baby', to realize that, at this particular juncture, the Committee was attempting to limit, or even eliminate, parts of the Wilson-Patten Sunday Beer Act of 1854, which laid restrictions on Sunday opening hours in public houses. He was writing an attack in 1855 on the attitudes that had been expressed in the 1853–4 parliamentary inquiry into Sunday drinking: the Committee he was attacking was in fact trying to modify the

195

1853–4 position. Many readers would understandably think that Dickens should have done his homework. Fair enough. And this would certainly have been true, were he still a parliamentary reporter or gathering evidence for a committee of public inquiry. What he was doing, however, even in his journalism, was creating that poetic drama Leavis spoke of, that imaginative take on the world, which centralized the freedom of the good working classes to make moral choices.

'The Great Baby' remains the most sublime rebuke to those parliamentarians and the 'Monomaniacs' (that is, the evangelical Christians) who 'have no other Idea of the People than a big-headed Baby, now to be flattered and now to be scolded, now to be sung to and now to be denounced to Old Boguey, now to be kissed and now to be whipped, but always to be kept in long clothes, and never under any circumstance to feel its legs and go about of itself'.

My favourite paragraph is a long apostrophe to the Reverend Temple Pharisee, rector of Camel-cum-Needle's-Eye, who has stepped out of his carriage to the Committee Door to give evidence about the shameful way in which working-class people enjoy themselves.

> As I stand in the pulpit, I can actually see the people, through the side windows of the building (when the heat of the weather renders it necessary to have them

open), walking. I have, on some occasions, heard them laughing. Whistling has reached my curate's ears (he is an industrious and well-meaning young man); but I cannot say I have heard it myself. – Is your church well frequented? No. I have no reason to complain of the Pew-portion of my flock who are eminently respectable; but, the Free Seats are comparatively deserted: which is the more emphatically deplorable, as there are not many of them. – Is there a Railway near the church? I regret to state that there is, and I hear the rush of trains, even while I am preaching. – Do you mean to say they do not slacken speed for your preaching? Not in the least. – Is there anything else near the church, to which you would call the Committee's attention? At the distance of a mile and a half and three rods (for my clerk has measured it by my direction), there is a common public house with tea-gardens, called The Glimpse of Green. In fine weather these gardens are filled with people on a Sunday evening. Frightful scenes take place there. Pipes are smoked; liquors mixed with hot water are drunk; shrimps are eaten; cockles are consumed; tea is swilled; ginger beer is loudly exploded. Young women with their young men; young men with their young women; married people with their children;

baskets, bundles, little chaises, wicker-work perambulators, every species of low abomination, is to be observed there. As the evening closes in, they all come straggling home together through the fields; and the vague sounds of merry conversation which then strike upon the ear, even at the further end of my dining-room (eight-and-thirty feet by twenty-seven), are most distressing.

It is one of Dickens's most impassioned journalistic pieces. 'Shrimps are eaten' is perhaps its most brilliant phrase. It establishes that the true purpose of the Lord's Day Observance Society and similar busybodies is the desire of the middle and upper classes, those who have large dining rooms, to limit and control the lives of the virtuous poor. Dickens took issue with the prison chaplain – 'the Reverend Single Swallow' – who claimed that drink was something that led to crime. He pointed out, which was surely a rather strong point, that drunks and criminals were unlikely to be restrained by closing pubs on Sundays – merely the harmless majority inconvenienced. In Dickens's pantomime vision of the world, it was easy, and necessary, to insist upon the incorrigibility of murderers, serious felons and the like. As easy as hissing and booing when the villain came onstage amid a puff of green smoke in the panto. ('Sloggins, when in solitary confinement, informed me, every morning for eight months, always with tears in his eyes, and uniformly at five minutes past eleven o'clock that he attributed his imprisonment to his having partaken of rum and water at a licensed house of entertainment called (I use his own words) the Wiry Tarrier.')

This is a good example of the way in which Dickens the Reformer, Dickens the Campaigner went into operation. You would look in vain for the detail of accurate political criticism of the actual, day-to-day Victorian scene in his works. His article 'Red Tape', for example, was attacking the Window Tax, *after* it had been abolished in 1851. Those tasked with the actual reform of the Civil Service in 1853 were more scathing in their criticisms of the existing system than Dickens was in *Little Dorrit*; and he can be shown in that novel to criticize those Tite Barnacles who in reality had either left the scene or were on the run; likewise, the workhouse system he attacked in *Oliver Twist* had been reformed three years before he wrote the book. The social abuses we meet in his novels are, for the most part, not evils that he wants abolished, so much as newly abolished evils that he is glad to see the back of. Yet how brilliant was Humphry House when he said that novel has 'the private emotional quality of a bad dream'. If we treat the novels as pieces of political polemic, we can ask such questions as when, precisely, they are supposed to be taking place, and point to individual alterations in the procedures of the Court of Chancery, or Poor Law Reform, or Sanitation, or railway-building as

199

evidence of Dickensian anachronisms. The novels, however, do not work on that level. Whether or when or how he got the details right, or wrong, his way of presenting the failing institutions and the failures of Charity was empathetic, imaginative, rather than forensic. Like the Christ of Mark's Gospel, he looks about him in anger at their hardness of heart. That still packs a powerful punch, even after the particular abuses or horrors anatomized – debtors' gaols or workhouses – have gone away. If you have seen the world through Dickens's eyes, parliaments or indeed any self-congratulatory democratic or elected body will seem like a national dustyard, inhabited by national dustmen. And, today, dustwomen.

Systems, whether political or religious, can never in the Dickens world respond to the central truth about life, which is personal, and only disabled by individuals – that is, as Mr Sleary says in *Hard Times*: 'there ith a love in the world, not all Thelf-interetht after all, but thomething very different'. [*HT* III 8] In the mind of Thomas Gradgrind, 'Facts alone are wanted in life.' [*HT* I 1] Gradgrind, who pursued a relentless, Benthamite, Utilitarian view of life – the way of life that John Stuart Mill was reared to by his monstrous father and which caused him, as he tells us in his *Autobiography*, mental and spiritual collapse when he had just grown up – comes to realize that none of the facts he has been bludgeoning into the heads of his pupils are actually true. The materialism, the ingrained belief in self-interest as the rule of the universe, the view of life that Samuel Smiles made into a bestselling guide to how to get on in life, and which Darwin mythologized into the science of how life itself came into being, is all – all based on an illusion. Gradgrind the Benthamite philosopher-schoolmaster and Bounderby the selfish banker are, like Scrooge and Dombey before his conversion, like Merdle in his hour of despair, worshippers of the false Victorian gods of Mammon, Competition, Survival of the Fittest. It is Sleary, the manager of a third-rate circus, who shines out as the fable unfolds, not as a great mystic or sage, but as a man who has discovered the one thing needful. Such figures are dotted about the Dickens universe: Mr Brownlow and, funnily enough, Nancy herself in most of her manifestations, Gabriel Varden, Captain Cuttle and Old Sol, Betty Higden, Canon Crisparkle, Newman Noggs, Joe Gargery . . . they are simply decent people, and their response to life – namely, that love is stronger than self-interest – is a recognition not of how things ought to be, but of how things are. Dickens is often described as sentimental, and that is because he is. In this, however, the belief that doing the decent and kindly thing is not merely our duty, but the way to a sane and happy life, is something he holds to be a simple truth. It is a Pelagian belief, of almost universal appeal and application.

'It seemth to prethent two thingth to a perthon, don't it, Thquire?' said Mr Sleary, musing as he looked down into the depths of his brandy and water: 'one, that there ith a love in the world, not all Thelf-interetht after all, but thomething very different; t'other, that it hath a way of ith own of calculating or not calculating, whith thomehow or another ith at leatht ath hard to give a name to, ath the wayth of the dogth ith!' [*HT* III 8]

Louisa Gradgrind had already made the same point to her father when she said, '"All that I know is, your philosophy and your teaching will not save me."' [*HT* II 12] We return to the conversion of Scrooge each year at Christmas because we share this Credo, or want to do so. We believe Dombey, who has learned love and gentleness, is not merely nicer but truer than the calculating businessman whom we meet in the first chapter of the novel. To discover, therefore, that Charles Dickens himself was not benign, not loving, not full to the brim with the milk of human kindness is therefore more disturbing than if the biographers had made similar discoveries about, let us say, Wagner or Rodin, or some of the other giants of the nineteenth century, where the impact of their vision does not, at first sight anyway, appear to require the acceptance of the unconquerable power of love.

This was thrown into even sharper relief when Dickens took to the road, and to the railroad, and to the ocean liner, and began his series of public readings.

The writer T. C. de Leon, who heard him in America, recorded:

> There are some far better readers; there are many more exact mimics; there are thousands of better actors; but the electric genius of the man fuses all into a magnetic amalgam that once touched cannot be let go until the battery stops working. There is something indescribable; a subtle essence of sympathy that can only be felt, not described, that puts him en rapport with the most antagonistic spirits and makes them his, while the spell is upon them.

The effect, especially when the *Carol* was read, was to draw the ineluctable connection between the man and the work. It was to suggest, overwhelmingly, that Dickens, who made perfect charity so attractive in his work and so moving in his public readings, was himself an embodiment of perfect charity. It was only with partial irony that the *New York Herald* referred to his return to America, to do the reading tour, as the Second Coming.

Dickens the passionate reformer, the benevolent promoter of Christmas, was also obsessively orderly

– neat and tidy to the border of mania, controlling, in his fantasy-life a detective strolling the streets. It should surprise no one, therefore, that, while he abhorred cruelty and tried to rescue the virtuous poor, he also had few qualms about punishing wrongdoers. In *Great Expectations*, set in the early decades of the nineteenth century, the lawyer's clerk took Pip on a visit to Newgate Gaol, and Pip/Dickens is able to remark to the reader:

> At that time jails were much neglected, and the period of exaggerated reaction consequent on all public wrongdoing – and which is always its heaviest and longest punishment – was still far off. So, felons were not lodged and fed better than soldiers (to say nothing of paupers), and seldom set fire to their prisons with the excusable object of improving the flavour of their soup. [*GE* 32]

Clearly, Pip speaks here with the voice of Dickens the journalist. There is nothing in the structure of the paragraph to suggest that Dickens distances himself, or his readers, in any way from this sentiment. To us, it seems as unsympathetic as Mr Bounderby's opinion that his workers expected to be 'set up in a coach and six, and to be fed on turtle soup and venison, with a gold spoon'. [*HT* I 11] One might accuse the Dickens who argued for prison reform in the 1840s, and for the abolition of capital punishment, and the Dickens who twenty years later defended the death penalty and called for harsher prisons, as a man who followed the familiar pattern of becoming more reactionary with age. The more probable explanation, however, is that Dickens, who had an imaginatively morbid fascination with violent crime and its punishment, and also had a tender heart, subscribed to both views at once. He wanted reform, of the more brutal prisons and of such monstrous phenomena as public executions; and he wanted punishment for the wicked. That is why he was a novelist and not an economist or a politician. G. M. Young was right to point out that Dickens was 'equally ready to denounce on the grounds of humanity all who left things alone, and on the grounds of liberty all who tried to make them better'.

In his remarkable essay 'Lying Awake', Dickens's mind filled with images of violence and death. The Paris Morgue 'comes back again at the head of a procession of ghost stories'. He remembered the joint hanging of Frederick and Maria Manning in 1849, outside Horsemonger Lane Gaol, and the 'two forms dangling on the top of the entrance gateway – the man's limp, loose suit of clothes as if the man had gone out of them; the woman's, a fine shape, so elaborately corseted and artfully dressed, that it was quite unchanged in its trim appearance as it slowly swung from side to side'.

Dickens had laid down his pen in the middle of composing *David Copperfield*, to join the crowd of 30,000 to witness this remarkable event. He had written two letters to *The Times*, protesting at the iniquity of public hanging. Convicted murderers, he suggested, should be kept from the public gaze and executed privately within the prison walls. (This reform was eventually brought to pass in 1868, nearly twenty years after he wrote the letters.) Douglas Jerrold, and his old radical friends of the 1840s, were appalled that Dickens now countenanced the idea of capital punishment, whether held in private or not. A part of Dickens, however, was at one with the crowds, the 'thieves, low prostitutes and vaga-bonds', fighting, whistling, joking brutally as the married murderers were brought out to the gallows. The Mannings were especially horrible people, who had murdered their lodger Patrick O'Connor. ('I never liked him so I finished him off with the ripping chisel,' Manning calmly told the jury. Maria, still evidently, to Dickens's eye, a fanciable woman, even when dangling from a rope, had ranted from the dock in her foreign (Belgian) accent and interrupted the judge.)

Dickens the moralist could write to *The Times*:

The horrors of the gibbet and the crime which brought the wretched murderers to it faded in my mind before the atro-cious bearing, looks and language of the assembled spectators. When I came upon the scene at midnight, the *shrillness* of the cries and howls that were raised from time to time, denoting that they came from a concourse of boys and girls already assembled in the best places made my blood run cold.

There is excitement pulsating through his denunciation. As a little boy, Dickens had loved it when his godfather Christopher Huffam walked with him through the streets of London at night. He had especially loved the crime-ridden area of Seven Dials – 'Good Heaven! What wild visions of prodigies of wickedness, want, and beggary arose in my mind out of that place!'

He deplored official leniency to ruffians, and felt that police and magistrates were devoted to the 'preserving of them as if they were Partridges'. ['The Ruffian', *UT* 30] Nor did Dickens believe that wicked people could be reformed or made better. There are good people and bad people, in Dickens's world, as in his novels. The repentance of the sinner, of which the Bible speaks, or the heart-searching inner reform of heedless or bad people, such as we meet in the pages of the great Russian novels, does not play much role in Dickens's fiction, with two big exceptions – the repentance of Scrooge, and the attempt made by Magwitch to put 'good' use to his fortune. No surprise then that, as far as he was concerned, criminals should not be rehabilitated. They should simply be punished.

> The generic Ruffian – honourable member for what is tenderly called the Rough Element – is either a Thief, or the companion of Thieves. When he infamously molests women coming out of chapel on Sunday evenings (for which I would have his back scarified often and deep) it is not only for the gratification of his pleasant instincts, but that there may be a confusion raised by which either he or his friends may profit, in the commission of highway robberies or in picking pockets. When he gets a police-constable down and kicks him helpless for life, it is because that constable once did his duty in bringing him to justice. When he rushes into the bar of a public-house and scoops an eye out of one of the company there, or bites his ear off, it is because the man he maims gives evidence against him. ['The Ruffian', *UT* 30]

Such language, while professing to deplore violence, is itself extremely violent. It is penned by Quilp. It is designed, like the language of Wardle's servant, the Fat Boy, in *Pickwick Papers*, to make the flesh creep.

Dickens's friend and (in some respects) mentor

Thomas Carlyle, the dedicatee, in 1854, of *Hard Times*, had in March 1850 published his *Latter-Day Pamphlet* on 'Model Prisons'. It was a diatribe against 'this universal syllabub of philanthropic twaddle!' Mrs Manning, in Carlyle's eyes, had been 'Not a heroic Judith, not a mother of the Gracchi now, but a hideous murderess, fit to be the mother of hyaenas!' Carlyle saw the reforming spirit of the nineteenth century as a substitute for the Christianity in which the governing class no longer truly believed the real law of the universe was '"Revenge", my friends! Revenge and the natural hatred of scoundrels, and the ineradicable tendency to *revancher* oneself upon them, and pay them what they have merited; this is forevermore intrinsically a correct, and even a divine feeling in the mind of every man.' It was this 'law' which led Carlyle to believe that 'By punishment, capital or other, by treadmilling and blind rigour, or by whitewashing and blind laxity, the extremely disagreeable offences of theft and murder must be kept down within limits.'

Dickens sided with Carlyle over the treadmill question. Making prisoners walk on a treadmill was a punishment only abolished in Britain by the Prisons Act of 1898. Those such as Elizabeth Fry, John Stuart Mill and Jeremy Bentham who had wanted prisons to be a place of personal rehabilitation did not persuade him. He complained that 'In an American state prison or house of correction, I found it difficult at first to persuade myself that I was really in a gaol: a place of ignominious punishment and endurance.' [*AN* 3]

Some English prisons, such as the one in Preston, had begun from the 1820s to follow the American pattern, opening workshops and teaching the prisoners useful skills. For Dickens, this muddled the essential purpose of a prison – to punish – with a spurious belief in human reformation. In his article 'Pet Prisoners' (1850) he deplored the decline in sheer punishment for its own sake, and its replacement with useful tasks: 'Is it no part of the legitimate consideration of this important point of work, to discover what kind of work the people always filtering through the gaols of large towns – the pickpocket, the sturdy vagrant, the habitual drunkard, and the begging-letter impostor – like least, and to give them that work to do in preference to any other?' He urged prison governors to impose work on the inmates that was 'badged and degraded as belonging to gaols only, and never done elsewhere'. [*SJ* p. 407]

By Carlyle's standards, Dickens was a softy. The Scotch Sage opined:

> Dickens was a good little fellow, and one of the most cheery innocent natures he had ever encountered. But . . . his theory of life was entirely wrong. He thought men ought to be buttered up, and the world made soft and accommodating for them, and all sorts of fellows have turkey for their

Christmas dinner. Commanding and controlling and punishing them he would give up without any misgivings in order to coax and soothe and delude them into doing right.

But this was the Dickens of *A Christmas Carol*, not the journalist who wrote the essay on 'The Ruffian'. Dickens the Ruffian, Dickens the Quilp, was a much tougher nut to crack – tougher than Carlyle, for whereas Carlyle was a tormented agnostic but at heart a Calvinistic puritan ranter, Dickens the cheery innocent was everlastingly linked to someone who at heart was not so very easily distinguishable from the violent criminals he so freely denounced. The would-be gentleman Pip is the heir, not of crazy old middle-class Miss Havisham, but of Magwitch.

> 'What were you brought up to be?'
> 'A warmint, dear boy.'
> He answered quite seriously, and used the word as if it denoted some profession.
> [*GE* 40]

Magwitch had been criminal ever since he was 'a ragged little creetur as much to be pitied as ever I see (not that I looked in the glass, for there warn't many insides of furnished houses known to me), I got the name of being hardened. "This is a terrible hardened one," they says to prison

211

wisitors, picking out me. "May be said to live in jails, this boy."' [*GE* 42]

Like Dickens, Magwitch is contemptuous of these visitors, who have tried to put into his hands Tracts he could not read. The 'cheery' Dickens has made this man loveable, while the complicated and tormented Dickens has, by making him the benefactor of the snobbish Pip, skewed all his preconceptions – about class, money, love even. For, in a twist of the plot that is as improbable as it is mythopoeically brilliant, Magwitch had been the associate of Compeyson, the public-school con artist who had, all those years ago, jilted Miss Havisham, broken her heart and started in train the whole emotional torment of the novel – Pip's social ambitions and inevitably unsatisfied love of Estella, who has been drained of the capacity for love by Miss Havisham; Pip's need for money to rise to a position that is all based on lies and illusion.

Magwitch, therefore, remains a 'warmint'. His one attempt at a good deed – to reward the little boy Pip for giving him that pork pie in the church-yard, by bestowing upon him a fortune made out of sheep-farming in Australia – does not really alter the fact that he is a warmint and always will be a warmint.

Hence – while professing on the one hand to believe in humane reforms, of schools and sewers and workhouses – Dickens's Carlylean belief in prison punishment at its best when it was most useless. In the case of juveniles, he was prepared to believe in the possibility of reform. He had praised the justice system of Massachusetts, whereby a young offender would be sent to a home and be taught a trade, rather than languishing in a common gaol. A similar motive guided him to rescue young girls from a life of crime and train them in Urania Cottage to be brides in Australia.

Although it is customary to speak of Dickens's reforming instincts, and of his charitable endeavours, it is hard to think of any writer who would have been less sympathetic to twenty-first-century ideas of human rights, or of welfare handed out by the state.

After a reading of *A Christmas Carol* in Sheffield in 1855, he made the pledge 'that to the earnestness of my aim and desire to do right by my readers, and to leave our imaginative and popular literature more closely associated than I found it at once with the private homes and public rights of the English people, I shall ever be faithful – to my death – in the principles which have won your approval'.

The English people, note. In *Bleak House* he despised Mrs Jellyby for her 'telescopic philanthropy', and her desire to help poor Africans, while neglecting her own children at home. (When her mission to Africa fails, she takes up the cause of feminism.) In 1865 there was a rebellion of the peasant workers in the planting district of Morant Bay, Jamaica. Twenty white people were killed and the courthouse was burned to the ground. A white clergyman is said to have had his tongue cut out. A black Member of the Assembly, Charles Price, was ripped open and his entrails torn out. The governor of Jamaica, Edward John Eyre, responded with the utmost severity. Over the next month more than 600 people were killed and 1,000 leaf-hut dwellings destroyed. Liberal opinion in England believed that Eyre had gone much too far, and figures such as Herbert Spencer and John Stuart Mill protested.

There was a robust response from the likes of Tennyson and Carlyle, and Dickens sided with them. 'The Jamaica insurrection is another hopeful piece of business,' he wrote.

> That platform sympathy with the black – or the Native or the Devil – afar off, and that platform indifference to our own countrymen at enormous odds in the midst of bloodshed and savagery, makes me stark wild. Only the other day, there was a meeting of jawbones of asses at Manchester to censure the Jamaica Governor for his manner of putting down the insurrection! So we are badgered about New Zealanders and Hottentots as if they were identical with men in clean shirts at Camberwell and were to be bound by pen and ink accordingly . . . But for the blacks in Jamaica being over-impatient and

before their time, the whites might have been exterminated without a previous hint or suspicion that there was anything amiss. *Laissez aller*, and Britons never, never, never!

The words make a twenty-first-century reader blush. It would be an incomplete picture of Dickens if we did not quote them. Nor can we say by way of mitigation that he lived in that alien world, the nineteenth century, since there were voices – highly articulate voices – raised in protest against Governor Eyre. The racism and insularity are of a piece with Dickens's belief that charity not only belongs and begins at home: it is a matter of individual kindness, individual virtue. Our obligation to relieve suffering when it is on our doorsteps is an absolute one. To worry about the plight of those miles from home is to be in danger of numbing our own capacity for charity, just as expecting the state to relieve the suffering of the poor can blind us to our own personal duty to do so.

Wordsworth's 'The Old Cumberland Beggar', composed 1797, published 1800, anticipates much of what Dickens stood for. The Beggar wanders the Cumberland countryside, scarcely lifting his eyes from the ground, in search of scraps and provender, and apparently relating neither to his outward surroundings nor to other people.

> But deem not this Man useless –
> Statesmen! ye
> Who are so restless in your wisdom, ye
> Who have a broom still ready in your
> hands
> To rid the world of nuisances.

In the poem Wordsworth dreads the Beggar being 'rescued' and institutionalized in some workhouse or place of protection for the poor:

> May never HOUSE, misnamed of
> INDUSTRY,
> Make him a captive!

The beggar at large, Wordsworth believes, provides a social function. Even among the very poor, he finds people not merely to help him materially, but to become capable of sympathy themselves. By traipsing from door to door, the 'useless' beggar:

> keeps alive
> The kindly mood in hearts which lapse
> of years,
> And that half-wisdom half-experience
> gives,
> Make slow to feel, and by sure steps
> resign
> To selfishness and cold oblivious cares.

216

Experience, the distracting business of being alive, makes Scrooges of all of us, Wordsworth almost says. The presence of an actual beggar, making actual demands on the sympathy of all who see him, keeps something alive, throughout the human community, which any number of charities or Poor Laws would not be able to provide. This, broadly, is the 'message' of Dickens's novels, as of his charitable endeavours. But much had happened to Britain since Wordsworth was a young man. The population had not merely exploded. It had become urban. One solitary old man, wandering from village to village in Cumberland in the late 1790s, might well have performed the morally and socially uplifting role ascribed to him by the poet. By the time Wordsworth died as Poet Laureate in 1850, however, the indigent poor had swollen in number. Betty Higden in *Our Mutual Friend* kept alive the Wordsworthian tradition – her individual acts of kindness to Sloppy and neighbours is allied to a dread of being taken to the workhouse. But how realistic was it to believe that the social ills of society could be cured by:

> that best portion of a good man's life,
> His little, nameless, unremembered acts
> Of kindness and of love.

Wordsworth's Member of Parliament, John Curwen, said in 1826, 'I once thought Great

217

Britain could produce [enough] corn for itself, but I now think otherwise.' The corn and other foodstuffs that were now, in post-Napoleonic times, being imported to Britain would, without the imposition of tariffs, have been cheaper than those produced by British farmers. The government was caught in the dilemma: reduce, or abolish, the tariffs, and let the poor eat – and thereby threaten the farmers and landowners with a potentially disastrous reduction in income. This was the debate that would culminate in the abolition of the Corn Laws in the mid-1840s.

Humphry House, writing in the high and palmy days of the foundation of the welfare state and the discovery of the advantages of a social democratic political system, is scornful of Betty Higden. He finds it 'hard to see any genuine tragedy' in the figure of a destitute old woman refusing help, for fear that she will be institutionalized. Her rejection of charity is, for House, merely 'stupid'. Seventy years after House formed these lofty judgements, Betty Higden's cussedness has a more heroic tinge.

For the twenty-first-century reader, regardless of their political persuasions – if any – the question is: how can sympathy, benevolence, the great Dickensian spirit of Christmas be converted into action, either in Dickens's country or in ours? Wordsworth prayed in 1800 that the Cumberland Beggar would never be made captive in a workhouse. The draconian, Malthusian New Poor Law of 1834, however, was trying to address a question which demanded more than the occasional Christmas turkey being taken to a delighted Bob Cratchit and Tiny Tim. The population had grown, and expert opinion, in and out of government, agreed with the Reverend Thomas Malthus's view that there was only a fixed amount of food available at any one time: therefore when the population grew, the poor were in trouble. Malthusian economics, moreover, taught that the more the wages of the poor were subsidized, the less money there would be: there being, in this wrong-headed view of things, only a fixed amount of money to pay wages or subsidies.

Plainly, the cost of subsidizing low wage-earners and paying for the indigent poor had rocketed. Poor Law administration in 1750 had been £619,000; in 1818 it was £8 million, more than thirteen shillings per head of the population of England and Wales. It was a problem that had to be addressed, in those days when not only was there a fixed Malthusian mindset at the heart of the executive, but there was also no political will for an income tax or any other sort of tax to fund a welfare system. Indeed, such a concept lay long in the political future, and one has to think oneself back, before such ideas took root, in order to understand the concepts and problems with which early- to mid-nineteenth-century Europeans were grappling. We know that from the late nineteenth century onwards, the concept of state welfare was developed by the Liberal Party. David Lloyd George, as chancellor of the exchequer, introduced the notion of an old-age pension paid for by national insurance, and the Independent Labour Party was waiting in the wings, and growing in popularity with its ideas, which scarcely existed in the time when Wordsworth was middle-aged and old, Dickens young and middle-aged.

The problems the Western world faces today vis-à-vis the economics of welfare – whether it is the question of American medical care for the poor, or reform of the benefits systems in European countries; and the problem of 'welfare dependency' versus the duty of a state to the most vulnerable in society – all these have come about because of the way in which our ancestors chose to grapple with a set of formidable problems.

Oliver Twist's 'Please, sir, I want some more!' in some senses says everything about the problem, but in others demonstrates the fact that Dickens existed in an alternative universe, determined in his imagination, as we now realize, by the actual workhouse next to which he grew up in Marylebone; and by his sense – quickened every day that he was walking to work at Warren's Blacking and dodging the street urchins, and working alongside the workhouse boys such as Bob Fagin – that the abyss of dependency, total poverty, absolute loss was a daily possibility. We have said that none of

Dickens's fellow novelists had been in this position, none of his fellow writers, but nor, of course, had any of the wiseacres we read in the histories of the Victorian age – not Bentham, not Dr Arnold, not Chadwick, not Gladstone or Derby or Cobden or Bright. Dickens had been there. They hadn't. He had grown up with parents who did midnight flits to avoid the bailiff. He had seen, with the beady, knowing eyes of the clever child, the fecklessness and hopelessness of his parents. He had, in all likelihood, seen such scenes as were quoted in our second chapter, of a dying woman giving birth on the pavement because she did not belong to the particular parish which administered that particular workhouse. He translated these experiences into the fairy-tale burlesque of Mr Bumble and Oliver and the Artful Dodger not because it was unreal to him, but because it was real.

Dickens's essay, first published in *Household Words* on 26 January 1856, entitled 'A Nightly Scene in London' is one of his finest pieces of writing. It finds him in Whitechapel on 5 November. On the pavement, against the wall of the workhouse, are five motionless bundles: 'Five great beehives, covered with rags.' He accosts the porter of the workhouse and is told that the place is full, there is no room for the women. 'The place is always full – every night.' Dickens turns then to the mounds of filthy rags, from one of which emerges 'the head of a young woman of three or four and twenty, as I should judge; gaunt with want, and foul with dirt; but not naturally ugly':

'Tell us', said I, stooping down, 'why are you lying here?'

'Because I can't get into the Workhouse.'

She spoke in a faint dull way, and had no curiosity or interest left. She looked dreamily at the black sky and the falling rain, but never looked at me or my companion.

'Were you here last night?'

'Yes. All last night. And the night afore too.'

'Do you know any of these others?'

'I know her next but one. She was here last night, and she told me she come out of Essex. I don't know no more of her.'

'You were here all last night, but you have not been here all day?'

'No. Not all day.'

'Where have you been all day?'

'About the streets.'

'What have you had to eat?'

'Nothing.'

Dickens gives her a shilling for food and lodging, which she says will be enough to see her through the night.

I put the money into her hand, and she feebly rose up and went away. She never

222

thanked me, never looked at me – melted away into the miserable night, in the strangest manner I ever saw. I have seen many strange things, but not one that has left a deeper impression on my memory than the dull impassive way in which that worn-out heap of misery took that piece of money, and was lost.

In 1906 David Lloyd George, commenting on his fellow radical Joseph Chamberlain's Tariff Reform, said that it had 'focussed the opera glasses of the rich on the miseries of the poor. Once you do that, there is plenty of kindness in the human heart.' That is not socialism, but Dickens would have totally approved.

One man alone, even so famous and influential a person as Charles Dickens, could not have supplied the needs of the Victorian poor, found cures for the sick children or salves for their wounded hearts. There is a danger that we should dismiss Dickens's charitable endeavours either as what is known to our generation as mere virtue signalling or as a piece of Victorian subterfuge. He was not a socialist, he railed against the institutions for not doing enough for the poor, and then when they tried to do something, he railed against them for their patronizing, interfering attitude. It would be easy to leave it there and merely to dismiss Dickens as confused about such matters; at worst, a humbug.

What I have tried to suggest in this chapter is that he was neither. He was not, primarily, an economist or a philanthropist; he was a great imaginative artist, responding to ills and abuses that were beyond his control, torn this way and that between naturally libertarian, individualist instincts and the sheer scale of the deprivation and need all around. We should utterly fail to understand him, though, and be completely unfair to his memory as a man, if we did not recognize how central Christian Charity was to him, as man and artist. His personal kindness and generosity were attested in dozens – hundreds – of examples. Hours of his time, which could have been spent on theatricals, or convivial dinners or walks or outings or journalism, as well as on the central business of his life, writing novels, were devoted to his charitable work. This is entirely of a piece with his art. *Great Expectations*, if you keep the true, the unhappy ending, is the story of what would happen to Dickens, or to any of us, if we sealed off the source of kindliness and goodness in our lives and pursued only success and worldly gain. *A Christmas Carol*, one of the most abidingly popular books ever written, reawakens in every reader the possibility of another life – not of the mystical side of Christianity, which meant precisely nothing to Dickens, but of its call to love one another.

Marley's Ghost was in torment:

'Oh! captive, bound and double-ironed,' cried the phantom, 'not to know, that ages of incessant labour by immortal creatures, for this earth must pass into eternity before the good of which it is susceptible is all developed. Not to know that any Christian spirit working kindly in its little sphere, whatever it may be, will find its mortal life too short for its vast means of usefulness . . .

'Why did I walk through crowds of fellow-beings with my eyes turned down, and never raise them to that blessed Star which led the Wise Men to a poor abode! Were there no poor homes to which its light would have conducted *me*?' [*CC* Stave 1]

In the workhouses and hospitals and ragged schools of London, from the 1820s to the 1860s, there were thousands of people who had met the author of those words, following that Star.

CHAPTER 5

THE MYSTERY OF
THE PUBLIC READINGS

A friend reports that, a day or two before his death, Dickens was discovered in the grounds at Gad's Hill re-enacting the murder of Nancy.

That ardent Dickensian, the poet Algernon Charles Swinburne, was right to say that *Great Expectations* and *David Copperfield* were 'his great twin masterpieces', and they were also the most closely autobiographical. They were parody autobiographies with, as we have observed, anything that was imaginatively inconvenient or aesthetically surplus to requirements, such as all his brothers and sisters, ruthlessly, deftly, excised. Yet we have come far enough in our pursuit of Dickens's mystery to realize that the self and selves he projected were very far from being in his control, and there were selves which, with that twinkle in the eye, he put on display without anyone else in the memory game being *au courant*. (Ralph Nickleby's breakfast is his breakfast; he is Quilp, etc.)

The readings do something else. In their

226

mesmeric, enchanting way, they bring forth a Dickens who had not perhaps ever been so forcefully or nakedly displayed. The American member of the public who was disappointed by them, because what he heard in the performance was not the Dickens he knew or the Dickensian characters he recognized, is a material witness here. 'That ain't the real Charles Dickens.' Well, no. But would the 'real Charles Dickens' please stand up? We are trying to make him do so in this book, but something tells me, reader, that you are going to be disappointed, and that, by the end, we shall be looking round and shall find that he has made his escape. We shall find that while the Dean and Chapter of Westminster Abbey have buried him as an Eminent Victorian with a Nation's Lamentation, the Real Charles Dickens, like a secret agent, has vanished into the Victorian crowd, one tall silk hat, one set of beard and whiskers, one frock coat, waistcoat and watch-chain among a million.

Vladimir Nabokov suggested that it was Dickens's *voice* that is the principal attraction in all his work: 'We just surrender ourselves to Dickens's voice – that is all . . . the enchanter interests me more than the yarn spinner or the teacher . . . this attitude seems to me the only way of keeping Dickens alive, above the reformer, above the penny novelette, above the sentimental trash, above the theatrical nonsense.'

This is right, but only if we interpret 'voice' in

that sentence to mean much more than it does in the case of many writers. The hypnotic power of the 'enchanter' and the control in that voice are indeed what cast their spell, even when the material being delivered in that voice is, or comes close to being, 'trash'. The real proof of this is that we yield to the enchantment, as when we are in the presence of a truly great performer on the stage, even when we can see it coming, and in some cases resist it or dislike it. The death of Paul Dombey is so schmaltzy that we simply refuse to be moved, but then, damn it, we read it and the tears well down our cheeks. Likewise, the Trial of Bardell v. Pickwick, which would be so unfunny if anyone else were narrating it, never fails to make us (me, anyway) laugh. Something similar happened to me when I was taken to see the great comedian Ken Dodd on the stage of the London Palladium – the ancient jokes, told by the equally ancient comedian, were surely not going to work, but within ten minutes I was laughing with the rest of the audience. Mind you, there are moments when the deep gulf fixed between us and the nineteenth century appears unbridgeable. One of Dickens's favourite set-piece readings – a favourite with himself and with audiences – was *Boots at the Holly-Tree Inn*. It is a story that, very loosely and broadly, Wes Anderson reworked to superb effect in his film *Moonrise Kingdom*: namely, two children in love who elope together, in the Dickensian case, described by the 'Boots' in a hotel on the Great North Road. In Anderson's treatment there is comedy, of course there is, but it is principally touching. One witness said that Dickens's embodiment of Boots was 'remarkable for ease, finish, and a thorough relish for the character. The swaying to and fro of the body, the half-closing of the eye, and the action of the head, when any point in the narrative is supposed to require particular emphasis to make clear . . . all assist to make it a perfect example of pure comedy acting.' For Dickens and his audiences, it was 'one roar'. The little girl in the story is not given so much as one line to speak – compare and contrast with the serious-minded, articulate and highly competent little girl in *Moonrise Kingdom*.

The ending, too, makes for uncomfortable reading or listening. Considering the fact that Dickens was on the road in the very year he had legally, and so publicly, separated from his wife Kate, the 'two opinions' of Boots do not seem as hilarious to us, perhaps, as they evidently did to both reader and audience: 'firstly, that there are not many couples on their way to be married, who are half as innocent as them two children; secondly, that it would be a jolly good thing for a great many couples on their way to be married, if they could only be stopped in time and brought back separate'.

We are in deep water when it comes to the readings. All the witnesses – especially those closest to him, such as George Dolby, Dickens's manager

229

in the last tours, both in Britain and America – attest their power, the fervour and frantic energy of them. The fact that he was found in his Kent garden re-enacting the death of Nancy, months after the reading tours had been discontinued because of ill health, is a demonstration of how vital a part of Dickens these performances were. And above all, what a reminder they were of Nabokov's point, about the voice being all.

And this, too, is why – to reiterate – the 'Dickens's Dream' idea of the characters being the chief or central part of the Dickens experience is inadequate. Take the famous public reading of Mrs Gamp, one of his best set-pieces – though never an especially popular one, strangely, with audiences; he dropped it after the 1858–9 tour. Mrs Gamp is, indeed, one of his most superb creations, and she stands out like a good deed in a naughty world, being almost the only undilutedly good thing in that (largely) failure of a novel, *Martin Chuzzlewit*. (Interesting, this. You could attribute the failure of *Martin Chuzzlewit* to the fact that Dickens had been writing too much and too fast, and that, after *Pickwick*, *Barnaby Rudge*, *Nicholas Nickleby* and *Oliver Twist*, it just was not possible to keep up the pace. But whereas all those previous books are good books, with many poor or sloppily composed intervals, *Martin Chuzzlewit* is actually a flop, a dud. The reason, perhaps, is that, whereas all his successful books feast on the rich material of his own childhood, this one – for its mythological base, its core – plunders the new experiences Dickens had had as a grown-up. Whereas the great fiction, so much of it, is concerned with the horror of imprisonment and the disgrace of loss, *Chuzzlewit* follows the Ben Jonsonian conceit of a rich man being sponged upon by all his relations: certainly an experience of which Dickens complained after the success of *Pickwick*, but one that in a strange way is, when handled by him, wearisome and unnourishing.) But in the middle of its tedium, up sprang Mrs Gamp. No one else could have created Mrs Gamp, nor – and this is the point – could anyone else have created her in the Dickensian way.

> 'Ah,' repeated Mrs Gamp, <u>for that was always a safe sentiment in cases of mourning</u> – 'ah! Dear! When Gamp was summonsed to his long home, and I see him a-lying in the hospital with a penny-piece on each eye, and his wooden leg under his left arm, I thought I should have fainted away. But I bore up.' [originally in *MC* 19]

The underlining is Dickens's own, in his prompt-copy, preserved in the Berg Collection in New York Public Library. And it is, of course, Dickens's voice. He never lets go of the puppet-strings, nor will he simply let us contemplate Mrs Gamp's voice describing her dead husband in the hospital. It is his own voice that wants us to understand what she is saying – namely, that the unscrupulous old woman has sold her husband's body to the surgeons. He adds: 'If certain whispers current in the Kingsgate Street circles had any truth in them, Mrs Gamp had borne up surprisingly, <u>and had indeed exerted such uncommon fortitude as to dispose of Mr Gamp's remains for the benefit of science.</u>' [*MC* 19]

The experience of reading Dickens, of falling under the spell of the enchanter, to use Nabokov's phrase, is to accept the habitual heavy irony of his language: '<u>The face of Mrs Gamp – the nose in particular – was somewhat red and swollen, and it was difficult to enjoy her society without becoming conscious of a smell of spirits.</u>' [*MC* 19]

No theatrical or cinematic version of Mrs Gamp could capture the Dickens voice, which is at least half the reading experience. We are not just confronted with the 'character', but with his rendition of her: it is the difference between seeing a cheap photograph of an old woman and seeing an oil painting of Rembrandt's mother. The same is true when Dickens is tub-thumping – 'Dead, Your Majesty . . . Dead, Right Reverends and Wrong Reverends of every order . . . And dying thus around us, every day.' [*BH* 47] (Oh, the pompous comma!) The same is true of the many meteorological and natural descriptions – the storm blowing over Yarmouth in Chapter 55 of *David Copperfield*, the sweltering heat of Marseilles at the opening of *Little Dorrit*, the fogs of *Bleak*

House, the many extraordinary evocations of the River Thames, especially in *Our Mutual Friend* and *The Old Curiosity Shop*, or, again in that novel, the descriptions of the slums on the outskirts of London gradually giving way to open country; or, in *The Old Curiosity Shop*, *Hard Times* and *Dombey and Son*, the appalled and vivid glimpses of England's industrial heartlands: 'Now, the clustered roofs, and piles of buildings, trembling with the working of engines, and dimly resounding with their shrieks and throbbings; the tall chimneys vomiting forth a black vapour, which hung in a dense ill-favoured cloud over the housetops and filled the air with gloom; the clank of hammers beating upon iron, the roar of busy streets and noisy crowds . . .' [OCS 43] Or Mr Dombey, passing through the same sort of country on the train: 'Louder and louder yet, it shrieks and cries as it comes tearing on resistless to the goal; and now its way, still like the way of Death, is strewn with ashes thickly.' [DS 20] There are many comparable moments in *Hard Times* where we see wind-blown, rain-lashed, smoke-choked Coketown through Dickens's eyes and hear it evoked by Dickens's voice, and no photographer or film director, however brilliant, could convey the actual prose of the enchanter, which fixes these scenes in our minds. It is untranslatable into another medium.

At the same time we recognize that Dickens, in his decision to perform some of his work in a series

233

of public readings, was making a step towards dramatizing his fiction. The readings, then, are an essential part of the Dickens mystery. His friend John Forster was opposed to his undertaking them. He saw it as a loss of dignity, and he also saw it as distracting Dickens from his prime purpose, which was to be a writer, not a public entertainer. In the months after he completed *Little Dorrit*, however, Dickens could not settle. His marital unhappiness had turned into an obsessive hell.

'I am incapable of rest. Much better to die, doing.' And he wrote to Forster from Gad's Hill:

> What do you think of my paying for this place, by reviving that old idea of some Readings from my books. The domestic unhappiness remains so strong upon me that I can't write, and (waking) can't rest, one minute. I have never known a moment's rest or content, since the last night of The Frozen Deep. I do suppose there never was a man so seized and rended by one Spirit. In this condition, though nothing can alter or soften it, I have a turning notion that the mere physical effort and change of the Readings would be good, as another means of bearing it.

Strong as his desire always was to make money, and desperate as he was to escape the hell into which marital collapse had plunged him – the fact that Dickens had caused the marriage collapse making it no less hellish – there is surely more going on, in this desire to do the readings, than mere restlessness. We would find it puzzling if Tolstoy (who scarcely ever spoke in public in his life) had given public readings of his novels; in a similar way, we think that Balzac being a one-man fiction factory, consuming endless cups of black coffee as the books poured from his pen, was sufficient; Balzac reading aloud would not have added anything to our understanding of his achievement, whereas Dickens performing from the podium . . . is different. In the case of Dickens on the road, enacting his characters, there is an aptness. In the case of all the other writers of the nineteenth century that I can think of, a reading aloud of the novels would simply be that – a reading aloud of the novels, and interesting as it would be to hear, say, Flaubert or Fontane reading, we would get just as much out of the experience if we read the book quietly to ourselves, or heard it on a 'talking book', read by an actor.

The Dickens readings were something in a different universe of experience. Actors ever since have tried to reconstruct the readings, but, if we attend their attempts, they only remind us of what we are missing, which is *Dickens*, not just reading from a text, but *being* these characters. And not just being the characters. He was being *Dickens* being the characters. You can't reproduce that. Though a minority of those who went to see and hear him came away disappointed, feeling that what they had heard was not 'their' Pickwick or Fagin or Scrooge, the majority were not merely 'enchanted' – the Nabokov word is inescapable, and the readings had something about them of a revivalist rally or a case of mass hypnotism – but also demonic. 'Much better to die, doing.' Dickens's family certainly felt, by the end, that the readings were killing him, and Edmund Wilson was only the most eloquent, but by no means the only, person who, contemplating that quite phenomenal roadshow – Dickens touring Britain and America for the readings – thought Dickens was releasing, without entirely controlling, dark forces inside him and his genius that were only implicit on the page, and which would eventually destroy him.

Dickens's career happened during the century when the population of Britain did not merely expand. It changed irrevocably. When he was born, it was primarily a rural population. By the time he was embarking on his public reading tours, it was largely urban. By 1841 nearly half the male labour force worked in industry. 'We cannot revert to rural felicity, to green fields, to rough and manly ignorant squires, to independent yeomanry, to ill supported and superstitious serf-like hinds,' said a Birmingham manufacturer in 1869.

Although the birthrate, rather mysteriously,

236

peaked and even began to fall by the end of Dickens's life, the population continued to grow, since mortality rates started to fall from the 1860s onwards, housing minimally improved, and the spending power of the working classes increased. (Of course by the standards of the twenty-first century, poverty was still severe, many were malnourished and lived with poor or non-existent kitchens or lavatories.)

There was, for the first time in history, an audience for popular entertainment to be numbered in the millions. Whereas the greatest contemporary novelists – the Brontë sisters, George Eliot, Thackeray in the 1840s onwards – could hope to be read by audiences of thousands, Dickens's reach was far broader and, with the beginning of the reading tours, in the last decade of his life, he was expanding his public all the time. The sixpenny ticket-holders probably included the semi-literate, if not the actually illiterate, as well as those who had been devotedly reading him in cheap serial form since the 1830s. He was pursuing, and achieving, a level of human popularity that was without parallel. There is nothing to compare it with – certainly nothing that pre-dates him – though the many accounts of the crowds who flocked to hear him, and of their ecstatic response to his voice, look forward to the twentieth-century reception of film stars and rock idols.

★　★　★

The public readings grew out of the Charitable Works, which were discussed in the last chapter. The first of them was given in Birmingham Town Hall two days after Christmas in 1853, when he read *A Christmas Carol* and *The Cricket on the Hearth* to raise funds for an adult educational establishment in the city. He stipulated that of the 2,500 seats in the hall, most should be reserved for the working classes, who paid sixpence for their tickets. He raised between £400 and £500. The response had been extraordinary. Kate and her sister Georgina had come with her husband to witness it.

Thereafter Dickens was deluged with invitations from all over Britain, to repeat the phenomenon. It was, in the early days, usually *A Christmas Carol* that audiences wanted. Subsequent readings were given in provincial towns and cities, usually for educational charities. At several venues in London, at Sherborne, at Reading, audience numbers were climbing towards the thousands; at Bradford, in Yorkshire, he had audiences of 3,700. He pledged in a speech in Sheffield – after reading the *Carol* – 'that to the earnestness of my aim and desire to do right by my readers, and to leave our imaginative and popular literature more closely associated than I found it at once with the private homes and public rights of the English people, I shall ever be faithful – to my death – in the principles which have won your approval'.

No one had ever seen anything like this in the

nineteenth century. A generation would pass in Britain before politicians (following Gladstone's example in the Midlothian Campaigns) went on the road to meet the crowds. (Incidentally, Gladstone was obviously influenced in his decision to go on what we call the 'campaign trail' in part by revivalist preachers, but also by the example of Dickens.) Dickens had drawn forth, and charmed, that new phenomenon, the great public. Over the next five years he gave a dozen or more charity readings, nearly always of the *Carol*, nearly always at Christmas time. It was in 1858 that he decided to turn professional.

Dickens's mimetic and histrionic gifts had been noted ever since boyhood. His father had made him perform turns. He learned to win his father's love not by obedience, but by playing the clown, singing songs and doing funny voices. Applause became a positive need, fed during youth and early manhood by theatricals.

As a boy at Wellington House Academy, his fellow schoolboys had noted his skill at mimicry and his adoption of false personae: they remembered him lurking round Drummond Street pretending to be a beggar, in order to con money out of old ladies, before running off down the street, convulsed with laughter. There had been the early attempts to become a professional actor – though, interestingly, the dramatic performances, something rather more elaborate than is usually associated with the amateur, had ceased, never to be repeated, after *The Frozen Deep*. In his theatrical productions – the lavish *Every Man in His Humour* and *Merry Wives*, as in *The Frozen Deep* itself – Dickens had, of course, been acting roles. In the readings he was acting not merely the 'characters' of Boots, Mrs Gamp and others; he was acting Charles Dickens. 'I have long held the opinion and have long acted on the opinion, that in these times whatever brings a public man and his public face to face, on terms of mutual confidence and respect, is a good thing.'

We stare, like the children's eyes in Yeats's poem 'Among School Children', 'in momentary wonder on/A sixty-year-old smiling public man'. Like his own children during the Christmas game, when they had no idea of the significance of 'Warren's Blacking', so suddenly brought into a memory game, we are not, as he claimed (and nor were his audiences), brought into 'mutual confidence' with Dickens. That is an illusion, a subterfuge. On the contrary, we confront mask after mask and have no idea of who the 'public man' really was. Perhaps the spruce, whiskery little figure pacing the lawn at Gad's, and murdering Nancy, all on his own, had no idea, either.

For whatever reason, after Nelly had entered his life, and after *The Frozen Deep*, the readings became a psychological necessity. The very things about the paid readings that John Forster found *infra dig* were those elements that drew

240

Dickens – they were 'common', vulgar, they made him like an actor. He was cleverly joining the Ternans' world while not joining it, for the readings were not held in theatres, had no props – beyond the reading desk and the book itself, which he scarcely needed because he performed the Boots or the Trial or the murder so often that he had them by heart. He was also doing something that was probably necessary, *for him*, in any relationship: he was competitively demonstrating that he could beat the Ternans at their own game. While Nelly was appearing in William Bayle Bernard's play *The Tide of Time* at the Haymarket and, in spring 1859, in John Palgrave Simpson's *The World and the Stage*, Dickens was packing in the crowds at St Martin's Hall. We can have no doubt that, if Nelly at this point in her career had become a star, and were the audiences for Dickens's readings small, it would have been the end both of the readings and of the relationship.

While he was finishing *A Tale of Two Cities* in 1859 he did a two-week provincial tour – Cambridge, Peterborough, Bradford, Nottingham, Oxford, Birmingham, Cheltenham, 'a new place every night'. At Oxford, the Prince of Wales came to hear him and the vice-chancellor of the university had asked him to stay the night, but Dickens refused – he had to rush on to the next town as soon as the reading was done.

These exhausting public readings formed part

of the pattern of Dickens's existence until three months before he died.

In his last completed novel, *Our Mutual Friend*, the ungainly workhouse boy Sloppy assists Betty Higden by turning her mangle, and helps out at her Minding-School (that is, a crèche for the babies and children of working mothers). Moreover, Sloppy reads to her the exciting crime reports in the newspapers. '"I do love a newspaper. You mightn't think it, but Sloppy is a beautiful reader of a newspaper. He do the Police in different voices."' [*OMF* I 16] An early typescript draft of T. S. Eliot's *The Waste Land* was titled 'HE DO THE POLICE IN DIFFERENT VOICES' and although he was persuaded not to use the quotation, it was central to his idea for the poem. In *The Three Voices of Poetry* (1953), Eliot again reverted to 'voices' in Dickens: 'You may remember that Mrs Cluppins, in the trial of the case of Bardell v. Pickwick, testified that "the voices was very loud, sir, and forced themselves upon my ear". "Well, Mrs Cluppins," said Sergeant Buzfuz, "you were not listening, but you heard the voices."' The modernist/symbolist use of 'voices', different 'characters' speaking alongside the authorial voice, and sometimes drowning it out, is central to the achievement of *The Waste Land*, as in the work of Eliot's friend and mentor Ezra Pound, especially *Personae*. Eliot, too, like Dickens, was a devotee of music hall and 'popular' entertainment.

Sloppy, reading aloud from the newspapers for a semi-literate audience, was far from unique in the mid- to late-nineteenth-century urban world. During the Crimean War the dispatches sent back to *The Times* by the pioneering war reporter William Howard Russell were read aloud in the market square of Hanley – one of the Pottery towns later incorporated into Stoke-on-Trent – by Samuel Taylor. This developed into his 'Literary and Musical Entertainments for the People', which he performed in the Town Hall. Those attending were charged a penny for admission. Between October 1857 and April 1858, nine Staffordshire towns were offered penny readings, with probably 60,000–70,000 attending. Penny readings became popular throughout the industrial towns of the British Midlands and the North. Joseph Chamberlain used to read Dickens aloud at Literary and Mechanics' Institutes in Birmingham, of which he was the radical mayor. Dickens, whose serialized fiction, from the beginning, had been on sale on station bookstalls alongside cheap journalism and penny dreadfuls, could see, as John Forster could not, how appropriate it was that he should pitch to huge live audiences. His first professional reading was of *The Cricket on the Hearth*, at St Martin's Hall on 29 April 1858. Nearly nine years later, he recalled in a letter to Robert Lytton on 17 April 1867:

When I first entered on this interpretation of myself . . . I was sustained by the hope that I could drop into some hearts, some new expression of the meaning of my books, that would touch them in a new way. To this hour, that purpose is so strong . . . that after hundreds of nights, I come with a feeling of perfect freshness to that little red table, and laugh and cry with my hearers, as if I had never stood there before.

The little red table was the reading table that he had designed himself, and which may be seen to this day at the Dickens Museum in Doughty Street. Before the table was made, Dickens accepted the pulpit lecterns that the various halls provided for his charitable readings. He gave exact instructions for the size and height of the desk. At first it was covered in greenish-grey material, with a fringe. On another small table stood a carafe of water and a tumbler. At a certain point of the 1860s, for some reason, he changed the colour of the table, which was covered with crimson velvet. Part of the routine was that he laid his gloves and his handkerchief on this little table before he began to read. It has been observed that the little table is still in remarkably good nick, given that it was taken across the Atlantic and hauled on and off trains. One reason for this is that it was usually covered with baize. Behind Dickens was a chocolate-coloured screen. This had a visual function – Dickens in his evening dress and the green or red table both stood out vividly against it. Also, it was meant to be an acoustic aid. Varied as Dickens's histrionic gifts were, his voice was not especially loud, and in performances that lasted two hours (with a ten-minute interval) great demand was laid on that voice.

At every venue, Dickens and his manager would inspect the stage and set up the props. If the stage was unsuitable – as, for example, it was in Shrewsbury in 1858 – Dickens would insist on alterations. On that occasion Dickens had worked out that he would be difficult to see, so his manager Arthur Smith set to work making a platform out of dining tables. They would then test the sound, and if the acoustics were really bad, they would, even at the last minute, ask for a change of venue. Then the lighting had to be set up. 'My servant has a screen of my own to be placed behind me, and assist the voice; also my own gas-fittings.' The gas fittings consisted of a high batten, suspended twelve feet above the platform and in front of the desk, supported by two vertical battens at either end, fixed with copper-wire guys. The battens had gas jets, one halfway up each vertical pipe and screened by green shades, and a row of gas jets along the top. Sometimes a metal reflector was used, placed just above the top rail. The lights would be low, and then, just before Dickens came onstage, they were turned up to full glare. On one occasion there was a gas leak, and during a reading in Belfast someone accidentally stood on a gas feeder-tube and extinguished all the lights.

Then there were the props – the book itself, the gloves and a paper-knife, which Dickens sometimes brandished. During a performance of Mrs Gamp in 1863, when the old lady is described as sitting close to the fender and sliding her nose backwards and forwards along its brass top, Dickens rubbed his own nose along the paper-knife.

The first manager engaged by Dickens for these carefully managed shows was the impresario Arthur Smith, described by Dickens as 'the best man of business I know'. 'Arthur is something between a Home Secretary and a furniture-dealer in Rathbone Place,' Dickens wrote. 'He is either always corresponding in the genteelest manner, or dragging rout-seats about without his coat.' Smith's practical skills were balanced by the good agent's ability to set the client at ease. Audiences would notice how Dickens shook, and how his legs trembled during performances. His nerves were stretched, and he absolutely could not do this roadshow without an efficient manager. Unfortunately, Smith fell ill in the summer of 1861 and died on 1 October. Dickens took on his assistant, Thomas Headland, and 'it is the simple fact that he has no notion of the requirements of such work as this'. The tours stopped. Dickens gave a short series of readings in London between

March and June 1862, and he repeated this season the following year. But with the inefficient Headland, he could not risk going further afield, particularly since, by now, his own health was failing. And these were years when, for at least some of the time, Nelly was in France – it has been persuasively supposed – having a child, or children.

This enabled that very great novel, *Our Mutual Friend*, to be written, and completed, between 1864 and 1865. That was the traumatic year of the Staplehurst train crash. And Dickens was also completing his second collection of occasional pieces entitled *The Uncommercial Traveller*.

It would have been logistically impossible, during that very busy time, to have resumed the readings, even had a suitable manager been available. Then, early in 1866, Dickens decided to resume them. He entered into negotiations with the agents Chappell in New Bond Street. They offered him £1,500 for a course of thirty readings in London and the provinces – £50 per reading – and undertook all the practical responsibilities for the tour and all the expenses of hotels, travel, etc. Dickens considered this would leave him enough time to continue as the editor of *All the Year Round*. The manager appointed to look after Dickens could not have been better chosen: it was George Dolby, whose book about the tours in the last years of the novelist's life is one of the best things ever written about Dickens.

Dolby was a bald, jolly, bewhiskered individual, just married and in his mid-thirties when he entered Dickens's life. They took to one another immediately. Their journeys together became a Pickwickian odyssey of shared jokes and confidences. Dolby, too, quickly realized that in taking on the novelist and the performer, he took on the delicate business of managing Dickens's 'image'. When the possibility of an American tour materialized, for example, Dickens wanted to bring Nelly. The likelihood of Nelly's presence failing to attract the notice of the gossips and journalists in New York was non-existent. On the American tour, as on the British, Nelly had to stay at home. The tours were all-male affairs, with Dickens's valet, Henry Scott, an invaluable addition:

> As a dresser he is perfect. In a quarter of an hour after I go into the retiring-room where all my clothes are airing and everything is set out neatly in its allotted place, I am ready, and then he goes softly out, and sits outside the door. In the morning, he is equally punctual, quiet and quick. He has his needles and thread, buttons and so forth, always at hand; and in travelling he is very systematic with the luggage.

Such was the success of the British readings that it was inevitable Dolby should plan an American tour. By the time Dolby set off to the States on a reconnaissance visit, in the summer of 1867, it was almost a fait accompli that Dickens would accede to the plan, much as he dreaded it. To Georgy, on 10 May, he compared himself being drawn to America as Charles Darnay, in *A Tale of Two Cities*, was drawn to his lodestone rock, Paris, and to William Wills he bluntly said that the attraction was money: the hope of making '£10,000 in a heap'. To Wills, the devoted editor of *Household Words* and later *All the Year Round*, Dickens was able to list the 'immense consideration' of paying his wife's income, and of having to finance his sons. 'You don't know what it is to look round the table and see reflected from every seat at it (where they sit) some horribly well remembered expression of inadaptability to anything.' Worries about money, especially money spent, lost or gained in the family, are never just about money. The fecklessness, uselessness, of his many children was quite largely something in Dickens's own head – he saw them becoming his father and mother all over again. Across their bright, prosperous, middle-class faces in the 1860s fell the shadow of the Marshalsea from forty years previously. Work, work, work – he alone could pay for it all. £10,000 in a heap. So he was drawn to the lodestone rock, his Calvary, his destined end; for somehow it was clear to him that the American tour would mark the beginning of his end.

After the first trip to the United States, he had

come to hate the place. He resented them pirating his works. In the Civil War he had sympathized, and more than sympathized, with the South, as did most English Liberals and Radicals. While hating the idea of slavery, they resented the idea of the Yankees imposing their will on the independent-minded, old-fashioned South. Palmerston, the (in some senses) Liberal foreign secretary and prime minister, had established a separate embassy for Texas in St James's.

Yet there are indications that even before he finally made up his mind about Dolby's planned American trip, Dickens was working his way in that direction. He rewrote a preface to *Martin Chuzzlewit*, softening his anti-American satires in that book. And when a boring Methodist pastor from Philadelphia asked to come to the offices of *All the Year Round* for an interview, Dickens said yes, in spite of being overwhelmed by work – writing, public readings in London, editing, and preparing a collected edition of his novels for the presses, the Library Edition, which, at the time of his death, had sold more than half a million copies in the UK alone and would make him a net profit of £6,250. He was at this time, as he wrote to Georgy on 10 May 1867 from the Wellington Street offices, so tired that 'I could hardly undress for bed'. But he saw the bore, Dr G. D. Carrow, and apologized to him and his American readers for the tone of his former 'bitter criticisms' of the American press.

Carrow in his clumsy way was rather a skilful interviewer. He remarked to Dickens that 'a man must have really loved a woman if he would fully interpret the secrets of a woman's heart'. Dickens was touched by this, and asked Carrow to expand. The clergyman cited the scene in *Bleak House* where the 'little woman' accepts her guardian marrying her off to the man she has secretly loved all along, Alan Woodcourt. Dickens seized both his hands and said, 'I see you understand me! And that is more precious to the author than fame or gold.' Asked point-blank whether he had loved a woman in this intimate way, Dickens exclaimed, 'You are correct, sir!'

The mutual-admiration society was intense. Dickens's understanding of the human heart was comparable only to 'that wonderful Galilean who knew the heart of all'.

The secrets of a woman's heart, however, weighed heavily on Dickens during 1867. They remain secret to us, even though it is clear that, in a very busy year for Dickens, Nelly had been neither happy nor well.

It was only in 1922, in New York, that there came up for sale a small pocket diary, purchased by the Berg brothers and now to be seen in their collection housed in the New York Public Library. This was none other than Dickens's appointment calendar, which he must have mislaid in New York in December 1867.

It is the closest documentary evidence in existence

of Dickens's hectic, secret life with Nelly. At this point in the story Nelly, twenty-eight years old, and her mother, sixty-five, had cottages in Slough, then a country village near Eton, easily reached by railway from London, Paddington, but quite a trek from Kent. The cottages had been leased by a Mr Tringham – that is, Dickens himself. The pocket book tells a story of Dickens constantly nipping to and from 'SL' and London, often at moments when he was assuring Georgy, back at Gad's, that the pressure of work was keeping him in London. While Georgy supposed him in London, he would in fact have visited the capital for a few hours of necessary work at 'off' – the office – only to return to SL. The first three months of 1867 were an exhausting series of journeys, to Liverpool, to Norwich, to Cambridge, to Ireland, for readings, followed by the return to SL. For the month of March, he never went to Gad's Hill once.

By the spring 'Mr Tringham' was house-hunting in the village-suburb of Peckham in South London. Now Peckham is part of the sprawling suburb of South London; then it was still a village in open country, but, crucially important, there was a new railway station at Peckham Rye, opened in 1865. Like Gad's Hill, it was on the London, Chatham and Dover line. Before the reader echoes Lady Bracknell and says, 'the line is immaterial', she should pause and consider how vital the coming of the railways was to the story of Dickens, as to nearly all the Victorians. But to him in particular. Without the railway, there could have been no public readings; nor could there have been his secret life with Nelly. His life would have been completely, unimaginably different.

April in the diary contains two of the most mysterious entries, about which the speculation of the biographers has been understandably frantic. It contains the information that 'N ill latter part of this month'. On 13 April, when Dickens spent the night in Slough, we read the word 'Arrival'. On 19 April, Wills, his trusted confidant about the Nelly affair, accompanied him to Slough, and it was the day after that when Dickens wrote in the pocket book the single word, enclosed in big square brackets, 'LOSS'. A baby? Opinions will remain forever divided. Claire Tomalin points out that the faithful Wills might have been brought to Slough in order to register the birth – and death? – of the child under an assumed name. But there is no evidence for this.

By May, Nelly's sister Fanny Trollope (herself a novelist now married to the brother of the more celebrated novelist Anthony) had arrived in England from Italy. Three years later, Dickens would be candid about his hatred of Fanny Trollope. A mutual friend, Frances Elliot, a Scottish heiress with literary aspirations, had evidently asked him about his relationship with the Ternan family. She knew Anthony and Tom Trollope (Fanny's husband), and Dickens wrote to her as follows:

The 'magic circle' consists of but one member. I don't in the least care for Mrs T. T. [Fanny] except her share in the story is (as far as I am concerned) a remembrance impossible to swallow. Therefore, and for magic sake, I scrupulously try to do her justice, and not to see her – out of my path – with a jaundiced vision . . .

I feel your affectionate letter truly and deeply, but it would be inexpressibly painful to N to think that you knew her history. She has no suspicion that your assertion of your friend against the opposite powers ever brought you to the knowledge of it. She would not believe that you could see her with my eyes, or know her with my mind. Such a presentation is impossible. It would distress her for the rest of her life. Thank you none the less, but it is quite out of the question. If she could bear that, she would not have the pride and self-reliance, which (mingled with the gentlest nature) has borne her alone [along?], through so much.

. . . Of course you will be very strictly on your guard, if you see Tom Trollope, or his wife, or both – to make no reference to me which either can piece into anything. She is infinitely sharper than the serpent's Tooth. Mind that.'

(Dickens and Mrs Ternan, who had played Desdemona to Kean's Othello and Portia to his Shylock, would have remembered all the anecdotage about the great actor, who had revived the tragic ending of *King Lear*. Perhaps she was even present on the legendary occasion when the great tragedian, in his frenzied rendition of the famous lines, made the inadvertent substitution – 'How sharper than a serpent's thanks it is to have a toothless child!')

Clearly, there was no love lost between Fanny Trollope and Dickens, and the elder sister had presumably seen how unhappy the relationship made Nelly, as such relationships are bound to do. Fanny came over to England at the end of May, without her husband. Her novel *Mabel's Progress* was being serialized in *All the Year Round*, but there is no record of her actually seeing much of Dickens – perhaps she dealt with Wills. In June, writing from Slough on Nelly's printed writing paper – with the monogram 'E. T.' at the top of the page – he warned Wills that the American trip was in the offing, if it could be possible for Nelly to accompany him. 'The Patient,. I ack. to be the gigantic difficulty.'

By June 'Mr Charles Tringham', that assiduous tenant of rented properties in villages within railway reach of the capital, had taken a house in Peckham in a row of villas close to Nunhead Cemetery called Linden Grove. Nelly's was called Windsor Lodge. By the time he paid the rates in January 1868, Mr Charles had become Mr Thomas Tringham; on another occasion, Mr Thomas Turnham. Probably this was Wills who was paying the bill and forgetting Dickens's pseudonym, since, when the rates were settled, Dickens was in America.

By the high summer the plans for Dickens and Nelly to go to America together in November were under way, and Fanny, who had returned to the Continent, was asking Nelly and their mother to come and stay with her in Florence. She arrived there, but with instructions that, if George Dolby felt it was possible, she should come back to England and follow Dickens to America in November. The code to be used, in telegraphs between Wills and Dickens, was 'Tel: all well means *You come*. Tel: Safe and well means *You don't come*.'

Before he set forth, he had a letter from Kate, his wife, wishing him well. He wrote back, on *All the Year Round* headed writing paper:

> My Dear Catherine,
> I am glad to receive your letter, and to accept and reciprocate your good wishes. Severely hard work lies before me; but that is not a new thing in my life, and I am content to go my way and do it.
> Affectionately Yours,
> Charles Dickens.

The last time he had crossed the Atlantic, it was a happier time; it had been with Kate. Now, four and a half months without Nelly stretched ahead. He sent her eleven letters during this period, as well as a cheque for £1,000 – all sent via Wills to whom (10 December) he confided, 'my spirits flutter woefully towards a certain place at which you dined one day not long before I left with the present writer and a third (most drearily missed) person'.

Dolby sailed on the *China* and arrived at Boston harbour on 23 October 1867. The point of starting in Boston was that it was supposedly a city where Dickens had many literary acquaintances – his publisher James T. Fields and his amusing, hospitable young wife in their house in Charles Street; Henry Wadsworth Longfellow, Louis Agassiz, Ralph Waldo Emerson, Oliver Wendell Holmes, Bret Harte, James Russell Lowell and others – and where he could spend two weeks of relaxation before the ardours of the readings commenced. Dolby secured Dickens an officer's cabin on the deck of the *Cuba*, but he left Liverpool with a sad heart, and he was going to be homesick, and ill, for most of the cold months he was away.

The idea that he might have been able to travel about America with Nelly, and for her not to be observed, was dispelled even before embarkation. Swarms of newspapermen were crowding the docks to watch the arrival of the *Cuba*. To avoid them, Dolby had arranged that the US Customs steamer the *Hamblin* should be put at Dickens's disposal; the steamer would meet the *Cuba* in the bay and come into harbour unobserved. It had been a difficult voyage, with rolling seas, and the *Cuba* had lost its way in the Bay of Fundy and then, as she approached Boston, got stuck in a mud bank for hours. By the time the *Hamblin* came ashore, the press were onto the ruse, and an exhausted Dickens and party were followed to their hotel, the Parker House. Even here, privacy proved impossible; the waiters left the doors of Dickens's private dining room open so that 'the promenaders of the corridor' could peep at him. 'These people have not in the least changed during the last five and twenty years – they are doing exactly now what they were doing then,' sighed Dickens. He was in a very bad way. Then Dolby told him that a crowd had assembled such as had never been seen before, the night before tickets for the first reading went on sale. Already, receipts amounted to $14,000 – nearly £2,000. This was at a date when a Congressman's annual salary was $7,500, (about $146,000 in today's money) and a surgeon-general in the US Army could hope to earn $960; a bricklayer's average take-home pay was $3 per week.

It was clear, then, even before the readings began, that they were to be a huge commercial success. This was not without its problems. From the outset, Dolby was criticized for not doing more to prevent the ticket touts from block-buying seats and selling them on at inflated prices. Having clocked up takings of more than $16,000 for the first four readings in New York, he discovered that touts were reselling tickets for $50 and more. At New Haven, Connecticut, the problem became so acute that an actual riot broke out. Touts from New York had reached the venue before Dolby's New York agents, and started to sell tickets for all the eight rows of the house. Dolby, when he read about it, made the eighteen-hour journey from Baltimore (which they happened to have reached on their leg of the tour) and actually cancelled the New Haven reading, refunding disgruntled ticket-holders only the price on the ticket. They made a heavy loss – but so did Dickens and Dolby ($2,600).

Wherever they went, the crowds were enormous, the response ecstatic.

It was not long, however, before Dickens, always prone to colds and catarrh, had gone down with what he called 'a real American' or 'American catarrh', and when the illness turned into influenza, Dolby cancelled the planned trips to Cincinnati, St Louis and Chicago. In spite of this, Dickens determinedly went on with the tour, taking in Washington DC, Rochester, Buffalo, Syracuse and Albany in the state of New York, Brooklyn as well as Manhattan (enormous audiences in Brooklyn at the Plymouth Church, where they queued all night for tickets, sleeping on the snowy sidewalks on mattresses). In four hours, in New York, Dolby sold $20,000 worth of tickets. Similar successes could be reported from Baltimore and Philadelphia, though for some reason Washington was slightly less appreciative.

At Washington, however, Dickens was able to go to the White House, where he and Dolby were amused by the notices: 'Please use the spitoons'. This was an interesting year in the United States. In 1867 President Andrew Johnson's secretary of state, William Seward, committed what was deemed to be 'Seward's Folly', purchasing Alaska from Russia for a mere $7.2 million. History would have been very different had this 'folly' not been committed!

The rather dull Andrew Johnson (a Democrat, Republican Lincoln's vice-president) had become president after Lincoln was assassinated in April 1865. Johnson was deemed by the House to be too lenient to the South, too much inclined to allow the Southern states to reform at their own pace and in their own way, and he was much hated by the Republicans. When he replaced Edwin M. Slate as secretary for war with Ulysses S. Grant, he was impeached, and only survived by a majority of one vote in the Senate. (It was Grant who had commanded the Yankee Army that received the surrender of Robert E. Lee at Appomattox, thereby bringing the Civil War to an end. Less than a week later, Lincoln had been assassinated.)

It was while the momentous impeachment

procedures were under way that Johnson received Dickens in the White House. Dickens told Fields:

> I was very much impressed by the President's face and manner. It is, in its way, one of the most remarkable faces I have ever seen. Not imaginative, but very powerful in its firmness (or, perhaps, obstinacy), strength of will, and steadiness of purpose. There is a reticence in it, too, curiously at variance with that first unfortunate speech of his. A man not to be turned or trifled with. A man (I should say) who must be killed to be got out of the way. His manner is perfectly composed. We looked at one another pretty hard. There was an air of chronic anxiety upon him, but not a crease or a ruffle in his dress, and his papers were as composed as himself.

How Dickens always loved neatness! Cleanliness, for him, was not next to godliness, it excelled godliness.

Before they had even reached Philadelphia, the agency gave Dickens a cheque for £10,000. While the Americans rewarded him, however, he was paying heavily in terms of his health. He suffered from a second bout of severe flu and by the time he had done readings in Baltimore, his appetite had all but deserted him, and he was sleeping only three or four hours out of twenty-four. Young as Dickens was – not quite yet fifty-six – Dolby must have wondered whether, by putting him through such a punishing schedule, he was going to kill the goose that laid the golden eggs. When his publisher, Fields, had come into Dickens's dressing-room after the first of the Boston readings (and no one but the valet and Dolby was normally admitted), the publisher had exclaimed, 'You have given me a new lease of life, for I have been so looking forward to this occasion, that I have had an idea all day that I should die at five minutes to eight tonight, and be deprived of a longing desire I have had to hear you read in my country for the last nineteen years.' It was a *façon de parler*, but one that revealed a sense of Dickens's fragility. The two men heartily embraced and drank champagne.

It was not, however, quite like that. Despite his initial depression in America, and his unwillingness to throw himself at first into the social life of Boston, and in spite of his perpetual catarrh and exhaustion, the readings transformed Dickens. They were a mind-altering, transformative narcotic.

During that evening's performance, while Dolby had been standing at the foot of the stairs, a member of the audience was seen lurching down them. Dolby offered him a hand, thinking he might be ill. The man burst out, '"Say, who's that man on the platform reading?" "Mr Charles Dickens," I replied. "But that ain't the real Charles Dickens, the man as wrote all them books I've been reading all these years.'"

Even though we did not hear the readings, and – despite, or because of, the many descriptions of them – if we find it slightly hard to imagine them, we sense that this man had seen something that the bluff Dolby had not. Dolby represents the man on the stairs, who shoved his hat on his head and stormed out into the night, as a comic character, the one man in the house who is not enjoying the show – like the figure in the Charles Addams cartoon who is laughing when everyone else is convulsed with fear by a horror movie. We know that the man had seen the disjunction. Whatever they were hearing from the stage, it was different from the experience of reading Dickens quietly, while turning the pages.

So on they went – Rhode Island, Rochester, the Falls of Tennessee, Buffalo, Niagara, New Bedford, Portland – in freezing weather, with Dickens often suffering from the catarrh, the sleepless nights, the fevers that were with him for most of the trip. Eventually they returned to Boston, took their affectionate farewell of the Bostonians before returning to New York, to address the Press Association dinner, with protestations that 'equally by my winter fireside and in the green English summer weather' Dickens would remember his American friends with 'the greatest gratitude, tenderness and consideration . . . God bless you and God bless the land in which I leave you.' It was an uncynical version of W. H. Auden's poem 'On the Circuit', about being on a lecture tour, moving from city to city, and turning from home with the sentiment 'God bless the USA, so large,/So friendly, and so rich'.

The quantity of loot being trousered both by Dickens and by Messrs Chappell of New Bond Street, London, was not lost on the US Customs, and the tax collectors demanded that Dickens and Dolby appear before a judge. Dolby argued that 'having the authority of head of the Internal Revenue Department . . . to the effect that neither Mr Dickens nor myself (as foreigners), added to which they were liable, added to which the Act of Congress distinctly stated that persons travelling for the purposes of giving "occasional lectures" were not liable for income tax'. The taxmen demanded 5 per cent of all Dickens's receipts for the lectures, which would have amounted to $12,000. Even while the porters were staggering aboard the *Russia* with the little reading desk and the rest of their enormous consignment of luggage, the taxmen were threatening Dickens and his agent with arrest, though in *Charles Dickens As I Knew Him* one senses Dolby exaggerating the danger of imminent arrest to improve his story. Regardless of who had right on their side, Dickens escaped the American tax authorities and, by the time he returned to England, he had clocked up personal earnings of more than £19,000, nearly twice the '£10,000 in a heap' that he had hoped to net.

There is a very good vignette in Dolby's account of the homecoming. He has already described the shock of the American man who did not feel that the Dickens on the stage was the 'real' Dickens. And he has depicted Dickens on the podium, Dickens on the railroads, Dickens being convivial with strangers, and Dickens among his literary cronies in Boston. They docked at Liverpool and 'After so long and rough a voyage, we deemed it inexpedient to travel the same night by the mail train, and so, remaining quietly in Liverpool', they stayed at one of Dickens's favourite hotels, the Adelphi.

> we continued our journey the following day. Reaching the Euston Square Station at about three in the afternoon, we parted from one another as if we had arrived there from one of our ordinary journeys. By arrangement, there were no friends to meet us at the station to give us welcome after our travels, and it was something almost ludicrous to see Mr Dickens walk out of the station, bag in hand, on his way to the Charing Cross Station and Gad's Hill, where of course his arrival had been made known by telegraph to his family.

Pause for a moment and watch the spruce, tired little man walking through Euston Station towards the stand where the hackney carriages stood waiting and the horses sniffed the afternoon air. Londoners who only know the hideous modern railway terminus can scarcely imagine how beautiful the Greek Revival Euston Station, completed in 1849, was. Dickens and the other passengers passed through a huge hall, flanked with pillars, towards the entrance arch, designed by Philip Hardwick and surmounted with two lodges (which is all that survives of the original design). Pevsner wrote that it was pride in the achievement of the railway line that led Hardwick to 'go all out for the sublime in his Doric display . . . Here was something as grandiose of its kind as anything the Greeks had ever accomplished. So it deserved the highest rhetoric available.' Betjeman added, 'To compare with Euston, there is nothing.'

Dickens, one of the most famous of the Victorians, was walking through one of the most sublime expressions of their aesthetic self-confidence. The Euston Road, which thronged with horse traffic, omnibuses, cabriolets, victorias, broughams, was a row of railway stations – with huge St Pancras, a red-brick cathedral, being erected 500 yards to the east even as he stood there beside the snorting Euston cab horses, and beyond St Pancras the twenty-year-old King's Cross with its huge stock-brick façade facing the road. It was modern London. Drummond Street, where the schoolboy Dickens had amused his chums from Wellington House Academy pretending to be a penniless beggar and cheeking the old ladies, was just behind the cab-stand where he stood. By now they had built all over the fields that he used to cross each morning in his walk from Camden Town. A few hundred yards to the north was the foetid terraced house in Bayham Street from whose narrow front hall the child had left each morning for his forty-minute walk southwards to Warren's Blacking, 30, Strand, during the year his father was in prison. The man whose performances on the stages of halls and theatres on two sides of the Atlantic held audiences enraptured, and whose books sold in the tens of thousands, had used experiences garnered in this neck of the woods half a century ago! No one seemed to notice him as he caught his cab. And if they had done so, which Dickens would it have been that they saw? The public performer? The secret, inexplicable imagination of the novelist? The tiny child in his 'poor white hat, little jacket, and corduroy trowsers' staring hungrily through the windows of pie-shops and making his equally anonymous journey through the pitiless streets of London?

The readings formed a part of Dickens's life from now onwards until a few months before his death. The readings. Nelly. And, eventually, the new novel, *The Mystery of Edwin Drood*. But that would not take form until the late summer of 1869. For fifteen months, against the familiar background of editing *All the Year Round* and writing shorter pieces for it, and attending to Gad's and trying to 'place' his children in their grown-up life, it was – the readings and Nelly.

We know that he had confided in the Fieldses, back in Boston, since Annie Fields, imagining his homecoming to England, wrote, 'I cannot help rehearsing in my mind the intense joy of his beloved – it is too much to face, even in one's imagination and too sacred. Yet I know today to be <u>the day</u> and these hours <u>his hours</u> – Surely the most painfully and joyfully intense of his whole life. And believe he is well once more. Tomorrow Gad's Hill!! Clearly, Dickens had not gone straight home to Gad's Hill. The valet Henry Scott was sent to Gad's with the luggage. If you had followed the novelist's cab from Euston, however, and seen him alight at King's Cross, that small, much-aged figure whom Dolby had watched disappearing into the crowds, you would know that he had taken the train straight to Peckham; for the next week, it was from Windsor Lodge that he commuted to the office in Wellington Street. The faithful Wills was keeping the periodical running smoothly. The separation from 'N' had indeed been painful, and it was clear that, whenever possible, during the next fifteen months, he would take her with him on the reading tours.

There is a nice conjunction, demonstrating his love for Nelly and the popularity of the readings, which resumed in the autumn, left behind in the memory of a shop assistant. The young man's name was Edward Young, and he worked at Dixon's, an emporium in Whitefriargate, Hull. Dickens entered the shop and, in the course of making a purchase – six pairs of ladies' black silk stockings – he asked Edward Young what he liked to do in the evenings. Young replied that he liked going to the theatre, and he liked dramatic readings, but that, unfortunately, the tickets for this evening's performance were sold out. As the two conversed, it was clear that Edward knew Dickens's works well. He was astonished when the customer wrote on a card and put it into his hand. The card was inscribed with the three words, 'Please Admit Bearer', and Edward realized only then who was writing the words. Dickens left the shop.

Such stories – of Dickens in shops, Dickens speaking to strangers – almost have something in them of the Resurrection narratives in the Gospels: the failure to recognize, followed by recognition on the part of the 'believer'. Fred Roe, in his day a relatively well-known artist, saw a watercolour drawing in the window of a junk shop in Seven Dials. He entered the shop and asked the proprietress, a stout party, how much she wanted for it. She replied, 'O, five shillin's.' After this exchange, Roe heard a voice from the back of the shop asking, 'May I look at the drawing?' He saw that it was Dickens, sitting in the rear of the shop with a notebook in his hand. He scanned the drawing for a moment, and then handed it back to Roe. 'T,' was all he said, meaning Turner. 'Yes,' said Roe. 'I congratulate you,' Dickens replied.

Seven Dials was a district that had obsessed Dickens all his life. It had been a nest of vice and crime at least since the eighteenth century, when Henry Fielding's brother tried to clear it up. Forster says that he had 'a profound attraction of repulsion to St Giles's' – the parish in which Seven Dials was found.

Fred Roe did not make the connection, but surely the junk shop in Seven Dials, where he found Dickens making notes in the 1860s, was in the neighbourhood of – or perhaps the very model for – Mr Venus's taxidermy shop in *Our Mutual Friend*. While writing the last, great, finished novel, Dickens told his illustrator, his young protégé Marcus Stone, that he was looking round for someone with a peculiar avocation, something 'very striking and unusual'. Stone had lately felt the need to find a taxidermist to stuff either a small dog or some pigeons (his accounts varied). He told Dickens about the taxidermist's shop in St Andrew's Street, Seven Dials, which he had lately visited. Dickens immediately accompanied Stone to the shop and 'with his unusually keen power of observation, was enabled during a very brief space to take mental notes of every detail that presented itself'. We see Dickens lurking in the junk shop with a notebook, accompanied by the young Stone. He was mentally sketching the shop for magnificent reuse as Mr Venus's shop – surely one of his most brilliant creations. Here we have the phenomenon of witnesses being themselves observed. They were not seeing *him*, it was the other way round, and Dickens was, moreover, in the case of the taxidermy shop, applying the transformative vision. The Shakespeare who gave us the description of the apothecary's shop in *Romeo and Juliet* must have been, in rather a comparable way, the unrecognized camera in the corner of the business, noticing and unnoticed.

The initial 1858 repertoire, when Dickens went professional and took the readings on the road, had been drawn solely from the *Christmas Books*. Little by little he had added the favourite set-pieces – Boots and Marigold, the death of Paul Dombey, the Trial of Bardell v. Pickwick. It was in 1863 that he had first tried 'alone, by myself, the *Oliver Twist* murder, but I have got something so horrible out of it that I am afraid to try it in public'. It is almost as if, in his private enactment of the murder of Nancy by Sikes, Dickens had summoned spirits from the vasty deep, and released a djinn from the bottle of whose sexually violent existence he had been scarcely aware; as if, in the words of T. S. Eliot's Sweeney:

> Any man has to, needs to, wants to
> Once in a lifetime, do a girl in.

271

(If this were a crime story, rather than a book about Charles Dickens, would we discover that a young woman in Hull had been found strangled with a pair of black silk stockings?) Dickens liked to joke about his 'murderous instincts'. 'I have a vague sensation,' he said, 'of being "wanted" as I walk about the streets.' The divided self who imagined he was a detective also imagined himself as the hunted criminal.

Five years after trying the *Oliver Twist* murder alone, he was planning his Farewell Tour of the British Isles, and decided that a 'powerful novelty' was essential to keep up ticket sales. It was then that he told Dolby he was going to include the murder of Nancy in the programme. Dolby was fiercely against it, and did all in his power to dissuade him – 'My reasons for this had reference not so much to the inappropriateness of the subject for Reading purposes – because I knew well that the sensational character of it would be a great attraction – as to the effect which the extra exertion might have on his constitution and the state of his health.'

Likewise, Dickens's family were against the inclusion of 'Sikes and Nancy' in a show meant to be amusing, and to be suitable for both sexes and all ages. Charley was working in the library at Gad's one warm afternoon in the summer of 1868 when he heard the sound of violence taking place outside in the garden. It sounded as if a tramp was beating his wife. The noise swelled, an alternation of brutal shouts and female screaming. Charley realized it was his duty to intervene and stepped outside the house, to find his father, at the other end of the meadow, murdering an imaginary Nancy with ferocious gestures.

Dickens asked his son what he thought.

'The finest thing I ever heard,' Charley replied, 'but don't do it.' You can imagine how Hitchcock would enjoy this scene. Norman Bates, dressed as his mother and 'doing' the voices, as 'she' instructs 'him' to murder the flighty young woman in the shower of their motel, is not the same story as 'Sikes and Nancy', but it is cognate.

Dickens decided to put it to the test by undertaking a reading before a select audience of 100 friends and acquaintances in St James's Hall, where he enacted 'Sikes and Nancy', which he by then had more or less by heart. All the guests were 'unmistakably pale and had horror-stricken faces', he was delighted to observe.

William Harness, who had been at Harrow with Byron and grew up to be a Shakespearean scholar, had been a receptive member of Dickens's private circle, and part of his audiences for years. Forster's *Life* carries an illustration of a group of them at 58 Lincoln's Inn Fields – Maclise the actor, Forster himself, Carlyle and others – listening to Dickens read aloud from *The Chimes* on 2 December 1844. Harness, upstage right, is so overcome with emotion that he has covered his face with both hands.

Twenty-four years on, and the old man, now nearly eighty, was still as satisfyingly suggestible. Harness told Dickens, 'I am bound to tell you that I had an almost irresistible impulse upon me to scream, and if anyone had cried out, I am certain I should have followed.'

Sir William Overend Priestley, 'the great ladies' doctor', had warned Dickens before the performance, 'My dear Dickens, you may rely upon it that if one woman cries out when you murder the girl, there will be a contagion of hysteria all over this place.' Better and better!

Another person present during that experimental reading was Mrs Keeley, a famous actress. Dickens asked her: should he include 'Sikes and Nancy' in the repertoire or no?

'Why, of course do it,' she replied. 'Having got at such an effect as that, it must be done. But,' rolling her large black eyes very slowly, and speaking very distinctly, 'the public have been looking for a sensation these last fifty years or so, and by Heaven they have got it!'

Between January 1869 and March 1870 Dickens would do no fewer than twenty-eight renditions of the murder of Nancy. It became an obsession. The only time Dickens lost his temper with Dolby was when the agent suggested that he maybe reduced the number of times he did his routine of publicly beating a young woman to death. Over a working supper one evening, they were drawing up a list of prospective readings to be performed over the next month in a variety of towns. When they had finished, Dolby noticed that the 'Murder' was taking precedence over everything else. He said:

> 'Look carefully through the towns you have given me and see if you note anything peculiar about them.'
> 'No', he replied, 'what is it?'
> 'Simply this,' I said, 'the success of this tour is assured in every way, so far as human probability is concerned. It therefore does not make a bit of difference which of the works you read, for (from what I have seen) the money is safe any way. I am saying this in the interest of your health.'

Dolby went on to say that readings from *David Copperfield*, the *Carol* and the rest 'will produce all the money we can take and you will be saved the pain of tearing yourself to pieces for three nights a week'.

But tearing himself to pieces was what Dickens needed to do.

> 'Have you finished?' he said angrily.
> 'I have said all I feel on that matter', was my reply.
> Bounding up from his chair, and throwing

his knife and fork on his plate (which he smashed to atoms), he exclaimed –

'Dolby! Your infernal caution will be your ruin one of these days!'

'Perhaps so, sir,' I said. 'In this case, I hope you will do me the justice to say it is exercised in your interest.'

I left the table, and proceeded to put my tour list in my writing-case. Turning round, I saw he was crying . . . and coming towards me, he embraced me affectionately, sobbing the while, 'Forgive me, Dolby! I really didn't mean it' . . .

Clearly he *had* 'meant it', or, to put it another way, clearly his attachment to the murder of Nancy was coming from a deep part of himself which neither Dolby, nor we, can understand.

Dickens told Wills that his performance of the murder had a transformative, destructive physical effect. 'My ordinary pulse is 72 and it runs up under this effort to 112. Besides which, it takes me ten or twelve minutes to get my mind back at all: I being in the meantime like the man who lost the fight.'

Dolby describes the mania for hearing the murder that swept through the towns on nights when it was known it would be performed. It was especially popular in Edinburgh. After it was complete, there would be total silence in the hall. Dickens would then go backstage, often walking with difficulty, and would be forced to lie on a sofa for some minutes before he once more became capable of speech. Then he would recover and 'after a glass of champagne he would go on the platform again for the final Reading'.

The parallels do not require emphasis, they are too obvious: Dolby is describing a post-ecstatic pause, such as might occur to a witch doctor recovering from frenzy, a spiritual medium coming out of a trance or, in a more homely and obvious analogy, in the quietness of post-coitum.

William Macready, Old Rugbeian, Garrick Club member, the grand old man of British theatre who had been his friend since Dickens was in his young manhood, and who had played opposite Nelly's mother as long ago as the 1820s, had thirty-five years as one of the greatest interpreters of Shakespeare known, since Garrick. His legendary farewell performance at Drury Lane on 26 February 1851 had been a performance of *Macbeth*. Macready was now living in frail retirement in Cheltenham. It was not one of the towns on Dolby's list, but for the sake of old friendship, and in homage to the stature of the tragedian, they arranged a 'command performance' in Cheltenham.

After the show, Dickens sent Dolby to the stalls to bring Macready back to the dressing-room. The old actor was very frail, and seemed to be struck dumb by the performance, 'as much excited . . . as if he had given it himself'. When he reached the retiring room, Macready stared speechlessly at Dickens, who urged Dolby to give Macready champagne. He refused, but pressed it on Dickens. 'Turning to Dickens, who had by this time placed him on a sofa, he said, in the manner peculiar to himself and with great hesitation, "You remember my best days, my dear boy? No! That's not it. Well, to make a long story short, all I have to say is – Two Macbeths!"'

The great tragedies of Shakespeare all involve murder, but in *Lear, Hamlet, Othello*, the killings are incidental to the theme; whereas in *Macbeth*, yes, the witch-haunted would-be king is driven on by ambition, but the play itself, 'steeped in so far', is really about murder. Blood and violence are of its essence. Macready had seen something not merely about 'Sikes and Nancy', but about Charles Dickens himself. The veil had been lifted, and then it had fallen again before the proscenium. That was what reduced them to the little silence, broken – as so often in the novelist's life and conversations – by him bursting out laughing. It 'so tickled Dickens that he burst out laughing'.

The inevitable happened at Chester in April 1869. Dickens had a minor stroke onstage. Nelly was in the audience. Frank Beard, his doctor, was summoned from London, and, although Dickens tried to make light of what happened, the medical advice was that the tour should be cancelled forthwith.

★   ★   ★

The connection between theatre and power, in particular between comic theatre and power, was probably not obvious until the twentieth century, when the mesmeric effects of the great dictators over mass audiences was put on display, and it was clear that such figures as Mussolini and Hitler had borrowed from Hollywood's box of tricks. One reason that Charlie Chaplin's *The Great Dictator* does not completely work as a piece of satire is that he was evidently too benign to realize that, in the decade or so before he decided to impersonate Hitler, Hitler had been impersonating him; the little tramp in baggy trousers, reduced to eating his own bootlaces as if they were spaghetti in *The Gold Rush*, hero of the 'Century of the Common Man', had more than a little in common with the outcast bum, tramping the streets of post-First World War Vienna and exuding self-pity from every paragraph of *Mein Kampf*. Both drew on the burlesque traditions of Grimaldi and the Victorian clowns, the pantomime tradition that was so large a part of Dickens's own inspiration and inheritance. One of the most intelligent analyses of the phenomenon is found in the character of Jerry Cobbold, the great comedian, in John Cowper Powys's *Jobber Skald/Weymouth Sands*. Jerry is not only a great comedian, he is also a power maniac, who has discovered, by his ability to manipulate crowds, how mass hysteria, and the incitement to mass violence, can operate.

The public readings do not explain anything,

but they show us the way that Dickens's power was capable of working. You simply can't envisage Thackeray or Trollope, popular as they were, having a comparable effect on audiences, still less – assuming that she had such hieratic skills – George Eliot. These popular novelists of the Victorian era were all working on a level different from that of Dickens. They were simply writers of various degrees of brilliance. The readings merely brought out what had been apparent from the first moment *Pickwick* moved from popularity to stratospheric bestsellerdom: onstage and on page, Dickens was not merely an artist. He was a mesmerist. It was his fascination with mesmeric power that would inspire his most ambitious novel, the one he left unfinished at his death, the one that killed him.

CHAPTER 6

THE MYSTERY OF EDWIN DROOD

'He was consumed with an enduring and almost angry thirst to excel'

D ickens recovered from the stroke, in April 1869, and as the summer progressed, he began to think about another novel. Dickens's American publisher, James T. Fields, and his wife Annie came over, together with Mr Childs, publisher of *The Philadelphia Public Ledger*, and his wife, in glorious June weather, and Dickens was determined to give them a real welcome. When the novel began to appear the following year, they realized that, during his kind tourist-guide views of London and Kent, he had been tracing the sites that would form the background to *The Mystery of Edwin Drood*. For example, as well as inviting the American friends to Gad's Hill, Dickens came up to London and took apartments at the St James's Hotel for himself and his daughters, so as to be able to guide his

American friends around the capital. In addition to the obvious sights, he escorted them to the postal sorting office, to give them some idea of the sheer, stupendous scale of London, its monstrous sprawl. And there were nocturnal tours of 'Horrible London', to make their flesh creep. He took them to the opium dens of Ratcliffe Highway and ended up in 'a place of resort for sailors of every nationality known as "Tiger Bay"'. Here they would be confronted by the sinister little den with which his new novel, seen through the eyes of an opium dream, would open.

The relationship between Victorian England and opium was a close one, and one that demonstrated parabolically the Victorians' capacity for double-think and double lives. They lived before antibiotics, before any pharmaceutical remedy against pain, bar a few simple drugs – and the greatest of these was opium. The 'opium dens' were low dives to be found in the region of the docks. The Ratcliffe Highway was a crime-ridden road cutting through the East End, connecting Limehouse to the City. The opium dens were really for the sailors coming off the ships, moored in Wapping and the other nearby docks. Middle-class people could purchase opiates, in those days before drug restrictions, at any pharmacy. There were no restrictions on the purchase of narcotics, and Dickens himself, in the last two or three years of his life, was heavily dosed with laudanum, the admixture of opium and alcohol that was, in those days before the invention of aspirin (by Bayer Pharmaceuticals in 1899), the commonest form of pain-relief. Dickens's letters reveal that he was opium-dependent, and it would be fascinating to know, as he devised the character of John Jasper, the opium-fiend and almost-certainly murderer of Edwin Drood, the extent to which his own experience of the drug was used directly when composing the story. Alethea Hayter, in her book *Opium and the Romantic Imagination*, was dismissive of the opium dream with which *The Mystery of Edwin Drood* begins. But I have heard Will Self, who has taken opium, assert the faithfulness with which Dickens described the vision, the confused sight of the spiky old bedpost transmogrifying into the cathedral spire.

An ancient English Cathedral Tower? How can the ancient English Cathedral Tower be here! The well-known massive grey square tower of its old Cathedral? How can that be here! There is no spike of rusty iron in the air, between the eye and it, from any point of the real prospect. What is the spike that intervenes, and who has set it up? Maybe it is set up by the Sultan's orders for the impaling of a horde of Turkish robbers, one by one. It is so, for cymbals clash, and the Sultan goes by to his palace in long procession. Ten thousand scimitars flash in the sunlight, and thrice ten thousand dancing-girls strew flowers. Then, follow white elephants caparisoned in countless gorgeous colours, and infinite in number and attendants. Still the Cathedral tower rises in the background, where it cannot be, and still no writhing figure is on the grim spike. Stay! Is the spike so low a thing as the rusty spike on the top of a post of an old bedstead that has tumbled all awry? Some vague period of drowsy laughter must be devoted to the consideration of this possibility.

Shaking from head to foot, the man whose scattered consciousness has thus fantastically pieced itself together, at length rises, supports his trembling frame upon his arms, and looks around. [*MED* 1]

Jasper's wheezing old 'supplier', Princess Puffer, says:

'Poor me, poor me, my head is so bad. Them two come in after ye. Ah, poor me, the business is slack, is slack! Few Chinamen about the Docks, and fewer Lascars, and no ships coming in, these say! Here's another ready for ye . . . .

'O me, O me, my lungs is weak, my lungs is bad! It's nearly ready for ye, deary. Ah, poor me, poor me, my poor hand shakes like to drop off! I see ye coming-to, and I ses to my poor self, "I'll have another ready for him, and he'll bear in mind the market price of opium, and pay according."' [*MED* 1]

The price of opium did, indeed, fall slightly after 1850 – from around 8d. to 6d. an ounce in the last decades of the nineteenth century. The numbers of deaths from opium poisoning rose slightly, but, compared with drug-related deaths today, they were nugatory, between 100 and 200 a year. The first attempts, by the Liberal government, to limit opium supply had come in 1868, with the Pharmacy Act stipulating that anyone buying arsenic, prussic acid and other poisons and narcotics must do so from a registered chemist, but the Victorians were still miles away from the modern system of narcotics control. Profits from the sort of opiates that could be bought over the counter at a pharmacy – of which J. Collis Browne's chlorodyne was the most popular – far exceeded anything that the proprietress of an 'opium den' could hope to make. (J. Collis Browne's profits were between £25,000 and £28,000 in the last decades of the nineteenth century.) It was decades after Dickens died that Bayer Pharmaceuticals, as well as perfecting the development of the aspirin, pioneered what it considered a purer synthetic opium derivative for medicinal use. It was so pleased with the result, a hero among cough remedies, that the firm gave it the name of Heroin.

Dickens belonged to the innocent days before the only people making profits from the sale of such narcotics were the gangsters. The calming and analgesic properties of opium were regarded as virtues, even though the effects of overindulgence had been celebrated in the writings of the Romantics, most notably Thomas De Quincey. The fact that Coleridge and De Quincey showed how to destroy your life with narcotics did not stop a wily and long-lived politician such as W. E. Gladstone adding a dash of laudanum to his coffee before making one of his notoriously boring speeches to the House of Commons. Dickens, however, while making what use he could of the actual effects, upon his own consciousness, of slight overindulgence, preferred to make the wicked John Jasper – habitual user of opium at home – the frequenter of the opium dens of Ratcliffe Highway.

Among the other sights that Dickens laid on for the American tourists was a visit to Canterbury, a short enough distance from his house in Kent. Having put up at the Fountain Hotel, they arrived at the cathedral just as the afternoon service was beginning – exactly as John Jasper, still bleary from the opium, arrives at Cloisterham Cathedral to sing Evensong in the first chapter of *Drood*. The Americans, and Dickens himself, were appalled by how 'mechanical and slipshod' the clergy were in their manner of conducting the service.

Afterwards, when a verger offered to show them

round the ancient building, Dickens dismissed the man and himself conducted the tour for his friends, 'in the most genial and learned style in the world'. He also conducted them around the town, and showed them 'Doctor Strong's' – the school attended by David Copperfield.

Directing his appreciative guests to the real-life sites of his fiction was something from which Dickens did not shy away. When in London, they had explored the Inn of Court where Pip is called upon by the old convict Magwitch, just as, when at Gad's Hill, he had taken them to walk on the marshes, and seen the churchyard with the babies' graves where Magwitch in chains first encounters Pip the child.

They could not have known at the time, but it must have dawned on them when they read the unfolding episodes of *The Mystery of Edwin Drood*, that the new novel was in many respects going to be a revisitation, not only of the geography, but also of the issues, of *Great Expectations*.

David Copperfield (1849–50), the benign version of his autobiography, was followed a decade later by the much more coherent, much more self-tormenting *Great Expectations*, in which, several layers of the carapace having been ripped off Dickens by falling in love with Nelly, the raw truth about his own ruthlessness, the impurity of his family hatreds, the psycho-bonds that drove his need for status and money, and the murky origins of his money – any money – had all been mythologized, projected, imaginatively realized. Of course, had Dickens fully known what he was doing, he could not have done it. A helpful course of cognitive therapy, such as our contemporaries might have urged upon a middle-aged man who had just visited such absolute mayhem on his wife and children, after Nelly and *The Frozen Deep*, would unquestionably have destroyed *Great Expectations*, made it, indeed, impossible for his imagination to operate at all. Perhaps that novel is the apogee of Dickens's achievement. It is the only novel in which there is no wasted paragraph, no waffle, no padding, no dud or redundant characters and *no illustrations*. It did not need illustrations because it is the most devastating and the most inward of all his psychodramas. Every page hits you like a heart attack. But how could he possibly have written it if he had completely known, as we strongly suspect, that biography unlocks the key of the myth? Pip owes his fortune to a violent criminal, not seen since childhood. The fact is unknown to himself, and the discovery is shattering. The author of this overpoweringly strong story, however, had to remain himself unaware that he owed the source of his wealth, the origin of his imaginative life and the capacity to translate it into gold, to a secret, violent criminal: not a 'warmint' who has turned his hand to sheep-farming in Australia, but a mysterious warmint called Charles Huffam Dickens. The other Dickens, the hairy bear in the forest, the secret twin he never knew and whom we glimpse only very occasionally, when, for example, he is practising the murder of a young prostitute as he walks around his shrubbery.

It is hard to think of any more powerful example of the truths explored in W. H. Auden's poem 'The Maze' (in some collections entitled 'The Labyrinth'):

> His absolute pre-supposition
> Is: – Man creates his own condition.
> This maze was not divinely built
> But is secreted by my guilt.
>
> The centre that I cannot find
> Is known to my unconscious mind;
> I have no reason to despair
> Because I am already there.

Dickens's insightful daughter saw the same truth when she said that her father was a wicked man, while she recognized, and loved, the complexity of characteristics that cohered in and around this wickedness.

Before he left for that last tour of the United States and docked at Boston harbour in November 1867, Dickens was about to publish, in *All the Year Round*, an article by Sir James Emerson on the murder of Dr George Parkman. This crime had been committed in 1849, and had been followed by court procedures that have been called the O. J. Simpson trial of the nineteenth century. More than 60,000 spectators filed into the Boston court to hear the trial of Dr John Webster, head of chemistry at the Massachusetts Medical College. He was accused of murdering the wealthy businessman and hospital benefactor Dr George Parkman. To this day, there are those who believe in Webster's innocence. One of the things that fascinated Dickens about the case was Webster's demeanour after his arrest and during the trial. He was quietly composed, and appeared to be sincerely convinced of his own innocence.

Dickens wrote home to Wilkie Collins on 12 January 1868:

> Being in Boston last Sunday, I took it into my head to go over the medical school, and survey the holes and corners in which that extraordinary murder was done by Webster. There was the furnace – stinking horribly, as if the dismembered pieces were still inside it – and there are all the grim spouts and sinks, and chemical appliances, and what not. At dinner, afterwards, Longfellow told me a terrific story. He dined with Webster within a year of the murder, one of a party of ten or twelve. As they sat at their wine, Webster suddenly ordered the lights to be turned out, and a bowl of some burning mineral

to be placed on the table, that the guests might see how ghostly it made them look. As each man stared at all the rest in the weird light, all were horrified to see Webster with a rope round his neck, holding it up, over the bowl, with his head, jerked on one side, and his tongue lolled out representing a man being hanged!

Poking into his life and character, I find (what I would have staked my head upon) that he was always a cruel man.

There were many things about Webster that would have caught Dickens's imagination. One was that he was a Micawber, a Dorrit, a man like Dickens's own father through whose fingers money simply leaked. Parkman had lent Webster money and wanted to be repaid. He discovered that Webster had run up debts elsewhere. Some valuable minerals that Webster had offered Parkman as a guarantee of his substantial loan had, it transpired, been mortgaged to another lender. The motive for killing the cold-hearted Scrooge-like Parkman was fairly clear, though it is less clear whether Webster would still have been obliged to repay the debt to Parkman's estate.

The central mystery of the trial, and one reason for the enthusiasm of the 60,000 ghouls who trooped into the courtroom to stare at Webster's impassive features, was that there was no body. Some body parts had been found in a laboratory in Dr Webster's department, and he appeared to have dismembered Parkman and burned some of him. In those relatively primitive days, when forensic medicine was in its infancy, it was not possible, initially, to establish beyond reasonable doubt that the body parts in the Massachusetts Medical College were indeed those of Dr Parkman. Nor could it be proved that Dr Webster had put them there, or dismembered the body. However, some gold in the cadaver's dentures, which were discovered among the charred remains, matched that of the Boston Brahmin's own false teeth; and his widow identified various body parts. The crucial evidence was given by the janitor, a dubious character who had made a nice little living supplying the Medical College with cadavers at $25 a time, but who was now rewarded with a staggering $3,000 for his evidence against Webster.

It was a case in which the judge created a precedent in US law. Hitherto, an American jury could not convict a suspected murderer in the absence of the victim's body. In this case the judge, Chief Justice Lemuel Shaw, ruled that the jury could convict, if they believed 'beyond reasonable doubt' that the body parts were those of Dr Parkman.

Webster was found guilty and he was publicly hanged. It was a story very much up Dickens's street, but what appeared to fascinate him most deeply was the murderer's state of mind. Webster had appeared to be not so much a hypocrite, when he professed his innocence, as a divided self. The mild-mannered professor of chemistry had perhaps been unaware, or scarcely aware, of the murderous capabilities of his darker self. The extent to which this case inspired Dickens's last novel has been questioned. The parallels are not so very close. That the Webster/Parkman case was one of the ingredients that fed into *The Mystery of Edwin Drood*, however, could not really be denied. We do not know, of course, for a certainty, how Dickens's book would have ended, but we know that he planned to write the story of a man who had committed a murder, while professing his own innocence. Like Dr John Webster, John Jasper, whose name is not so dissimilar, was ardent in his expressions of a wish to pursue the murderer. Like the body of Dr Parkman, the body of Edwin Drood is, in the surviving pages of the novel, never discovered. Like John Webster, John Jasper was, Dickens said, destined in the last section of the completed novel to have confessed to the crime he had committed, and the final part of the book was to have been an exploration of the divided self of a killer. One obvious influence upon the way Dickens came to the story of the Parkman murder, as the gestation of his own last novel developed, was *The Moonstone*, the 1868 novel written by his friend Wilkie Collins. In that story, Franklin Blake removes the moonstone from its hiding place while he is under the influence of opium. Once the effects of the drug wear off, he has no recollection of having stolen the jewel.

Dickens all but alluded to this story in *The Mystery of Edwin Drood* when describing the headmistress of the girls' academy in Cloisterham: 'As, in some cases of drunkenness, and in others of animal magnetism, there are two states of consciousness which never clash, but each of which pursues its separate course as though it were continuous instead of broken (thus if I hide my watch when I am drunk, I must be drunk again before I can remember where) so Miss Twinkleton has two distinct and separate phases of being.' [*MED* 3]

Double-selves, divided personalities, and the psychological theories of those who believed in animal magnetism, all these preoccupations weighed on that divided self, Charles Dickens, as he undertook his final novel.

The Mystery of Edwin Drood would seem to suggest that there are more sick souls, more false selves, in the world – or, anyway, in the imagined cathedral town of Cloisterham – than healthy ones, and that wholeness, an integrated personality that is happy in its own skin, not at war with itself, is the exception rather than the rule. The disrupted torn self inflicts terrible damage, on its other self or selves and on other people. But the divided self is also a source of creativity. Dickens could see that the gallery of characters who had been buzzing out of his head ever since 'Boz' first ventured into print had not come from a calm, happy place, but from a cauldron of self-contradiction and

294

self-reproach, a bubbling confusion of moral centres. The capacity to create fiction was an artistic way of describing the capacity to self-deceive. The creative urge was the artistic way of describing the urge that used, battered and, if necessary, destroyed the loves of those closest to him. It has been rightly said that the murderer in Dickens's last novel is himself a kind of novelist. He is shaping his own story.

Just as Mr Quilp[en], in the early days of Dickens's marriage, derived his pantomimic strength from the demonic, cruel side of Dickens's own nature, and from Dickens's personal hatred of his wife, so the psychopathic villainy of John Jasper, in the unfinished novel, stems from Dickens's own possessive sexual fantasies about his much younger mistress, Nelly. Any lover with a much younger partner is tormented by the possibility that the young one will eventually find a mate of a similar age. The fear that he was approaching death did not diminish this torture for Dickens: on the contrary. The knowledge that Nelly, an attractive young woman, would undoubtedly find a mate after his own departure from the scene fed into the imaginative maelstrom that led to *The Mystery of Edwin Drood*.

The key to the plot of this last novel, however, which unravelled a good while before he died – indeed, as we shall see, the unravelling of the novel was one of the things that killed Dickens – is

Mesmer's idea of animal magnetism. Jasper, obsessed by desire for the schoolgirl Rosa Bud, attempts to mesmerize her during their music lessons together, and she, overpowered by the sexually predatory nature of his feelings, is forced to run away and seek hiding in London.

We began with the Mystery of Fifteen Pounds Thirteen Shillings and Ninepence, and we followed a perhaps too-sensational version of events, which took Dickens from Gad's Hill to Peckham, where he spent his last fully cognizant hours with Nelly Ternan. But let's have second thoughts. Let's tell a different story. Let's accept the version given out by Georgy Hogarth. We cannot prove that Dickens went to Peckham on that June day, had a seizure and needed to be brought home to die a respectable death in Gad's Hill. We might not wish to gather behind the cloak of respectability that his family drew around Dickens's last days; but we will accept the verdict of the housemaid who was sent to fetch the doctor, that, at the very end, Dickens certainly was at home. This, though, is simply to quibble about the kind of death that doctors write about when they sign death certificates; the bodily death that Dickens clearly felt creeping over him as he planned *The Mystery of Edwin Drood*. (The contract drawn up with his publishers makes provision for the book being unfinished at the hour of his death.)

There are, in any event, versions of the story of his bodily death, other than the version that took him to Peckham and had him suffering from a stroke in poor Nelly's house; and there are other keys to his Mystery. In the story that became the official version, and which could well be the true one, Dickens, on Wednesday 8 June, did something he never normally did. He wrote all day, rather than finishing work at lunchtime. After his luncheon at Gad's Hill that day, he returned to the Swiss chalet. If this was the case, we must conclude that he was writing the last pages he would ever compose. Either way, whether Dickens was at Peckham in the arms of Nelly or sitting in the chalet at Gad's Hill fervently and frantically writing against the clock, the overpowering importance of sex, in his life and in his fiction, was inescapable. The story of 'Fifteen Pounds, Thirteen Shillings and Ninepence' would take us some way to recognizing the centrality to his life, in that last decade, of Nelly Ternan. More than that, the existence of Nelly reminds us of the centrality of sex, of women, of the sexual passions he could never openly write about. *The Mystery of Edwin Drood*, more than any of Dickens's books, concerns itself with clumsily, scarcely buried sexuality.

At the little female academy run in the cathedral town of Cloisterham by Miss Twinkleton there is an annual ceremony in which she takes leave of her boarders before they go home for their holidays. As the girls gathered round, Miss Twinkleton said, "'Ladies, another revolving year had brought us round to that festive period at which the first

297

feelings of our nature bounded in our" – Miss Twinkleton was annually going to add "bosoms", but annually stopped on the brink of that expression and substituted "hearts".' [*MED* 13]

Dickens had been stopping on the brink of 'bosoms' all his professional career, and substituting 'hearts': in his writing, that is to say, if not in his life. He had been teetering on the edge of writing about sex – for example, in the story of Little Em'ly's seduction by Steerforth – and then stepping back again. The fact that he did not write overtly, very often, about sexual passion should not make us suppose that the books allow us to forget sex. On the contrary. Quilp's desire to seduce the pure child-woman Nell Trent, having fathered another child-woman, 'the Marchioness', on Sally Brass (though in the final published version he expunged any such suggestion); Sikes's brutal relationship with Nancy the prostitute, ending in her being clubbed to death; Mr Carker's wish to seduce the wife of his employer, and Edith Dombey's willingness to elope with Carker to punish her husband; Lady Dedlock's aching, depressive yearning for the dead copywriter, as she sits trapped in a sexless marriage; Pip's masochistic adoration of Estella – these and dozens more examples shout to us about sex, sexlessness, desire and the inability to live without sex and be happy; or to live with it and find satisfaction.

Rather than inventing figures such as Balzac's

Valérie Marneffe (who in *La Comédie humaine* overtly uses sex as a form of self-promotion, but is in fact as sexually frustrated as the Dickensian figures just named, as are all the characters in the sex-soaked *Cousine Bette*), Dickens gave to his readers sentimental, sexless heroines like Dora and Agnes in *David Copperfield*. As his writing career drew to a close, however, he seemed to approach the subject that so concerned him with such subliminal violence – sex – more nearly. The scene he repeated again and again on the stage, during the public readings, was the savage murder of Nancy the prostitute in *Oliver Twist*. Arthur Clennam in *Little Dorrit* enjoys a repetition, with the eponymous heroine, of Dick Swiveller's cosy relationship with the dwarfish 'Marchioness', while the actual sexual passions occur in the margins of the story – with Miss Wade's elopement with Tattycoram, or in the unmentionable life of the prostitute encountered on the Iron Bridge in the middle of the night. In the penultimate novel, however – *Our Mutual Friend* – the sexual impulse is much nearer the surface of the story. Bella Wilfer is the closest we ever get to a woman describing and embracing her sexual feeling and achieving satisfaction: her awareness of her father's sexual frustration in his own marriage, and her pity for him, and her quasi-incestuous secret 'dates' with her father before she finds an evidently satisfactory mate in *Our Mutual Friend* are all recognizably messages

299

from the real world of sexual life, as opposed to the fantasy world of toy doll-women like Dora Copperfield. Bradley Headstone, in the same novel, is driven to attempting a murder because of his frenzied sexual jealousy of Eugene Wrayburn and Lizzie Hexam.

In the unfinished novel Dickens returned to this very theme, with his story of John Jasper, the choirmaster who, violently jealous of his nephew Edwin Drood, and of Drood's rival Neville Landless, contrives a cunning and dastardly scheme whereby he will kill Drood, and Landless will hang for the murder. Jasper longs to possess Rosa Bud, and believes that Drood will have her – not even for the asking, but as the result of an absurd pact, made by their respective fathers when Edwin and Rosa were young children. In this story, of a young woman who is envied by all her fellow teenagers because she is engaged to be married, but who secretly does not love her young man and yearns to be free; of a young woman who excites the darker, possibly violent passions of her music master, the saturnine John Jasper, and who is instantaneously loved, on their first encounter, by the Asiatic Neville Landless, there is a fourth man who is preoccupied with her to the point of obsession – and an almost blatantly obscene obsession at that. This figure is, of course, her creator.

Not content to give her the suggestive name of Rosa Bud, Dickens allows her fiancé to call her by the synonymous nickname of Pussy. When

300

Edwin Drood playfully tries to kiss the verger's wife, Mrs Tope, who acts as his uncle's housekeeper, he exclaims, "'Give me a kiss, because it is Pussy's birthday'" and she replies, "'I'd Pussy you, young man, if I was Pussy as you call her . . . Your uncle's too much wrapt up in you, that's where it is. He makes so much of you, that it's my opinion you think only to call your Pussys by the dozen, to make 'em come.'" [*MED* 2]

The double-entendre here is not between Edwin Drood and his uncle's housekeeper; it is between Dickens and his more sophisticated readers. The old Podsnappian convention persists that there is going to be nothing in his novels, as they are read aloud in the cosy family circle, which could bring a blush to the cheek of a young person. (And, of course, even this famous Podsnappery is itself a subversive piece of flagellant filth; one remembers that one of Dickens's most fervent admirers was the poet Swinburne.)

Even without conjuring up the image of Charles Dickens very nearly dying of sexual excess in Peckham, therefore, we can follow, in the last book he wrote and never finished, a comparable journey in his imagination as he plotted, and wrote, *The Mystery of Edwin Drood*.

We have also observed that at the heart of Dickens's last novel is the idea of animal magnetism, as espoused by Franz Anton Mesmer, and, by extension, the possibility of 'Mesmerism' – that is, of

301

one human being exercising hypnotic power for good or ill over another: in practice, such power nearly always being exercised by a man over a woman. Fred Kaplan, who wrote so well about Dickens and Mesmerism, reminded readers that 'in late Dickens, to love another is to have power over that other, and to give that other power over you. It is to enter into a special kind of subject–operator relationship.' If Mesmerism is a metaphor (while also being an actual practice followed in the eighteenth and nineteenth centuries), then it speaks volumes that Dickens was able to practise Mesmerism on his wife when they were still a sexually active couple. When she accepted, at least to some degree, the 'subject–operator' nature of the relationship; when she grew out of this, and questioned it, she could be discarded as an obviously 'difficult customer', especially since he had found, in the much younger Nelly, the perfect submissive.

Not only did Dickens practise Mesmerism, but he also read widely in related subjects. Only months after his death, when his library was put up for sale, purchasers could have found such titles as Count de Gablis's *A Diverting History of the Rosicrucian Doctrine of Spirits: Sylphs, Salamanders, Gnomes and Daemons* (1714), John Abercrombie's *Inquiries Concerning the Intellectual Powers and the Investigation of Truth* (1840) and, above all, John Elliotson's *Human Physiology* (1835–40). Elliotson was the key pioneer of

302

Mesmerism in Victorian England, and his *On Numerous Cases of Surgical Operations without Pain in the Mesmeric State* (1843) bears on the flyleaf – as the auctioneer and the punters would have noted, when it went under the hammer – the inscription 'To Charles Dickens, from his sincere friend, John Elliotson'.

Like many ideas originating on the European land-mass, especially with the French-speaking parts of Europe – most notably the emergent theories of evolution – Mesmerism had failed to take hold in England during the long period of the Revolution (1789) and the subsequent wars. It had been in 1779 that Franz Anton Mesmer, having fled Vienna, had published, in French, and in Paris, *Mémoire sur la découverte du magnétisme animal*. Though it sounds to us like mumbo-jumbo, as nearly all science does fifty years after it has been accepted as truth, Mesmer's theory has been seen by historians of Ideas as being deeply in tune with the Enlightenment and with revolutionary times. This was chiefly because Mesmer was an out-and-out materialist. Having 'discovered' the 'fluid' in the universe, he could discard the spiritual influence of God, or the Absolute Good, on the soul. He was, therefore, a progressive, and those who embraced his theories in Britain were nearly all, likewise, seen as political radicals. (Most enthusiasts for Mesmerism in Britain were, for example, vociferous abolitionists in the slavery question.)

Mesmer's was the era when, beginning with

chemistry and the experiments of Joseph Priestley in England, and Antoine Lavoisier in France, modern science, properly speaking, began. The discovery of the elements, and the composition of matter, made an almost immediate technological difference to the world. Having discovered the chemical property of water, it was almost no time before it became possible to see the technological power of steam. The magnetic property of iron was no longer a mystery – it was something that could be demonstrated and explained in terms of chemistry and physics. From H_2O to steam engines was a short step: within decades of the chemists' theoretical studies there were mechanized factories; the Luddites were trying to put back the clock and destroy the spinning jenny and the powered loom; and railroads were steaming across the fields and plains of Europe and America. A new world had dawned.

Mesmer believed it was possible to explain and categorize the human psyche in rather the way that it was possible to classify the inanimate universe. His 'discovery' of animal magnetism led to two propositions. First, there is a magnetic 'fluid' in the universe. Mechanical laws, working in an alternate ebb and flow, control 'a mutual influence between the Heavenly Bodies and the Earth'. Animate Bodies partake of this fluid. Second, because it was now possible for science to identify the ebb and flow of this fluid, it was also possible to create a new theory about the power and influence of people upon one another. When one human being exercised power over another, they were exercising animal magnetism. It was possible, moreover, to demonstrate this power in a hypnotic manner.

Mesmer's ideas, like many other scientific ideas – for example, all the ideas of Cuvier or Lamarck about evolution – were held at arm's length, or ignored, by the British intellectual community for most of the half-century that began with the American Revolution and included the French Revolution. It was only, really, in the late 1830s that either the evolutionary idea or the animal-magnetism idea got much of an airing in Britain, and most British medical opinion was decidedly suspicious of the idea of animal magnetism.

An exception was John Elliotson, who held the Chair of the Principles and Practice of Medicine at the newly founded University College, in London, and who began to do mesmeric experiments on the wards of University College Hospital. Most notably with a pair of sisters named O'key.

Elizabeth and Jane O'key were a pair of epileptic housemaids, unusually small and – just the way Dickens liked them – undeveloped and child-like. Elizabeth, dubbed the 'prima donna of the mesmeric stage', displayed 'no evidence of her having made any approach towards puberty'. She was pale, sickly and melancholy; her hands were covered with warts, which she picked, so they were always raw and bleeding.

Having initially supported his friend Elliotson,

Thomas Wakley, pioneer coroner who exposed the evils of Victorian epidemics and the scandal of disease among the urban poor, founder-editor of *The Lancet* and a political radical, came to have his doubts as Elliotson, in putting the O'key sisters through their paces, lowered the tone of scientific experiment to that of vaudeville – and bawdy vaudeville at that. Elliotson chose to make his mesmeric experiments on the O'keys public, to avoid the implication that he was exercising an un-wholesome power over vulnerable young females in private. This only led to the implication, in *The Lancet* and elsewhere, that the experiments were salacious. Both sisters, but especially Elizabeth, when placed under the mesmeric spell, became roguish with members of the usually all-male audience, addressing the Marquess of Anglesey, for example, as 'white trowsers', to the general amusement of the other observers. The O'keys, under the mesmeric influence, could lift heavy weights and display extraordinary telepathic powers; when blindfolded or when their line of sight was hidden by screens, they could tell how many fingers Dr Elliotson was holding up; there were many, rather footling, experiments, involving coins and pieces of metal, which were almost in the nature of conjuring tricks.

Elliotson came to believe that it was possible to use mesmerism as an anaesthetic, and to conduct surgical operations painlessly upon bodies who had been mesmerized. He also believed that his subjects, especially the O'keys, entered mysteriously into clairvoyant knowledge when under the influence. When Elizabeth O'key was led into the men's ward of the University College Hospital, she asked hysterically why 'Great Jacky', the 'angel of death', was sitting on one of the patients' beds. Then, having shuddered, she moved to another bed where she found 'little Jacky'. The man on whose bed Great Jacky had been seen died that night; the companion of 'little Jacky' 'escaped scarcely with his life'. It was at this point that the hospital authorities insisted upon Elliotson discontinuing his mesmeric experiments, and he forthwith resigned. On the very next day, 28 December 1838, at 6.30 p.m., Elliotson and Dickens dined together.

Elliotson became the godfather to Dickens's second son. In accepting this role, Elliotson, a bachelor agnostic, made clear that he regarded his part in the child's life as supplementary to Dickens's bodily role.

> I shall be delighted to become father in God to your little bo peep. I should, however, have been compelled to forego this delight had you not absolved me from religious duties & everything vulgar – For nothing could I teach him in the vulgar tongue – nor would I have spoiled him for arithmetic by teaching him that three are one & one is three or defaced his views on

the majesty of God by assuring him that the maker of the Universe once came down & got a little jewess in the family way.

As we saw in the chapter on Charity, Dickens never had much truck with the Christian orthodoxies, and indeed joined the Unitarian Church, a body that has, since the eighteenth century, discounted the central doctrines of God's Incarnation, the divinity of Christ, and the Trinity, preferring to concentrate on the moral and social requirements of the New Testament, kindliness, forbearance and concern for the poor. There was, however, one clergyman in Elliotson's circle, the Reverend Chauncy Hare Townshend, and he was so enchanted by Dickens that he actually composed a sonnet 'To the Author of Oliver Twist, Nicholas Nickleby & c'. Dickens became a frequent attendant at the mesmeric demonstrations not only of Elliotson, at his premises at 37 Conduit Street, but also of Townshend. Only the pressure of work would keep him away, as when he apologized for non-attendance on 6 January 1842 – he explained that he was in the process of 'murdering that poor child': that is, finishing off Little Nell in *The Old Curiosity Shop.*

Townshend's book of 1840, *The Facts of Mesmerism*, could have been describing the obvious appeal of the fad to Dickens himself when he said, 'Even the swimmer, who learns at length to surmount the boisterous surf, or to stem the adverse stream, will revel in the consciousness of awakened power. How much more must the mental enthusiast riot in the display of energies so long concealed, so wondrously developed.' Townshend, indubitably homosexual, longed to mesmerize Dickens himself, a plea that Dickens always refused – on the grounds that it might cause him headaches and interfere with his work. Clearly, the real reason was that Dickens did not wish to surrender himself to another's power. He recognized that Townshend – who became a good friend – had prodigious mesmeric power, which extended not only to the human race. The mesmeric cleric, in the intervals of obsession with a fifteen-year-old Belgian, Alexis, whom Dickens nicknamed the magnetic boy, put on the most astonishing mesmeric demonstrations, ranging from Alexis's clairvoyant powers to Townshend's own capacity to hypnotize not only human beings, but also birds and animals. Under Townshend's spiritual powers, tom tits and nightingales fell into trances and allowed themselves to be handled and tossed about like balls. Dickens, naturally, believed it was possible to develop comparable capacities of control within himself.

The following year, 1842, Dickens took his wife to America, by which time he had already learned – from Townshend and from Elliotson himself – how to perform as a mesmeric operator. Soon after he arrived in Boston, Dickens, presumably with an introduction from the London practitioners in the cult, was invited by an American mesmerist, Dr Collyer, to witness his cases.

Not long after this, while in Pittsburgh, Dickens 'magnetized' his wife Kate in the presence of two witnesses. Within six minutes of passes about her head with his hands, Kate became hysterical. She then fell asleep. Dickens found he could wake her easily, as taught by Elliotson and Townshend, by transverse movements of his thumbs over her eyebrows, and by blowing gently on her face.

The 'success' of this first experiment in animal magnetism slightly shocked him. Writing to his friend William Macready – Dickens recommended him to consult Elliotson and take mesmeric cures for his own weak health – the novelist assured the great actor that he wished him to be the witness 'of many, many happy times' when Dickens was able to cast this spell over Kate. Indeed, on their return from America he would often mesmerize his wife and other members of the family or friends. Not all his subjects were women. Macready himself recalled, 'I did not quite like it, but assented: was very nervous, and found the fixedness of the position – eyes, limbs, and entire frame – very unpleasant, and the nervousness at first painful. Reasoned myself out of it, and then felt it could not effect me.'

Mesmerism as metaphor: surrender of the will: clearly, the submission of the mesmeric subjects

310

to their operator was not overtly sexual, or even a metaphor for sex alone. Where this is leading us is closer to the understanding of the way Dickens operated – operates – as an artist. John Keats did not like poetry that has a design upon us. Well, the novels of Charles Dickens have a design upon us all right, and there is never going to be any doubt about who is in control. Every reader accepts him on his or her own terms or finds him repellent. Dickens wooed/wowed the crowds in his lifetime, and this is the way that his books still operate. This is where Mesmerism fits into the picture of Dickens as an Artist. This is the point of emphasizing the emblematic significance of Mesmerism in Dickens's range of performance tricks.

The sexual element, if not to the fore, was undoubtedly strong in all this. Witness the fact that Wakley and others found something obviously unsavoury about Elliotson's public demonstrations of how he could make the apparently not-yet-pubescent O'keys pass into hysterics, swooning, crying aloud, and so forth.

Dickens, likewise, though prepared to mesmerize, either literally or metaphorically, his children or his friends, found it most exciting to perform the bag of tricks on women. Clearly the most dramatic example of this occurred during his long Italian journey with his wife and children, in the autumn of 1844.

★ ★ ★

In the course of the journey Dickens had befriended a Swiss banker by the name of Emile de la Rue, and his small, beautiful, child-like, nervous English wife. Another little child-woman on the edge of nervous collapse. You can sense Dickens becoming too excited. As they travelled through Italy, the Dickenses and the de la Rues pitched up together in various places, including Genoa and Rome. Dickens's intimacy with Mme de la Rue caused Kate enormous distress. It is not entirely clear whether Dickens slept with Mme de la Rue. What was on display, and what was apparently tolerated by her husband, was Dickens's desire for absolute control over a young, vulnerable woman who was suffering, in the diagnosis of a late-twentieth-century psychiatrist, from 'a hysterical conversion-cum-catatonic syndrome or demonic hallucinations and abnormal posturing and contortion'. He told M. de la Rue that 'Kitty Clive, the actress, had said to Garrick (crying at his Lear) that she believed he could act a gridiron; while he (Dickens) had a perfect conviction that he could magnetize a frying-pan.'

Mme de la Rue, 'a most affectionate and excellent little woman', suffered from nervous tics and hallucinations. She constantly found herself on a green hillside, with a blue sky above her head. She suffered from appalling pain, and was under the impression that stones were being hurled at her by unseen hands. (In *The Mystery of Edwin Drood*, the alcoholic stonemason Durdles pays the street urchin 'Deputy' ('Winks') to pelt him with stones as a way of guiding him home when he is hopelessly inebriated.) Dickens undertook to cure his 'patient' by mesmerism.

Mme de la Rue was his most successful 'patient'. At Genoa, Kate became so disturbed by the amount of time Dickens was spending in Mme de la Rue's bedroom at all hours of day and night that it was expedient for the novelist to take his family away for a while, in the hope of calming his wife's 'unreasonable' behaviour. Thirteen years later, in 1857, when he was in the process of separating from Kate, Dickens wrote to M. de la Rue:

> Between ourselves . . . I don't get on better in these later times with a certain poor lady you know of than I did in the earlier Peschiere days. Much worse. Much worse! Neither do the children, elder or younger. Neither can she get on with herself, or be anything other than unhappy. (She has been excruciatingly jealous of, and has obtained proof of my being on the most intimate terms with, at least fifteen thousand women of various conditions of life since we left Genoa.) Please to respect me for this vast experience.

Back in 1844, when they returned to Rome, the de la Rues joined the Dickenses in the Hotel Meloni. One night Kate woke up to find Dickens

313

striding up and down their bedroom with all the candles ablaze. He had just come from Mme de la Rue's bedroom, where he had been mesmerizing her and trying to calm her night fears. He had found her 'rolled into an apparently insensible ball, by tic on the brain'. Within half an hour of submitting to Dickens's will, the 'excellent little woman' was sleeping as calmly as a happy child.

Contemporary theories about animal magnetism lay at the core of *The Mystery of Edwin Drood*. John Jasper exercised just such mesmeric force over Rosa Bud as Dickens had utilized in the bedroom of Mme de la Rue.

As Rosa Bud explained to her friend Helena, the Asiatic new girl at Miss Twinkleton's academy:

> He has made a slave of me with his looks. He has forced me to understand him, without his saying a word; and he has forced me to keep silence, without his uttering a threat. When I play, he never moves his eyes from my hands. When I sing, he never moves his eyes from my lips. When he corrects me, and strikes a note, or a chord, or plays a passage, he himself is in the sounds, whispering that he pursues me as a lover, and commanding me to keep his secret. [*MED* 7]

Helena Landless is going to be the physical protectress of the vulnerable Pussy. 'The lustrous gipsy-face drooped over the clinging arms and bosom, and the wild black hair fell down protectingly over the childish form.' [*MED* 7] No shyness here about the word 'bosom'. Landless, the surname of Pussy's protectress, and of Helena's brother who falls instantly in love with Rosa at first sight, is an unusual name. It must have been suggested by the name of Nelly – Ellen Lawless Ternan. The relationship between Jasper and Rosa Bud reflects the 'dark' side of Dickens's possessive love for his much younger mistress. The fantasy that took shape in the form of this particular fiction was created by Dickens's preoccupations in the last year of his life. His fictions had long been fed by the thought of older men taking child-brides or tiny female companions who were not as sexless as they appeared, or child-women – as in the case of the doll's dressmaker upbraiding her drunken father, or Little Nell restraining her grandfather's calamitous gambling habits – who had reversed their roles. At the same time, there had also been the story of Miss Wade rescuing Tattycoram from the smothering possessive love of the Meagles (Dickens recognizing the negative and repellent nature of the benignant, jolly old charitable figures in his fictions).

We misunderstand the word 'Life' if we think that the 'Life' of Charles Dickens is one of two things. One is the prosaic, outward surface of his life, the events that actually occurred to him, and in which he was involved – in Dickens's case, the childhood in Chatham and London; the horrors of Warren's Blacking warehouse and the Marshalsea; the marriage to Catherine Hogarth; the public and charitable involvements of his hyper-energetic life. Secondly, the 'Life' of a novelist could be the uses to which the novelist put these experiences – John Dickens in the Marshalsea, turning into Mr Dorrit. Clearly, in a rough and ready sort of way, this is what happens in the 'Life' of a novelist, and almost all biographies of novelists do indeed consist of this juxtaposition of supposedly 'real' experiences and the reproduction of these experiences in fictive form.

So, in a book such as Michael Painter's two-volume biography of Marcel Proust, we watch the patient assembly of the 'originals' from which the imaginative author fashioned the fictional Baron de Charlus, Mme de Guermantes, and so forth.

Actually, what is happening in the 'Life' of a novelist is something much less straightforward than this, and the reductive attempt to draw the connections between 'real' and fictional life leads to various levels of clumsiness. Who, in a sense, cares that Sherlock Holmes might or might not have been based on a particular teacher at Edinburgh encountered during Conan Doyle's medical training? This tells us precisely nothing about Sherlock Holmes, who is an immortal figure – unlike the dead and (all but – save by Conan Doyle obsessives) forgotten 'original'.

316

Clearly, unless a writer is composing works of science fiction or what is shelved by the booksellers under 'fantasy', the real world will be used as a canvas, the world as actually encountered by the writer. A sense of place was important to Dickens, and he evoked town and landscape with unforgettable clarity. A certain type of reader will always be interested in visiting the places that appear to have inspired their favourite novelists. Is Pemberley Chatsworth? What was the original of Mansfield Park? Sometimes the identification of imagined place and its original in real life becomes so powerfully confused that the 'real' place is actually subsumed in the imaginary: witness Illiers in Normandy being renamed Combray. Presumably it is only a matter of time before Laugharne in South Wales becomes the Llareggub of *Under Milk Wood*.

Although the mental processes that lead to these identifications are easily traceable – and Dickens positively encouraged them, as we have seen, pointing out the site of Dr Strong's school at Canterbury, or the staircase in the Temple where Magwitch visits Pip – this seems an odd way of reading both geography and fiction. Within months of Dickens's death, the Gradgrindian Dickensians were out in the streets of Rochester with their notebooks. Pass a generation, and the whole of the novel had been mapped out, with almost reproving attention to the alterations made by the primary imagination of a novelist to the

317

topographical facts. In Chapter 4 of *Drood*, for example, we encounter the gloriously absurd figure of the local auctioneer Mr Sapsea, the 'purest Jackass in Cloisterham', who thinks of himself as a distinguished appendage to the Dean and Chapter and concludes the auction-sales 'with an air of bestowing a benediction on the assembled brokers, which leaves the real Dean – a modest and worthy gentleman – far behind'. [*MED* 4] Sapsea lives in lodgings over the High Street in an old building near Nuns' House, where Rosa Bud goes to school. 'Over the doorway is a wooden effigy, about half life-size, representing Mr Sapsea's father, in a curly wig and toga, in the act of selling.' [*MED* 4] The second issue of *The Dickensian* (1906) contains an article by Mr Woodford Sowray, which informed readers that 'there was a figure in Rochester; but I found that it did not stand over the doorway of the ancient three-gabled house in the High Street, as described in *Edwin Drood*, but that its actual position was over the door of a house further on in the direction of Chatham . . . that the house when the story was written was occupied by a Mr Batten, a builder (now dead) who was at one time mayor of the city and that in the course of alterations to the house the effigy was removed'. [*SJ* p. 304] Arthur J. Cox, who edited the Penguin edition of the novel in 1974, pointed out that Dickens claimed this 'ancient three-gabled house' as Uncle Pumblechook's premises in *Great*

Expectations. As we noted when Dickens was showing his American publishers the Inns of Court, Canterbury and Rochester, he himself enjoyed this tracing of the Dickensian 'originals' and the 'actual' sites of his stories.

In a sense, the 'real' wooden figure, however, and the 'real' three-gabled house ceased to exist even before they were demolished, not as physical entities, of course, but as Dickensian originals.

The antiquarian, faddist interest in identifying individual buildings or streets in Rochester that might have been 'used' in the composition of the novel only, in any event, go a little way to helping us understand why Rochester, a city just down the road from Gad's Hill where the book was being composed, should have any significance in our reading of the story at all.

The question is not whether this wooden figure, or that house, can be identified as the models for Cloisterham, Dickens's imagined city. The question is where all this stuff is coming from – what are the wells from which he is drawing water? Cloisterham is the Rochester of Dickens's childhood. In Chapter 3 he informed us that 'For sufficient reasons, which this narrative will itself unfold as it advances, a fictitious name must be bestowed upon the old cathedral town.' [*MED* 3] It is the world as he knew it before he was transported to the hell of premature adulthood in London and had to confront his father's bankruptcy, the debtors' gaol, the blacking factory, the London crowds, the Fall. But it is also a story that concerns itself with the problems of personal identity. At the beginning of the story, Jasper is 'the man whose scattered consciousness has thus fantastically pieced itself together' [*MED* 1] as he comes round from an opium trip. The stone-mason who teaches him how to bury and dispose of human remains 'often speaks of himself in the third person; perhaps, being a little misty as to his own identity'. [*MED* 4] The young people are still finding themselves, and the older figures in the book – except those such as the jackass Sapsea, who are fixed, like so many Dickensian characters, in caricatures of themselves – dance in a disturbing state of flux. They are by no means who they appear to be.

The story takes place before the railway came to 'Cloisterham' (that is, pre-1840), in the benevolent prelapsarian world of Mr Pickwick and his friends, who visited Rochester in 1837.

In *The Mystery of Edwin Drood*, however, the imagination of Dickens was moving in other directions. It is a story of murder, sexual jealousy, hatred.

Dickens had told his friend Forster, 'I have a very curious and new idea for my new story; not a communicable idea (or the interest of the book would be gone) but a very strong one, though difficult to work.' Many theories have been propounded, both about what Dickens intended to be 'very curious and new' about his story, and about how the plot would have evolved, had he lived to complete the story. 'Datchery', the stranger who arrives in Chapter 18 in the old cathedral town, with his shock of white (in a later chapter, grey) hair and his clear intention to investigate John Jasper's activities, will surely turn out to be someone in disguise?

The 'curious and new' fantasy was fed with the knowledge of Dickens's own approaching death. When he died, he would lose control over Nelly. Her young body would become the possession of another man. Dickens could not guess that Nelly herself would concoct the most stupendous of fictions out of her own life, re-creating herself aged thirty as a woman of eighteen, marrying a young man and bearing his children, and recalling Dickens, as she brazenly did, as a man who had befriended her when she was a mere child.

When Princess Puffer, the mysterious old proprietress of the opium den, meets her client John Jasper after a long gap, a gap in which Edwin Drood has supposedly been murdered, she asks him:

> 'Who was they as died, deary?'
> 'A relative.'
> 'Died of what, lovey?'
> 'Probably, Death.' [*MED* 23]

That was what was staring Dickens in the face as he wrote this last, triumphant chapter.

321

A resurrection chapter for, in the previous hundred pages, he and the book had already died, and it was only in this final chapter – writing, writing, writing in the Swiss chalet in that last week of his life – that from a dull day and a grey sky had suddenly flared a glory.

The death certificate tells us that Dickens died on 9 June 1870. Readers of *The Mystery of Edwin Drood* could see that he had actually died several months earlier.

The novel had been a new departure. In July 1869, Dickens had written to Forster, 'What should you think of the idea of a story beginning in this way? – Two people, boy and girl, or very young, going apart from one another, pledged to be married after many years – at the end of the book. The interest to arise out of the tracing of their several ways and the impossibility of what will be done with the impending fate.'

Had he written this book, Dickens would indeed have been changing course quite dramatically as a novelist. For such a story to succeed, he would have needed to trace the inner life of the characters; and to tell the inner life, moreover, not of a child, or of one of his self-projections, such as David Copperfield or Pip, but of two people, one of them a woman, exploring their emotions. George Eliot could have written that book, but it is so different in theme from any of Dickens's previous imaginative interests that one wonders where such an idea could have come from. Nelly?

A month later, Dickens had changed his idea. Forster reveals to us that the idea was the story of a man murdering his nephew. By the time Dickens set to work, the two themes – the young people, committed by some arrangement to be married, but both unwilling; and the uncle-murderer – have melded, and we have the story that occupies the opening instalment of *The Mystery of Edwin Drood*. John Jasper, the lugubrious twenty-six-year-old opium addict, who works as the director of music in a cathedral town, is the uncle of the scarcely younger Edwin Drood. Drood, twenty, destined for a career in business in Asia, not unlike Arthur Clennam in *Little Dorrit*, is betrothed to Rosa Bud, Jasper's pupil, and, as we discover, is the object of Jasper's fervent and quite unwanted desire.

It would seem that Dickens had seldom, if ever, plotted his novels in advance in this way. There had never, therefore, been a novel that depended so much upon plot. We have already explored two of the ways in which Dickens was going to handle the double plot: it was to be by making John Jasper a mesmerist. By setting himself the task of telling the story twice, first as a narrative of his own, and then again, in the words of Jasper in his prison cell, Dickens was plotting a modernist, almost Nabokovian narrative structure, which would indeed have been something quite new in his fiction.

He was exhausted, ill and dosing himself frequently with laudanum throughout the period of the novel's planning and composition. I am completely convinced by Robert Tracy's analysis:

> Lay Precentor of Cloisterham Cathedral and opium addict John Jasper's art is music, but he is also inventing a plot and writing a book about a murder that has not yet taken place. As a character in *The Mystery of Edwin Drood*, he is writing a variorum version of the novel in which he appears, attempting to control its plot and define some of its characters. Jasper as novelist is a projection of Dickens himself, who has imagined so many crimes and murdered so many characters in so many novels.

Anxiety that he was not going to be able to pull off the feat of writing Jasper's final version of the story contributed to Dickens's illness, there is no doubt. W. H. Wills wrote, 'The anxiety (about the novel) and excitement materially contributed to his sudden and premature death.'

Jasper had planned the murder from before the beginning of the novel. His expressions of love and affection for his beloved Ned are the merest hypocrisy. His obsession with Rosa Bud means that he is determined to possess her and, even if this proves impossible, to prevent Ned from doing so. The crucial plot detail here is

Jasper's ignorance of the fact that Rosa and Edwin have in fact agreed that they should *not* become lovers, still less get married, but they have decided to keep this fact a secret.

The arrival of Neville Landless allows Jasper the chance to create an even more complicated plot for his 'novel', as well as yet another subject for his evil mesmeric machinations. In the scene where Edwin Drood and Landless quarrel, we can watch Jasper actually manipulating the row, charging their glasses with what they believe to be mulled wine. After they have quarrelled and then fought, and Landless has staggered out into the night, he tells Canon Crisparkle, truthfully, 'I have had a very little indeed to drink.' [*MED* 8] We have noted – what was unseen by the two young men – that Jasper had prepared them mulled wine: 'It seems to require much mixing and compounding.' [*MED* 8] Clearly, from the moment Landless arrived at Cloisterham and displayed his fiery temperament, Jasper sees that he can use him. He works his mesmeric powers on Landless, either to commit the murder himself, or to believe that he has done so with his heavy stick. Quite how the plot would have been explained, had Dickens lived to write the confession in the prison cell, we do not know.

In any event, the novel begins to unravel. The unravelling happens after Jasper writes to Canon Crisparkle, 'My dear boy is murdered.' [*MED* 16] In precisely the same way that Webster reacted to the murder of George Parkman, Jasper expresses himself determined to unmask the murderer. We must assume either that he is simply lying or that, as a divided self, he does not fully appreciate whereof his opium-crazed self is capable.

Dickens must have realized with a panicking, sinking heart that he has written only four parts of a twelve-part serial, and most of the story has already been told. He had killed Edwin Drood off much too early. Unless he were to be writing a Wilkie Collins-type mystery novel, or a modern detective story – which he surely *was not* trying to do – Edwin Drood should have stayed around much longer. How on earth is Dickens going to bulk out his story for eight more episodes?

From now onwards, we see the novel disintegrate. He resorts to the feeble device of making a mysterious stranger arrive in Cloisterham. Datchery is clearly someone in disguise – perhaps Bazzard, the law clerk who is working for Mr Grewgious – though some ingenious readers suppose he is actually Helena Landless. Not for one moment, not for one sentence, does the 'character' of Datchery ring true, and 'his' arrival, even more than the sudden change in Mr Boffin's character in *Our Mutual Friend*, seems like one of those lurching plot-reversals that Dickens intruded into sagging narratives, rather as a desperate cook, preparing mayonnaise, watches the mixture curdle beneath his spoon and must resort to beating up a new egg yolk and adding the mixture as before.

The mixture as before, in the case of *The Mystery of Edwin Drood*, is tired, sad stuff. By the time Rosa Bud has run away to London and the quarters of Mr Grewgious, she finds herself, not in *The Mystery of Edwin Drood*, but in London's legal quarter, wandering at large in a Dickens-land, in what could be discarded pages of *Bleak House*. The disgruntled old landlady Mrs Billickin ('Unless your mind is prepared for the stairs, it will lead to inevitable disappointment' [*MED* 22]) is simply a rent-a-Dickens character, devoid of true comedy or interest. He was writing on autopilot when he came up with her. The writing is flat, the story is going nowhere, and any reader by the time they have reached Chapter 22 of the story would have the sense that the author had in fact already died.

But then came the prophetically entitled Chapter 23, 'The Dawn Again'. Jasper renews his acquaintance with Princess Puffer, and in his opium dream, like Macbeth or Raskolnikov, he revisits his crimes. '"I did it here hundreds of thousands of times. What do I say? I did it millions and billions of times. I did it so often, and through such vast expanses of time, that when it was really done, it seemed not worth the doing, it was done so soon."' [*MED* 23]

Like Durdles, the boozy stonemason, Dickens was 'perhaps a little misty as to his own identity'. [*MED* 4] Jasper and Dickens together arrive in an opium-crazed climax to a horrified contemplation of their past. In the final pages that

Dickens was writing in the chalet in those last days, our belief in the novel revives. We glimpse something of the masterpiece that was lost when he died. Jasper returns to Cloisterham, leaving behind his other self in the opium den, but Princess Puffer, on this occasion, pursues him. She meets the improbable Datchery and is directed into the old cathedral.

All unconscious of her presence, he [Jasper] chants and sings. She grins when he is most musically fervid, and – yes, Mr Datchery sees her do it! – shakes her fist at him behind the pillar's friendly shelter.

Mr Datchery looks again, to convince himself. Yes, again! As ugly and withered as one of the fantastic carvings on the under brackets of the stall seats, as malignant as the Evil One, as hard as the big brass eagle holding the sacred books upon his wings (and, according to the sculptor's representation of his ferocious attributes, not at all converted by them), she hugs herself in her lean arms, and then shakes both fists at the leader of the Choir.

In that last hour in the chalet, Dickens had returned to form. The glorious sunset, as red as his favourite flower, the potted scarlet geranium, blazed in the heavens.

★　　★　　★

328

Atmospherics and character are two of the ingredients we encounter in all the great Dickensian fictions. I use the word 'atmospherics' to convey the *mise en scène*, the weather, the language-music in which the whole is described, a language that is playful, intense, observant and always in control. The characters who burst into the scene, in any of the great novels and stories, all speak in their own highly distinctive language, but they cannot escape being described by the Dickensian voice, which is so much a part of our reading experience. This is true even in *Bleak House* where there are two narrative voices, Esther Summerson's and Dickens's own, and where, so often, Esther finds her pen being guided by Dickens, creating turns of phrase and perceptions of which the somewhat vapid Esther would never, herself, have been capable.

The Mystery of Edwin Drood is strong in atmosphere and it has a small but powerful set of characters. Because Dickens died before he finished writing it – died twice, in my submission, Dickens the writer dying several weeks before Dickens the man – it has been inevitable that so many attempts have been made to propose for the novel. For a certain type of reader, the plot predominates, and the question of whether John Jasper did or did not kill his nephew – and if he did not, who did – becomes the method not merely of creating a plausible ending for the novel, but also of reading that part of it which we have received from Dickens's own hand.

Now, although Dickens's novels do have story-lines and plots, and they need the plots to stop them being mere series of incidents, like *The Pickwick Papers*, we do not particularly care about their plot-lines as such. The extraordinarily improbable series of coincidences, for example, that enable Oliver Twist, after a stray encounter in the street with an old man whose pocket he was supposed to be picking on Fagin's behalf, to find that the old man is Mr Brownlow, who keeps a drawing of Oliver's mother hanging on his walls – she having been the love of his life. Quite how Oliver relates to Mr Brownlow or, even more improbably, to Monks, the villain who is trying to kill him (in fact, his brother), is not what we remember when we have closed the book. We remember the Artful Dodger, Fagin's lair, and Nancy and Bill Sikes. And the same is true of all the books, even those stories such as *Great Expectations* and *A Tale of Two Cities* where so very much hangs on the plot. (Charles Darnay who loves Lucie Manette is really the Marquis St Evrémonde – but what we remember is Dr Manette's obsessive inability to escape his time in the Bastille; and Mme Defarge's knitting as the tumbrils roll through Paris.)

We do not know whether Dickens, who told his son Charley that John Jasper had, quite definitely, committed the murder, would have changed the plot, had he lived; or whether Edwin Drood, who appears to be dead in the surviving pages of the novel, might not have returned, like John Harmon in *Our Mutual Friend*, either disguised or openly. We do not know whether Dickens was intending to borrow from his friend Wilkie Collins's plot in *The Moonstone* and have the crime committed while under the influence, in this case, of opium, which induces amnesia until the narcotic repossesses the perpetrator's brain.

None of these things can be known. And in some senses, they are beside the point. What we have are the surviving six monthly parts (out of the projected twelve). Dickens had seen Numbers 1–3 through publication and corrected the proofs of Number 4, and Numbers 5 and 6 were altered after his death, restoring cuts, in book form, that had been deemed necessary for serial use. And what these surviving pages reveal is that for the first four episodes or so, Dickens was writing at the very height of his powers. He had never created more tense 'atmospherics'. He had returned to the Rochester of his childhood. The old hag whom we met in the wonderful opening pages – in the opium den – Her Royal Highness the Princess Puffer – has now come down to Cloisterham from London in pursuit of John Jasper. Dickens does not tell us how she got there, or whether he had forgotten that the railways have not yet reached Cloisterham. Rochester, and the marshes, and the glittering Medway, had always been the scene of the lost Eden, the time of innocent walks with his father John Dickens, of relative prosperity working

331

in Chatham dockyards, of a certain degree of schooling, and of the family being of containable size before his poor parents found themselves, like the old woman who lived in a shoe, the mother and father of more children than it was possible to cope with. The railways in Dickens had always been symbols of the cruel, modern world intruding into Pickwickian innocence, thundering its man-made earthquake through Staggs's Gardens, where 'a bran-new Tavern, redolent of fresh mortar and size, and fronting nothing at all, had taken for its sign The Railway Arms . . . the old-established Ham and Beef Shop had become the Railway Eating House'. [DS 6] The railway brought loss of innocence, and since the Staplehurst crash it brought fear, and the possibility of destruction. It was an emblem of unhappy death, and the possible instrument of Dickens's – and Nelly's – exposure to the public. In an essay in *All the Year Round* of a decade since, 30 June 1860, Rochester had been 'Dullborough', 'my boyhood's home . . . Most of us come from Dullborough.' Cloisterham had seemed more picturesque than Dullborough, but it had first come before our eyes in an opium trance. At the beginning of the Cloisterham myth it was still out of reach of the corrupting railroad, but by the time it had run into difficulties, it had become possible for the serpent to enter Eden and the old purveyor of wickedness from the Ratcliffe Highway to present at the innocent place. Old Puffer is the Angel of Death. 'Died of what, lovey?' 'Probably, Death.' [*MED* 23]

So now the novel was never going to be finished.

The eyelid drooped, but flickered. There was still life in the body as they lifted it from the floor to the sofa. 'At death', Larkin averred, 'you break up: the bits that were you/Start speeding away from each other for ever.'

In Dickens's view of things, this process could begin long before the moment of death. The 'bits that were you' could, indeed, coexist with bits that were not 'you' at all, or were a different 'you' who was able to lead a separate life from the conscious 'you'. In his final novel, he chose to write about the phenomenon of the divided self, in the context of a gruesome murder story. The phenomenon, however, was not external to himself. He had always been a divided self – the victim-child and the Infant Phenomenon who exacted a cruel revenge on his hapless parents; a lovelorn romantic and a domestic tyrant; a worshipper of feminine purity who had probably somehow managed to contract venereal disease and who certainly liked to pace the streets of Paris and London, eyeing up the trade. His oeuvre abounds in divided selves of one sort or another, or of doubles – such as Edward Carson and Charles Darnay in *A Tale of Two Cities* or the many paired siblings or twins, from the Cheerybles in *Nicholas Nickleby* to the Flintwinches in *Little Dorrit*. Now the complicated juggling act, of keeping his divided selves from ever coming to know one another, had ended, and he was drifting towards the peaceful Garden of Proserpine.

By the time Katey returned from London to Gad's Hill, having told her mother the news that Charles Dickens was dying, the death-scene was finally assembled in the dining room. She brought with her Frank Beard and her sister Mamie. Nelly was already there, having been summoned back from Peckham, presumably by Georgina.

'Directly we entered the house,' Katey remembered, 'I could hear my father's deep breathing. All through the night we watched him, taking it in turns to place hot bricks at his feet, which were so cold. But he did not stir.'

The next day, 9 June, was the fifth anniversary of the Staplehurst train smash. Charley arrived in the morning, with Dr Russell Reynolds who, upon examining the unconscious patient, told them all what they knew already. No hope. All day the door was open, leading into the conservatory where bright-red geraniums, Dickens's favourite flower, could be glimpsed, together with vivid blue lobelia. Light flooded into the room. His eyes could no longer be dazzled. Just before six in the evening he gave a deep sigh, and a single tear rose to his right eye and trickled down his cheek. Dickens was dead.

CHAPTER 7

THE MYSTERY OF
CHARLES DICKENS

Dickens was dead: to begin with. There is no doubt whatever, about that . . . Old Dickens was as dead as a doornail. With death, the oyster shell stayed firmly closed, and the pearl that, in this book, we have tried to prise out was, for the time being at any rate, left hidden. There he lay, ceasing at once to be the lover of Nelly, or the creative divided self who had made the novels, the wicked-virtuous monster recalled later by his children, the Enchanter who could mesmerize crowds of thousands by his readings, leaving behind for ever the sickly factory boy who had stared with bewildered and potentially vengeful eye upon a cruel, bloody England, and now Charles Dickens was ready to change into an Eminent Victorian. Dead, my lords and gentlemen. Dead, Right Reverends and Wrong Reverends of every order. Sir John Everett Millais, the establishment painter par excellence, arrived on the very day to sketch his corpse.

Much to ponder here! Millais, whose painting *Christ in the House of His Parents* had been so furiously (and rather unaccountably) denounced by Dickens as a work of blasphemy, was now, twenty years on, stepping over the threshold of Gad's Hill. No longer a young firebrand, but the essence of respectability; frock-coated, pomaded, an adornment of the Royal Academy, and well on his way to the baronetcy that he had conformed so ardently to achieve: a Podsnap among painters. Those who kept alive in their hearts the flame of rebellion against Victorian England, such as William Morris and John Ruskin, deplored Millais, who had left them for a riband to stick in his coat. He had diluted art with commerce, and his sentimental painting *Bubbles* would be used as a commercial advertisement for soft soap. Highly appropriate. He understood the whole duty of man in a commercial country. Dickens, in his last novel, had mocked the vain pomposities of cathedral monuments: the tax inspector '"Departed Assessed Taxes;" introducing a vase and towel, standing on what might represent the cake of soap. "Former pastrycook and Muffin-maker, much respected."' [*MED* 5] Now they were going to sarcophagize and memorialize Dickens. Katey regretted that Sir John, the Royal Academician, had not asked for the bandage to be removed from Dickens's chin, for, 'it marred the calm appearance of my father's countenance'. But since when had his face ever been calm? Mrs Storey, in reconstructing the scene, said that the face in death 'was observed by more than one to resemble Tennyson'.

Of course. Between one whiskery great man and another, who would presume to distinguish? Whether it had been Darwin or Gladstone or Herbert Spencer lying there, who would have minded, for what was about to happen was that, in taking him as their own, they would neuter him and use him as a vehicle for collective self-congratulation.

Dickens had let it be known that he wished to be buried in the little churchyard at Shorne, on the edge of the marshes immortalized in *Great Expectations*, and the family accordingly began to make the arrangements. Given the picture of cathedral life in *The Mystery of Edwin Drood*, there was a certain dusty, mouldy and unconscious graveyard humour in the fact that the Dean and Chapter of Rochester quickly muscled in on the act and wished to reclaim their local son for their own vaults, among the nuns, abbots, distinguished muffin-makers and undistinguished bishops of Rochester. "'There's a old 'un under the seventh pillar on the left as you go down the broken steps of the little underground chapel as formerly was; I make him out (so fur as I've made him out yet) to be one of them old 'uns with a crook. To judge from the size of the passages in the walls, and of the steps and doors, by which they come and went, them crooks must have been a good deal in the way of the old 'uns!'" [*MED* 5]: thus Stony Durdles.

Millais brought with him the sculptor Thomas

Woolner, who took a death-mask, later to be fashioned into a sculpture, an unlikeness that did in marble what Millais had achieved with a pencil, an eminence who could have been the Chancellor of the Duchy of Lancaster or the Bishop of Sodor and Man.

But while plans were afoot to bury the Great Victorian in his nearest cathedral, and the Victorian pieties were being trotted out, something had happened that was quite unlike the death of most other writers. 'It is an event world-wide,' Carlyle said, 'a unique of talents suddenly extinct.'

Carlo Dickens e morto, an Italian newspaper eloquently telegraphed, and Mary Cowden Clarke (Mistress Quickly in his production of *The Merry Wives of Windsor*), reading the words in Genoa, felt that 'the sun seemed suddenly blotted out'.

The Times, huffing and puffing with full-throated portentousness, and entirely forgetful of the number of occasions on which it had denounced him, pontificated that 'Westminster Abbey is the peculiar resting place of English literary genius; and among those whose sacred dust lies there, or whose names are recorded on the walls, very few are more worthy than Charles Dickens of such a home.'

The Dean of Westminster, Arthur Penrhyn Stanley, had met Dickens with the poet Frederick Locker-Lampson, best known for his anthology-piece 'Mabel'. Dean Stanley sent a message via

338

Locker-Lampson to the Dickens family, conveying the gracious sentiment that he was 'prepared to receive any communication from the family respecting the burial'.

Back at Rochester, Stony Durdles had been at work with his hammer, to find an area beneath the ancient stone floors that could accommodate another coffin.

'I take my hammer, and I tap.' (Here he strikes the pavement, and the attentive Deputy skirmishes at a rather wider range, as supposing that his head may be in requisition.) 'I tap, tap, tap. Solid! I go on tapping. Solid still! Tap again. Holloa! Hollow! Tap again, persevering. Solid in hollow! Tap, tap, tap, to try it better. Solid in hollow; and inside solid, hollow again! There you are! Old 'un crumbled away in stone coffin, in vault!'

'Astonishing!'

'I have even done this,' says Durdles, drawing out his two-foot rule (Deputy meanwhile skirmishing nearer, as suspecting that Treasure may be about to be discovered, which may somehow lead to his own enrichment, and the delicious treat of the discoverers being hanged by the neck, on his evidence, until they are dead). 'Say that hammer of mine's a wall – my work. Two; four; and two is six,' measuring on the pavement. 'Six foot inside that wall is Mrs Sapsea.'

'Not really Mrs Sapsea?'

'Say Mrs Sapsea. Her wall's thicker, but say Mrs Sapsea. Durdles taps, that wall represented by that hammer, and says, after good sounding: "Something betwixt us!" Sure enough, some rubbish has been left in that same six-foot space by Durdles's men!'

Jasper opines that such accuracy 'is a gift.'

'I wouldn't have it at a gift,' returns Durdles, by no means receiving the observation in good part. 'I worked it out for myself. Durdles comes by *his* knowledge through grubbing deep for it, and having it up by the roots when it don't want to come.' [*MED* 5]

But now the Dickens children had a better offer. Durdles had the grave already dug and open in St Mary's Chapel, in Rochester Cathedral, when the plan changed once more. Neither the small country churchyard that their father had actually wanted, nor the cathedral that he had depicted with such gruesome comedy in his final book, was to receive all that had been mortal of the Great English Worthy. Arthur Penrhyn Stanley, cousin of 'The King of Lancashire', Lord Derby, and son-in-law of that Lord Elgin who had brought back the Parthenon Marbles to the British Museum,

340

also husband of Queen Victoria's beloved friend and lady-in-waiting Lady Augusta, had signalled that he was prepared to receive a communication. So a communication was sent, and the family, via John Forster, conveyed that they would like to bury Dickens in the Abbey, on condition that there were only two coaches full of mourners, that there should be no plumes, trappings of funereal pomp of any kind, and that the time of the interment should be kept secret. The dean agreed to these conditions, perhaps thinking of Oliver Twist's unhappy time as an undertaker's mute, sleeping under the counter at Mr Sowerberry's establishment and staring with terror at the shadowy coffins as he tried to sleep. 'An unfinished coffin on black tressels, which stood in the middle of the shop, looked so gloomy and death-like that a cold tremble came over him, every time his eyes wandered in the direction of the dismal object.' [*OT* 5]

Somewhere in the vicinity of Gad's, perhaps in Rochester, perhaps nearer at hand, 'Coffin-plates, elm-chips, bright-headed nails, and shreds of black cloth, lay scattered on the floor' [*OT* 5] as someone or another made the coffin. And at six o'clock in the morning on 14 June, that receptacle, now filled up, left Gad's for the station at Higham. How often, when living, Dickens had taken this trip, as often as not alighting at Peckham Rye to see Nelly, or whizzing on to Charing Cross Station, a short walk from the offices of *Household Words* in Wellington Street.

Now he rattled along to Charing Cross in his coffin. When it arrived at the terminus, it was carried into a hearse and three carriages followed, not the two the family had originally specified as a maximum. In the first were the four children who were still alive and still in England – Charley, Old Etonian and failed businessman, at present making a mess of editing *Household Words*; Harry the barrister; Mamie; and Katey Collins, who would one day be the person who revealed Dickens's Secret Life to the world. In the next carriage was the purveyor of the official version, biographer John Forster, who had known Dickens since the Doughty Street days, the early triumphant Pickwickian days; he shared the carriage with Charley's wife; with Georgy, who had also been with Dickens ever since the days of Doughty Street and had been his companion to the very last; and with his sister Letitia, four years Charles's junior, who had been a little child when their father was taken into the Marshalsea, but whose eyes had seen it all: the hilarity of the aunts and the parents clapping and laughing as the infant Charles entertained them with songs and imitations; the ignominy of her twelve-year-old brother setting out to Warren's Blacking warehouse; the success of Boz; the holidays in Broadstairs when she and her husband stayed with Charles as he laboured on *Barnaby Rudge*; and later holidays on the Isle of Wight, when, at Lady Swinburne's house at Bonchurch, the company had screamed with excitement at Dickens's skill as a conjuror, and Lady Swinburne's strange flame-headed little boy, with an enormous head, Algernon Charles, had clapped and cheered. In the third carriage were Frank Beard, Wilkie Collins with his brother Charles (Katey's gay painter-husband) and the family solicitor, Frederic Ouvry, in whose house at Walham Green there had been an amateur performance of *The Frozen Deep*, followed by a glorious afternoon, 'quaffing great goblets of champagne'. Twelve years later, Ouvry had penned Dickens's will, leaving £1,000 to Nelly.

Twelve mourners, that was all. They reached the Abbey, to which the public had not been admitted, at nine o'clock, and the coffin was carried through the west door, up the nave and into Poets' Corner in the South Transept. Claire Tomalin, in her book *The Invisible Woman*, wondered if, behind a pillar, and standing apart from the others, Nelly stood to watch the burial. I so hope that was the case.

The dean noted:

> It was a beautiful summer morning, and the effect of the almost silent and solitary funeral, in the vast space of the Abbey, of this famous writer, whose interment, had it been known, would have drawn thousands to the Abbey, was very striking. As the small procession quitted the Church I asked Mr Forster, as it would be a great

disappointment to the public, whether he would allow the grave to be open for the remainder of that day. He said, 'Yes; now my work is over, and you may do what you like.' The usual service was at ten o'clock. At eleven o'clock there arrived reporters from every newspaper in London, requesting to know when the funeral would take place. I told them it was over. Meantime the rumour had spread, and during that day there were thousands of people who came to see the grave. Every class of the community was present, dropping in flowers, verses and memorials of every kind, and some of them quite poor people, shedding tears.

Dean Stanley, imaginative, clever man, got it right. The National Valhalla was indeed the place in which to enshrine the mortal remains. A pompous public funeral, however, and the musical rites of a church in which Dickens did not really believe, would have been entirely inappropriate. Stanley respected the family's wish for a quiet burial, and acknowledged the public's need to pay tribute to the novelist.

Privately, Dean Stanley would have perhaps empathized with the perception of G. K. Chesterton that 'Even if we are not interested in Dickens as a great event in English literature, we must still be interested in him as a great event in English history . . . He did what no English statesman, perhaps, has really done; he called out the people. He was popular in a sense of which we moderns have not even a notion.' Stanley, after all, as well as being an aristocrat and a member of the Establishment, had known the terrors of English childhood, when his parents had sent him to the brutal world of Rugby School in 1829, thirteen years old, short of stature, frail, and clad, by his heedless innocent mother, in a blue coat with many buttons, grey trousers, adorned by a pink watch-ribbon. The boys immediately nicknamed him Nancy, and he was destined to be a character in a novel, *Tom Brown's Schooldays*. Thomas Hughes did not even bother to change his name – little Arthur, who dares to kneel down to say his prayers before getting into his cold dormitory bed. The sheer misery of being a child, and its terror . . . . No reader of Dickens, regardless of class, can miss this, nor can any reader respond to it in a purely 'literary' way.

Gwen Watkins ended one of the best twentieth-century expositions of the mystery – *Dickens in Search of Himself* – with these words:

John Carey [in *The Violent Effigy*] sees Dickens as 'essentially a comic writer', but it would be true to say that he is essentially a tragic writer, since in all but a few of his books he shows us what it feels like to be, or to have been, a child who can never find what it has never been given, its birthright of love. He has illuminated for us the sufferings of the empty heart, but it is from his own heart that the light streams.

Reading these words of Gwen Watkins, written in 1987, I am looking once again at my eight- or nine-year-old self, painfully thin, my bottom and back covered in the bruises and welts inflicted by a sadist teacher, sitting in a classroom with twenty or so other little boys. In retrospect, it is hard to believe that these children are sitting there in the 1960s. John F. Kennedy is president of the US, and the Beatles have told the world that 'All You Need is Love'. But there we sit, indistinguishable, really, from Victorian, or at least Edwardian, children. The pictures on the wall – a print of *General Gordon's Last Stand*, taken from George William Joy's painting, which hangs in Leeds City Art Gallery, and a portrait of Lord Roberts dating from the time of the Boer War – can give us no indication that we are in fact living in a country whose Empire is all but dismantled. Mephy, the teacher who is in charge of the stationery cupboard, as well as the English master, has been round the class making sure that each ceramic ink-pot, the size of a small eggcup, has been filled with viscous blue ink, and that each child has in front of him the wooden pen-holder, fixed with a steel nib, with which we write our lessons. No ballpoint pens for us – and the felt-tipped pen had not been heard of.

The idea of our all being at that school was not, in the minds of our mothers and fathers at least, to punish us for being born, though we could have been forgiven for thinking so. We were among the privileged few, the privately educated. We had been taken away from our families aged seven, and for the last few years had been living in what was in effect a concentration camp run by sexual perverts. There were, however, bright lights. The English lessons were among them, even though – unlike my elder brother, who doted on our teacher – I found Mephy, real name F. N. Sweet, sinister. He was not the teacher who molested us, but by this stage I distrusted all grown-ups, and the skill with which Mephy impersonated Fagin, in particular, also Wackford Squeers, was all too convincing. For the writing part of the lesson was over and we opened our books to excerpts from *Oliver Twist* and *Nicholas Nickleby*.

He was called Mephy because, in the remote past – decades before any of us arrived at the school, or, indeed, on the earth – he had had red hair. Mephistopheles, the Red Devil. Mephy. Now he was shaven bald, and his nobbly old head was as pale as the white stubble that sprang from it. His craggy face was framed with tortoiseshell spectacles when he read aloud, or, more often, simply recited, for he knew some of the scenes by heart – Fagin teaching the urchins how to pick pockets, or Wackford Squeers teaching the Dotheboys pupils how to read and write. 'We go upon the practical mode of teaching, Nickleby; the regular education system. C-l-e-a-n, clean, verb active, to make bright, to scour. W-i-n-, win, d-e-r, der, winder, a casement. When a boy knows this out of a book, he goes and does it.' [*NN* 8]

There was something truly thrilling/horrific about the way in which Mephy, with enormous strides, paced about the room pretending to be Fagin, while also making his left hand enact that of the Artful Dodger, snatching handkerchiefs from the pocket of his capacious oatmeal tweed coat. Mephy's voice was croaky, and rather harsh. He was not a kind teacher, and we were ruled as fiercely in his lessons as in all the others. Indeed, for he must have known the true character of our headmaster and his appalling wife and daughter, he seemed entirely to endorse the regime. My father believed Mephy was a jailbird, attributing his pallor to the fact that he had been behind bars, but while he might have been in prison (one assumes for the usual reasons in those days – but perhaps he had been a 'conshie'), his cheeks had had decades of the fresh air of Great Malvern to get a little bloom into them and they remained ashen-white.

Yet without those lessons, and that introduction to Dickens, my spirit would have gone under. We were not given the whole of *Oliver Twist* or *Nicholas Nickleby* to read, but little school editions, composed of a few chapters. Dickens brought me redemption at that time, in part because his books, what tiny fragments of them I had experienced, were compulsive reading. Apart from these little Dickensian extract-books, I found reading distasteful. The school forbade us to read any book that was not in the school library, and the only fiction on offer there was either by G. A. Henty or by Captain W. E. Johns (*With Kitchener in the Sudan* or *Biggles*). I have remained counter-suggestible to this day and scarcely ever manage to finish books that have been recommended to me. Henty and *Biggles* were unreadable. One of the many occasions when I was thrashed, by a headmaster who was visibly masturbating, usually inside his trousers, but not always inside, as he did it – an activity that was mysterious to me: what on earth was he *doing*? – was for reading a book that I had brought back to school in my suitcase, *The Adventures of Tom Sawyer*. The distaste, and horror, one felt while these punishments went on was exacerbated by the knowledge that those of us who had proved attractive to the headmaster – and we were wise enough to know that these gratuitous canings were in their repellent way a form of special treatment, reserved for favourites – would have to endure persecution from the man's wife and daughter. The tortures they dreamed up – discovering your least-favourite dish, making you eat it until you vomited, and then making you eat the vomit; locking you in a cage and, after a few hours, assembling an audience of the other boys to wait until you wet yourself – were far worse, really, than the antics of the paedophile headmaster. He, presumably, was out of control, unlike the womenfolk of his household: the wife – who was the daughter of the headmaster of Harrow, a rather beautiful woman in a gipsy kind of way – was hideously in control of herself and of everyone else, while the daughter, a plump, plain girl, would have enjoyed life could she have gone back a few decades and crossed the Continent to gain employment as a concentration-camp guard.

Only later, when time mercifully moved on and I went to a school for older children, where no such horrors were experienced, did I devote my evenings to reading the novels in their entirety and, indeed, I think I read the whole of Dickens then, with the exception of *Pickwick* – a book for which I was not ready. Only much later in life, in my forties, did I discover it, now one of my very favourites. I can still remember my astonishment when another teenaged boy, seeing me absorbed in one of the novels, expressed the view that they were not 'realistic'. Up to that point, this idea had not occurred to me. Nearly all the grown-ups in my family, and among the teaching staff, appeared to me like Dickensian 'characters', repeating their leitmotifs and showing no inclination to escape self-parody. Having passed into a more pretentious phase of readership, in which I supposed that Dickens's way of depicting human character was too crude to be able to arrive at the truth, I discovered, as already mentioned, the judgement of Elizabeth Bowen/Iseult in *Eva Trout* and came to my senses again. Had I known it, I would have echoed George Santayana: 'When people say that Dickens exaggerates, it seems to me that they can have no eyes and no ears. They probably only have notions of what things and people are; they accept them conventionally at their diplomatic value.'

My adolescence took place twenty and more years after the ending of the Second World War, but the BBC in those days still occasionally broadcast on British radio extracts from the programmes that had been popular years before we were born. *Round the Horne. The Navy Lark. The Glums. ITMA.* 'It's bein' so cheerful, that keeps me goin'', 'Can I do yer now, Sir?' and the gales of audience laughter. Those who exploded with mirth were living on minimal rations, hearing almost every month the news that their young menfolk were dying in the most terrible battles all over the world, while they themselves made their way to poorly paid work through the rubble and ruin of bombed-out cities, and their way home in the evening through blacked out-streets. 'The great thing abaht the Blitz is – it takes yer mind off the war.' (A storm of merriment, as they contemplated, or rather did not contemplate, the destruction of their houses, possessions and loved ones.)

Since those terrible times, for reasons too obvious to expound, the Western world has realized that none of this will quite 'do'. That generation who came home from the wars, to all the countries of the world, and 'never talked about it' were, we can now suspect, suffering from PTSD. As, presumably, have all the soldiers and sailors the world has ever known. Those who torment children – which, by modern standards, includes the high proportion of those who have ever taught them since the beginning of time (if by 'torment' you mean impose corporal punishment) – are made the objects of public hatred, suspended from their posts. Their victims are offered therapy. Many of those who suffered sexual and physical abuse as children are very often afflicted for life, so those of us who did so are encouraged to think that this is true of us all.

It is certainly not part of my task in this book to pronounce upon whether any of this is a good thing or a bad thing. This book, however, is about a man who was able to draw forth tears and laughter from readers and audiences to a prodigious degree. His work has passages of lyricism, descriptive force, comedy and pathos that have no parallels in the English language. It has been the surely rather obvious contention of this book that this all sprang from the inner, hidden fount of Dickens's own suffering, and the reason he meant so much to his contemporaries – and survives, meaning so much to us – is that we respond to him differently. We respond to him because he has been there before us, though nothing or almost nothing gives a hint of this, unless it is the twinkle that Henry Fielding Dickens saw in his father's eye during that last Christmas.

Certainly when I look at my own childhood, which had moments of abject terror and hopelessness, I realize that Dickens not only helped me through those moments – walled up, aged seven to thirteen, in an establishment that made the existence of the pupils at Dotheboys seem actually enviable – but also helped me in my horror-stricken recollection of those times. He performed, as Gwen Watkins says, the function of the tragedian, if that is to provide *katharsis* through fear and pity. Yet John Carey was surely right to say that Dickens did so, not by writing tragedy, but by writing comedy. I survived my own childhood traumas by realizing that my tormentors were not only figures of pure horror, but also that they were as comic as Wackford Squeers, as grotesque as Fagin, though as cruel as Mr Murdstone.

Katharsis through tears, but not through tears alone: that was what Dickens offered – offers – me, and millions upon millions of readers. That is why of all the nineteenth-century English writers, in prose or rhyme, he has remained the most popular. The streets of Mumbai and Lagos, the *banlieue* of Paris and Brussels, the housing estates of wrecked Britain and the Badlands of American cities are

353

still scenes where terror and violence are the daily experience of the child. And every week, somewhere around the world, a prelate, a youth leader, an esteemed teacher, now advanced in years, is brought into the dock and made to answer for what he 'did' to children, all those years ago.

Philip Larkin, to judge from his letters, read Dickens pretty frequently, throughout his life, despite his misgivings.

> Better the Dickens you know than the Dickens you don't know – on the whole I enjoyed [*Great Expectations*]. But I should like to say something about this 'irrepressible vitality', this 'throwing a handful of characters on the fire when it burns low', in fact the whole Dickens method – it strikes me as being less ebullient, creative, vital, than hectic, nervy, panic-stricken. If he were a person I should say 'you don't have to entertain me, you know. I'm quite happy sitting here.' This jerking of your attention, with queer names, queer characters, aggressive rhythms, piling on adjectives – seems to me to betray basic insecurity in his relation with the reader. How serenely Trollope, for instance, compares. I say in all seriousness that, say what you like about Dickens as an entertainer, he cannot be considered a real writer at all; not a real

novelist. His is the garish, gaslit, melodramatic barn (writing that phrase makes me wonder if I'm right!) where the yokels gape: outside is the calm, measureless world, where the characters of Eliot, Trollope, Austen, Hardy (most of them) and Lawrence (some of them) have their being. However, I much enjoyed G. E. & may try another soon.

Any intelligent reader can see immediately what Larkin is saying here, they can recognize the phenomenon he is describing, though – as a matter of personal preference – we might prefer every second spent in the garish, gaslit barn with the Enchanter to the 'serene' grown-ups who were Larkin's preferred reading. And the Larkinian judgement is what we should expect from one who, with his other friends in what came to be known as 'The Movement', eschewed mythology, legend, 'style', the 'difficult'; who professed to prefer jazz to Beethoven. (Perhaps really did. *How could anyone?*)

The novelists Larkin lists – certainly those who were more or less Dickens's contemporaries – are the sorts of writer who take us on a journey, either by telling us a story, or by speaking of a world outside ourselves, or – as in the case of Tolstoy – suggesting the spiritual or intellectual journey of the protagonists. At its most basic, this type of narrative keeps us turning the pages by making us wonder what will happen next. Trollope, however thin the gruel he served up, was the absolute master of making us know what would happen next. It is like the pappy experience of being addicted to a TV soap and, when a writer has the skill to the advanced degree it was possessed by Anthony Trollope, it is not to be sneezed at.

Dickens did not aim for this effect, any more than he was trying to depict, as Larkin seems to think (probably rightly; George Eliot, Trollope and co. were trying), the realistic nineteenth-century world, if by that is meant the middle- and upper-class world of hunts, castles, dinners, parliaments and cathedrals.

There is, of course, another category of writer altogether, and that is the stylist, the inventor of their own world. They include the creators of fantasy such as Hesse or Bulgakov, or those who are so linguistically acrobatic that we abide in their world – Nabokov, Firbank – even though it is not, obviously at any rate, trying to tell us anything about the world outside 'the barn'.

One easily sees why a leading light in 'The Movement' – everyday language, a blokeish suspicion of foreign culture or special effects – would fight shy of much of this sort of thing unless it came clearly labelled. (Larkin's friend Kingsley Amis, for example, was a keen aficionado of science fiction.) I would put into this category – of authors whom we read not because they provide us with a mirror on the world, but because they create a theatrical show, a firework display, a mannered, perfectly formed 'world' inhabiting its own stylistic universe – figures as diverse as P. G. Wodehouse, Raymond Chandler or, among the poets, Wallace Stevens, and – in spite of Larkin finding her to inhabit the 'calm measureless world' – Jane Austen, for I'd submit that we read her more because of her 'voice' than because she depicts the 'world', still less the 'world which is the world of all of us'.

If forced to say that Dickens was one or the other sort of writer – this mannered second sort who creates, by language or other effect, their own world, and the others, who take us on a journey through what purports to be the real world – we should surely place Dickens with the mannerists, with the stylists. He sure as heck isn't a realist – is he? 'His is the garish, gaslit, melodramatic barn (writing that phrase makes me wonder if I'm right!) where the yokels gape.'

This book has been written by a gaping yokel who now feels the need to explain what happens when we become absorbed in a Dickens novel, or find ourselves at large in 'the Dickens world'.

To answer Philip Larkin, I am going back to that open grave in Westminster Abbey, where the crowds filed past. Walking there, I recollect my own friendship with the poet. When we attended John Betjeman's memorial service in the Abbey together, Larkin told me that he expected it would not be long before he, too, had a service there in

357

his honour. It was his way of saying he was dying, which he was, but my first thought was – 'You must be joking.' His gloomy bachelor poems, about stubbing out cigarettes in lonely rented rooms, or playing jazz records in his mother's front parlour in Leicester, were accomplished with a technical skill that was awe-inspiring, but . . . the Abbey? How wrong I was, as, a couple of years later, I stood there with thousands of other people, to whom Philip Larkin's poetry – of loss and loneliness, of unbelief, of social fear, of being 'fucked up' by their parents, and of not being able to sustain satisfactory relationships, however hard you try 'talking in bed'; above all, his poems that confront the ignominy of old age and the finality of death – all spoke to a post-religious generation in the most direct way possible.

So, to the two categories of book – the ones that take us on a journey, and the mannerists/stylists who delight us with their pyrotechnic skills – we need to add at least one other category: the writers who have been there before us and, seemingly, for us: the ones whose experiences make sense of our experiences, or whose books hold up a redemptive mirror to our own lives.

That Larkin is such a writer does not need explanation. That Dickens is one such, however, while jerking our attention with queer names and queer characters – this tangle needs a little bit of teasing out. That is what this book has tried to do.

★　　★　　★

If Dickens remains immortal, it is, among other reasons, for his profound understanding of the inner child who remains with all of us until we die. Clearly, however, he had a special status in his own times, different in kind from that enjoyed by any other writer, however popular. Even at the time, those who considered themselves grown-up were inclined to patronize his achievement.

The vulgarity of Dickens, his appeal to the yokels, that is not in doubt. 'My dearest Georgy,' he wrote on 29 August 1858, from Dublin:

> The success at Belfast has been equal to the success here. Enormous! I think them a better audience on the whole than Dublin, and the personal affection there, was something overwhelming. I wish you and the dear girls could have seen the people look at me in the street – or heard them ask me, as I hurried to the hotel after the reading last night to 'do me the honor to shake hands Misther Dickens and God bless you, Sir; not ounly for the light you have been to me this night; but for the light you've been in mee house, Sir (and God love your face!) this many a year' . . . I have never seen men go in to cry so undisguisedly as they did at that reading yesterday afternoon. They made no attempt whatever to hide it, and certainly cried more than the women. As to the Boots at night – and

Mrs Gamp too – it was just one roar with me and them. For they made me laugh so, that sometimes I could not compose my face to go on.

The nineteenth century was a problem, a solution for which its wisest heads sought a solution: socialism, or a return to Catholicism, or an embrace of science, or what not. Dickens did not provide that solution, but he provided what was comparable to the mythologies of a pre-literate age. It is not an original thing to say. G. K. Chesterton, more than a hundred years ago, wrote, 'Dickens was a mythologist rather than a novelist; he was the last of the great mythologists and perhaps the greatest.'

There was no need for him to write a detailed documentary about the law. The Case of Jarndyce and Jarndyce, and the fog-bound Court of Chancery, a mythologized version of the 'real' thing, spoke louder than what is normally meant by satire. Likewise, the Circumlocution Office and Sir Tite Barnacle, the mythologized version of bureaucracy. Because mythology, we can see it everywhere in post-Dickensian settings, which are quite different from Victorian society. His prisons, his heartless bureaucracies, his impenetrable and unending legal procedures were Kafkaesque before Kafka was conceived.

His contemporary readership picked up on this, and saw that Dickens was doing more than a journalist or a political campaigner could do. He was, among other things, making the optimistic assertion that in spite of the dehumanizing effects of overcrowding, industry, cities, political systems, every man, woman and child goes on being not only an individual, but, potentially, a comic individual. There are many tears, some of them wrung from us so gratuitously that we protest even as they flow, in the pages of Dickens. The overwhelming message, however, is something that used to be considered very British: the default position of a sane person is to find life funny, rather than the reverse.

The Victorians, creators of a human horror story that was horrific in a way only they knew how to make worse – slums, treadmills, racist imperialism, the lot – understood this, with their music halls, their usually unfunny humorous periodicals, their pantomimes and vaudevilles, their excruciating Gilbert and Sullivan. When Dickens grates upon the modern ear, he does so because he is so inescapably a man of his own times, a representative of them, the most imaginative and inventive such representative, but one who cannot escape their often alien outlook – his wish for criminals' backs to be scarified, the racism of his response to the Governor Eyre incident, so blatant as to have almost a quality of innocence.

When they put him in his grave and left it open for thousands to stream past, that is what the crowds were responding to. In the three most

361

overtly political of the novels, *Barnaby Rudge*, *A Tale of Two Cities* and *Hard Times*, he had confronted the phenomenon of the crowd and power. In the first two, he looked back to moments in the previous century when mass hysteria dehumanized men and women, leading to behaviour of which, merely as individuals, they would have been incapable. Some of his finest writing is to be found both among his descriptions of the Gordon Riots in *Barnaby Rudge* and of the convulsions of revolution in France in *A Tale of Two Cities*. The Victorians shared Dickens's dread of the same thing happening again, should crowd-mania possess the ever-swollen populace. The population of Coketown, the disgruntled industrial proletariat, likewise sends shivers into the middle-class bosom. 'Whenever a Coke-towner felt he was ill-used – that is to say, whenever he was not left entirely alone, and it was proposed to hold him accountable for the consequences of any of his acts – he was sure to come out with the awful menace, that he would "sooner pitch his property into the Atlantic". This had terrified the Home Secretary within an inch of his life, on several occasions.' [*HT* II 1].

Dickens's response, to the proletariat struggle, as to those destitute and threatened with the workhouse, is broadly consistent – namely, that it was his function, as a charitable citizen and as an artist, to continue asserting the value and distinctiveness of every individual. Hence the great tragedy of

Betty Higden – I am with Swinburne there, considering it one of Dickens's finest moments.

One of the clergymen in the Abbey at the time of Dickens's funeral was the Reverend William Benham, then teaching history at Queen's College, Harley Street, one of the first schools founded for the education of girls in Victorian London, by Benham's mentor, F. D. Maurice. He later became the vicar of Margate, where he was also chairman of the Schools Board in the town. It was in 1877 that the Reverend George Wharton Robinson became the headmaster of Margate High School, and brought his young wife to live with him there. Her mother had died the previous year. The new bride, to celebrate her life with her young schoolmaster husband, had already lost a lot of age, and by the 1881 census she would have become a mere twenty-eight years old, two years younger than her husband. In their wedding certificate of 1876, neither husband nor wife supplied an age, and the prosaic truth – that she had been thirty-seven when she married her much younger husband – was something that was perfectly easily concealed. In spite of illness in the year before their wedding, she was robust enough to bear two children: Geoffrey, born when simple fact would have declared her to be approaching her fortieth birthday, and the second, Gladys, long after that unheeded anniversary was past.

In spite of the couple both being ill – George

would eventually resign his headmastership for nervous reasons, and she was 'frail' – they ran their school with brio and imagination. Mrs Robinson organized plays and concerts, and helped with productions at Margate's Theatre Royal – *Romeo and Juliet*, Wilkie Collins's *The New Magdalen* and *Alive or Dead?*, a dramatized version of *The Mystery of Edwin Drood*. Nobody thought to enquire into the Mystery of Mrs Robinson, and, indeed, there was no reason to suppose that there was one. No one needed to know that her own father, as a not very successful actor, had appeared at the Theatre Royal Margate, or that, during the 1840s, the most famous novelist in Britain had frequently come over from Broadstairs to attend productions there.

Everyone loved Dickens, didn't they? There was nothing suspicious about Mrs Robinson reading aloud from the novels to the children in her husband's school. It was a badge of pride for the school that Mrs Robinson – who, being now only in her twenties, must have been a mere child when she knew the famous man – had been acquainted with the writer and was able to ask his sister-in-law, Miss Georgina Hogarth, to present the prizes at Margate High School.

But for Mrs Robinson, all was not well. She was troubled in her conscience. And when she got to know the Reverend George Benham – visitor to the school in his capacity as chair of the Schools Board, as well as vicar of Margate – she began to

364

confide in him. The story all tumbled out. After the years had passed, Benham, a keen Dickensian, met a fellow enthusiast who told him he was planning to write a biography. Benham repeated what Mrs Robinson had told him. It was indiscreet, but she had not been making a formal confession, so there was no exact breach of professional decorum. Perhaps he felt the truth ought to be told; perhaps, learned and devout man though he was, he was a blabbermouth who simply could not keep the story to himself: that she had been Dickens's mistress; that he had set her up in a house; that he visited her two or three days a week; that, even during his lifetime, she had felt deep remorse about the relationship, and that her remorse had made them both miserable; and that now 'she loathed the very thought of his intimacy'.

Yet the mesmerist from beyond the grave still worked his enchantment, and even after admitting her true story to Canon Benham, she appeared on the stage of the Theatre Royal Margate in a comedietta entitled *Orange Blossoms*, rounding the evening off with an impersonation of Mrs Jarley, the waxworks proprietress in *The Old Curiosity Shop*.

Those who know the story of the novel will know that Little Nell and her grandfather were on the run from the evil attentions of the dwarfish villain, Daniel Quilp. Quilp has been bleeding the grandfather dry, because the silly old man is addicted to gambling and goes to Quilp for loans he cannot repay. As a result, Quilp is now the virtual owner of The Old Shop. But, more than that, he wants to possess Nell body and soul. Carnal knowledge of the little woman-child.

The quill-pen of the dark, dwarfish, demonic little novelist had invented the story of Quilp and Nell long before our Nelly was known to the demonic Dickens. Nell had 'loathed the very thought of his intimacy' more than a decade before Nelly made that fateful journey to Manchester to take part in *The Frozen Deep*. Yet both Nelly Robinson and, now, Canon Benham, as he sat in the audience, must have had strange thoughts as they re-enacted the scene: Nell taking her cue from Mrs Jarley, the waxworks proprietress, and identifying the wax figures for the visitors.

The waxworks were played by the children, one of whom was Nelly's son Geoffrey, who knew nothing of his mother's story until the 1920s when he was working as a second-hand bookseller in Slough. By then he had been through the First World War – wounded at Mons, posted to Persia on a secret expedition and, at the end of the war and after, in charge of a refugee camp for two years in the Persian port of Enzeli. It might be thought that beside the sufferings Geoffrey witnessed during those years, the discovery of the truth about his mother was shattering. He consulted Henry Dickens, by then a judge, who confirmed it was all true: that Nelly had been the novelist's mistress, and that the age on her death certificate, sixty-five, was – like so much in the Dickensian world – a work of fancy.

One asks oneself whether her husband was also made privy to the secret and whether it had a comparably devastating effect. In March 1886, George Wharton Robinson presided over a charitable reading called 'An Evening with Charles Dickens'. Almost immediately afterwards, this hitherto healthy man of thirty-six suffered an unspecified type of nervous collapse. They sold the school and began to run into financial difficulties, living in a modest way, moving from modest flat to modest flat in Bayswater: Artesian Road, Sutherland Avenue and Maida Vale. In 1888, Robinson removed his name from *Crockford's Clerical Directory*, implying that he no longer considered himself a clergyman, or that, perhaps, he had lost his faith. Perhaps, more shattering than to lose his faith in the Almighty, he had lost his faith in Nelly.

She did her best to keep them afloat, offering lessons in French and elocution. Those who met the couple in those straitened times remembered that 'George made of himself an absolute doormat to Ellen'. Eventually, much to her sister Fanny's dismay, she sold her only substantial asset, the house in Ampthill Square that Dickens had bought for her in 1860. At least with the proceeds she could ensure that Geoffrey and Gladys would be financially secure. Geoffrey lived until 1959. Gladys survived until 1973, protesting to anyone who would listen, before she sank into senility, that the relationship between her mother and Dickens had been blameless.

Those who find Dickens garish, vulgar, unrealistic, are those who consider 'realistic' to be synonymous with 'real'. Much as they might enjoy Dickens, they are never going to do so as richly as those who see that he was a visionary – 'His flexibility is that of a richly poetic art of the world.' It is touching that one of the presentations enacted by Nelly Robinson and the children on the stage at Margate should have been that of her near-namesake Nell Trent among Mrs Jarley's waxworks.

> 'Never go into the company of a filthy Punch any more,' said Mrs Jarley, 'after this.'
> 'I never saw any wax-work, ma'am,' said Nell. 'Is it funnier than Punch?' [. . .]
> 'It isn't funny at all,' repeated Mrs Jarley. 'It's calm and – what's that word again – critical? – no – classical, that's it – it's calm and classical. No low beatings and knockings about, no jokings and squeakings like your precious Punches, but always the same, with a constantly unchanging air of coldness and gentility.' [*OCS* 27]

Did the last eight words of that sentence describe Nelly's marriage? Did the years in

Peckham, and Slough, and France – the secret years that, when she was speaking to Mr Benham, she so much repented – did they not return as richer, happier memories?

Little Nell was trained by Mrs Jarley to give the commentaries upon the waxwork display to the visitors, and she became very good at it, able to excite the trippers with her descriptions of 'Jasper Packlemerton of atrocious memory, who courted and married fourteen wives, and destroyed them all, by tickling the soles of their feet when they were sleeping in the consciousness of innocence and virtue'. [*OCS* 28] The waxworks themselves, however, were as adaptable as the commentary, and when they were being displayed, for example, to schoolgirls, their proprietress was capable of changing their identity. When the girls looked at what was supposed to be Mary, Queen of Scots, 'in a dark wig, white shirt-collar, and male attire, was such a complete image of Lord Byron that the young ladies quite screamed when they saw it'. [*OCS* 28] Likewise, 'Mrs Jarley had been at great pains to conciliate, by altering the face and costume of Mr Grimaldi as clown to represent Mr Lindley Murray as he appeared when engaged in the composition of his English Grammar, and turning a murderess of great renown into Mrs Hannah More.' [*OCS* 29] Hannah More had been a writer and bluestocking on the outer edges of Dr Johnson's circle, and in all likelihood the children at Mr Robinson's High School in Margate used the English grammar composed by the American Quaker Lindley Murray. By making the children enact this scene, Nelly was playfully realizing how easy it was for people, as well as for waxworks, to assume other masks and identities, to become the person other people wanted you to be. Behind the respectable face of the grammarian, however, there grinned out the face of Grimaldi the mesmeric clown.

LIST OF ABBREVIATIONS

The works of Dickens are readily available. There seemed no good reason to cite page numbers from one edition rather than another. I have therefore included in the body of the text a reference to the book number (where appropriate) and chapter number of the relevant Dickensian work.

I have used the following abbreviations:

AN – American Notes
ATTC – A Tale of Two Cities
BH – Bleak House
CC – A Christmas Carol
CS – Christmas Stories
DC – David Copperfield
DS – Dombey and Son
GE – Great Expectations
HM – The Haunted Man and the Ghost's Bargain
HT – Hard Times
LD – Little Dorrit
LOL – The Life of Our Lord
MC – Martin Chuzzlewit
MED – The Mystery of Edwin Drood

NN – Nicholas Nickleby

OCS – The Old Curiosity Shop

OMF – Our Mutual Friend

OT – Oliver Twist

Pilgrim – the twelve-volume edition of *The Letters of Charles Dickens*, edited by Graham Storey, Kathleen Tillotson et al.

PP – The Posthumous Papers of the Pickwick Club

RP – Reprinted Pieces

SB – Sketches by Boz

SJ – Selected Journalism 1850–1870

TC – The Chimes

UT – The Uncommercial Traveller